THE DIARY OF A MEDICAL OFFICER DURING THE GREAT INDIAN MUTINY.

THE DIARY OF A MEDICAL OFFICER DURING THE GREAT INDIAN MUTINY OF 1857

WRITTEN BY
JAMES WISE, M.D.

The Naval & Military Press Ltd

Published by
The Naval & Military Press Ltd

INTRODUCTION.

My acquaintance with Doctor James Wise dates as far back as 1860, when he was civil surgeon of Chittagong. He was a rare good man, both mentally and physically. In personal appearance he was strikingly handsome—a tall, soldier-like, fair man, of over six feet in height, with hair and moustache of an auburn hue and bright kindly blue eyes. There was a goodness, a *bonhomie*, a cordial simplicity about him that was irresistibly attractive, and which must have aided him greatly in his profession as a medical man. Quiet and somewhat reserved in manner, there was under-running a strong sense of humour, and, above all, in everything he did, he was thorough. I should take James Wise to be a good type of the great Scandinavian race of Scotsmen who have done so much to establish our Indian Empire.

The Diary which is here published has no literary pretensions. It is simply what it professes to be—a daily record of events, and is put forward, primarily no doubt, to satisfy the affectionate longings of those to whom the writer was near and dear; but these pages have, besides, an undoubted value and interest, as an addition to contemporary history. A journal like this, full of detail, and with a strong dash of personal adventure, cannot fail to be interesting, even to the casual reader, but is specially valuable as the faithful record of an eye-witness during this now far-distant and almost forgotten period of English trial, and as such cannot but be useful in arriving at a correct solution of the historical problems connected with the Indian Mutiny. The story of this great struggle is now an old one, and in our zeal for good works—in the introduction of representative government among a people unfit to govern—in delivering them from the evils of an opium slavery, from which they do not suffer—in teaching them Anglo-Saxon roots and the Gospel of Herbert Spencer, to the detriment of the faith of their fathers—we English people have forgotten the tide of blood which less than half a century ago swept over the land and shook the foundations of our rule in India. The history of that great struggle is as a tale that is told, and the lesson which it taught has been learnt, not by the victors, but by the vanquished. I think therefore that in this time of oblivion it is not unfitting that these diaries, the simple testimony of one who is now dead and has nothing to gain or to lose any more, should be placed before the British public, to help them to weigh and consider the importance and difficulties of the great Indian problem—to enable people to realize how unstable are the foundations on which we seek to superimpose a fabric of utopian government, the inexpediency of which is fully recognized by most of the able men who help to administer our great Eastern dominion, and so (if it may be) put a drag on our over-hasty work of reform.

Doctor Wise was born on the 18th June, 1834. He went to India as a surgeon in the service of the East India Company in 1856, and being appointed after landing in Calcutta to serve as surgeon with the Artillery at Meerut, he joined and took charge of his duties there shortly before the outbreak of the Mutiny.

On the 9th May, 1857, a number of men belonging to the 3rd Regiment of Native Cavalry stationed at Meerut, who had been sentenced to imprisonment for refusing to make use of the cartridges served out to them, were degraded and fettered at a public parade of the garrison, and were marched off to gaol cursing the injustice of the English power. On the next day their regiment, the 3rd Native Cavalry, broke into open mutiny, stormed the gaol, released their imprisoned comrades, and then, joined by the greater part of the other native troops in the station, they took the road to Delhi, where at that time the King of Delhi, the descendant of the Great Mogul, from whom we had wrested the empire, lived as a pensioner on our bounty. To him went the mutineers. They wanted a head, and sought naturally to find their leader in the descendant of their ancient kings. The troops at Delhi joined the Meerut mutineers. The King of Delhi placed himself at their head. English blood was shed; the sword was drawn and the scabbard thrown away. Here Doctor Wise takes up the story, and the Diary commences with the march of our English troops from Meerut to concentrate on Delhi; and so I leave my dear friend, regretting that he is not alive to tell his own story with his lips.

T. H. LEWIN.

NOTE.—The term "Pandy" or "the Pandys" is used throughout this journal to denote the mutineers—*i.e.* the revolted soldiers of the East India Company's Service. The name "Pandy" is a common patronymic among Hindoos, and it was as common to find a native soldier called "Pandy" as in an English regiment it would be to find Brown or Smith. Hence, the term "Pandy" was adopted by English people as a generic title for the dark-skinned soldier of India, and Dr. Wise speaks habitually of "Pandy" as we do nowadays of "Tommy Atkins."

T. H. L.

THE DIARY OF A MEDICAL OFFICER DURING THE GREAT INDIAN MUTINY.

MAY 27th, 1857. At ten p.m. we started from Meerut a body of about 1,100 men, consisting of 400 of H.M. 60th Rifles, 80 of the 3rd battalion 3rd company of Foot Artillery, 50 of the 1st troop 1st brigade of Horse Artillery, 100 recruits with two large siege guns, 200 of H.M. 6th Dragoon Guards, and 150 of the Sappers and Miners. The 60th commanded by Colonel Jones, the company by Major Scott, Horse Artillery by Major Tombs, both, however, under Lieutenant-Colonel Murray Mackenzie; the recruits by Captain A. Light, the 6th Dragoons by Colonel Custance, and the Sappers by Lieutenant Geneste. The commander was Brigadier A. Wilson; his staff consisting of Captain E. B. Johnson, staff officer; Captain Hamilton, quartermaster; Lieutenant Waterfield, commissariat officer. The night of starting I was ordered to remain in medical charge of rear-guard, consisting of Captain Light's recruits, and company squadron of the Carabiniers. Our duty was, of course, to push on all stragglers. Our delays were, therefore, frequent. Camels' burdens upsetting, hackeries losing their wheels, etc. The night was cool, a great deal of lightning in distance. About daybreak came up with our advanced portion. They had just arrived at the encamping ground at the tenth mile from cantonment. After sleeping for about an hour, waiting for the baggage to advance, we were suddenly awoke by a violent shower of rain. It only continued a few minutes, being succeeded by a dust storm which made us sorry figures on our arrival in camp.

May 28th. Except for a copious supply of water our camp was bad, being so crowded. On our arrival found the tents almost pitched; all the baggage safe. Drs. Mackinnon, Smyth, and myself stay in the same tent. We three have charge of the Artillery. With the Rifles are Surgeon Lucas, Assistant-Surgeons Biddle and Duff. With the Carabiniers, Assistant-Surgeon Moore. Slept for about an hour after arrival, being very tired, and, except a few minutes now and then on the roadside, had none during the night. At the mess we have breakfast, tiffin, and dinner. This day was intensely warm, beyond anything I ever felt. Being under canvas without a breath of wind, is at this season far from desirable. Dr. Mackinnon, though a very old campaigner, could not sleep on that account; it makes little difference to me. From morning to night the perspiration was pouring incessantly. The sad news arrived this afternoon of the death of the Commander-in-Chief, General Anson. He was approaching Delhi from Umballa, and had reached Karnal when he died. This will cause delay. General Barnard, a Crimean campaigner, is likely to succeed him. From Meerut we hear that the depôt was flooded by the storm last night. A good joke is told of one of the volunteers. Behind the school of instruction there is a small wicket at which there was always a rifle sentry. This man thought he saw something and fired, this was in the direction of one of the bastions in which there was a guard of volunteers. One of these out of compliment fired at the rifleman in return, and a volunteer in the opposite bastion threw his gun up in air and fell, as he thought, mortally wounded. On being carried towards hospital and being examined, nothing was found the matter. Another volunteer let his firelock off by mistake, setting fire to a tattee in the magazine. It was fortunately discovered in time and extinguished. Struck our tents at ten p.m., starting at eleven. After some delay at starting got on very smoothly. Not with vanguard, but ordered to keep beside the Brigadier.

May 29th. Night cooler than last. Crossed the canal at four a.m. Although little known of at home, it is one of the largest undertakings in the world. The road crosses by a very fine bridge. Stopped about twenty miles from Meerut. Passed a village burned to the ground and a large bungalow. In the courtyard the furniture, etc., were found half burned. Camping ground much larger than yesterday's, situated in rice fields. A report arose this afternoon that a body of four hundred troops were encamped about four miles from this. The Irregular Cavalry, under Captain Hall, went out to reconnoitre, but saw no one. The place of our encampment is called Maradunggun. Started at eleven p.m. My horse was so restless that I was obliged to walk the whole distance.

It is said the 10th N.I. at Futtehgurh have revolted and are on their way to Delhi, so we were in expectation of coming up with them, but were disappointed.

May 30th. Our march stopped about 3.30 a.m., the Brigadier going forward with a company of Rifles to reconnoitre the bridge across the Hindan. Captain Hall's men started the evening before and occupied it. The Sepoys must have been on it lately, as cartridges were found. One man was caught on the bridge, not knowing who approached. He said he was a Sowar of the King of Delhi sent with a letter to the chief of a neighbouring village. This was found on his person with the royal seal. As daylight broke, the camp was marked out. The front is covered by the river Hindan, now fordable in many places; on the left the high-road to Delhi, at the junction of the Meerut and Allygurh roads; our right is covered by a large mud village. Not a man said to be on this side the Jumna. The river is crossed by a cast-iron suspension bridge. All remained quiet during forenoon. Day cooler than usual; strong breeze blowing. About five p.m. our outposts came in, reporting the approach of a body of irregular horse, followed by clouds of dust, advancing from Delhi. All our troops immediately turned out, but before they got out of camp a round shot was fired, which was aimed at Lieutenant Moore and two other officers of the Carabiniers. It struck the ground on the other side of the river and bounded over their heads. The second that came passed through and through camp, hitting the Dragoon hospital, passing through Captain Hall's tent, and killed two doolie bearers sitting smoking. The Horse Artillery were on the right, Major Scott's battery in the centre, and the Rifles and Carabiniers crossed by the bridge. The position of the natives was on the other side of the river, in front of a village, their guns being posted among trees. A squadron of Carabiniers were what they kept firing at, but only succeeded in wounding one or two men. The Horse Artillery crossed the river, advancing at the gallop, although the enemy were firing grape, which fell short. Major Tombs turned their flank, and poured in a continuous discharge of grape. The Rifles soon advancing up the road, began to fire, and the enemy were driven from their guns by their charging. The guns were spiked, and the gunners bolted. Behind the cannon was a small tope of trees; in this there was an ammunition waggon, which, while surrounded by the 60th, blew up, throwing men, horses, etc., in all directions, killing about half a dozen, and wounding about the same number. A slow match is said by some to have been laid when they perceived their guns were lost; others that a havildar of the 11th N.I. set fire to it himself. The main body of the enemy were by this time far on their retreat, but behind were numerous stragglers, who were shot down and sabred. For want of a sufficiency of cavalry they did not consider it safe to charge, but the troop kept up the pursuit until stopped by sunset, and two burning villages they fired on their retreat. This was about three miles, or eight from Delhi. The number of guns captured were two 24-pounders, two 18 and one 10-inch howitzers. A number of sandbags, trenching tools, and ammunition were taken. What their object was is uncertain. Probably they intended to throw up a battery to command the bridge, not knowing of our arrival; or expected to remain unseen, place their guns in position, and open upon us in the morning. This will be a damper on their courage, but they deserve credit for coming out so far (eleven miles) and attacking us. The number of killed are—6th Dragoon Guards, four killed, three wounded; 60th Rifles, ten killed, about fifteen wounded; Artillery, three killed, eight wounded; one bhistie and two doolie bearers—total, twenty killed, twenty-six wounded. Poor Captain Andrews, of the Rifles, was blown to pieces at the head of his company. Lieutenant De Bourbel, of the Carabiniers was wounded in the hand while charging a man; he will lose three fingers by it. Busy until twelve p.m. assisting Dr. Moore. Had three amputations of thighs; he performed two. One was Sergeant Mackenzie; he died from loss of blood and from the shock of the operation. The other was a bhistie, who also died soon after. The bearer's leg that I amputated is getting on well, although he lost a great deal of blood.

May 31st. All quiet during night. About seven a.m. a report of men advancing arose, but turned out untrue. A party of the Rifles were sent out to burn some villages on the Delhi road. Yesterday when the firing commenced the camp followers and many servants made for the village on the right, Ghazi-u-din-nagar, but the inhabitants turned out with latties, etc., and drove them back. Many, however, were seen going off to Meerut as fast as possible. About two p.m. the alarm was sounded, and all the troops immediately turned out. The Horse Artillery went off at the gallop in the same direction as yesterday. The firing soon became very warm. The enemy were posted on a ridge with a mud village in their centre Their position strong, with numerous heavy 18-pounders. Their firing was exceedingly good. Colonel Mackenzie said that he had never seen better from natives, and that if the troops had not had a bank in front of them with the guns peering over, scarcely a man would have been spared. Poor Lieutenant Perkins was killed while crossing the river by a shell, which took away the top of his head. Death must have been instantaneous. The Rifles marched over the bridge and were soon peppering them at a village. One squadron of Dragoons supported Captain Light's 18-pounders, which were sent out, it being found that the 6-pounders of the troops could not commit sufficient execution. Another troop kept moving about in rear of Major Scott's battery, and the Horse Artillery to protect them. These Dragoons were a favourite mark for the enemies' guns, but from their moving about the range could not be got. The Rifles found some hard fighting in the village, but the great heat told more on our men than the bullets. After about one hour and a half heavy firing, the enemy retired in good order towards Delhi, with three guns, which they turned and fired at us and then galloped on. Captain Napier, of the Rifles, received a gunshot wound of thigh, fracturing thigh. Poor Lieutenant Moore, of the 6th Dragoons, was severely wounded at back of head by gunshot. He was sensible on admission. His helmet was cloven in, and the outer table depressed. Ball had not lodged. The Dragoons had no opportunity of charging. The escapes were miraculous. A round shot took away the butts of three carbines, while the Dragoons were patrolling. Two of the Carabiniers were drowned, one in following some Sepoys who took to the river, he plunged in after them where the water was deep and never rose. The other tried to make a short cut into camp, dashed into the river, and perished. Yesterday the enemy consisted principally of men from the 38th N.I. and the 45th. To-day, of the 38th and 20th N.I.; they were dressed in white clothes. The casualties by the sun are almost as great as by bullet. Two of the Dragoons were brought in dead, and four or five affected. Two of the Troop Horse Artillery died soon after coming in, and three more are still alive. The Rifles had a great many struck down. Two of their officers were affected and staggered like drunken men. The enemy are said to be commanded by a European, who is known by his appearance and the colour of his beard. Some say he is one of our artillery who escaped from the prison in Meerut. During the night several villages were in flames towards Delhi. The fire was bright, and illuminated all the sky.

June 1st. A great deal of firing during the night, said to be at Delhi, heavy guns being now and then audible. Some say it was the Sepoys murdering the 3rd L.C. for not assisting them yesterday. It appears that their master of ordnance—formerly a clerk in the commissariat—was killed yesterday. About seven a.m. the Ghoorkhas 2nd battalion came in from Bolundshureen, having been ordered in by the Brigadier. They were enthusiastically cheered in by the troops in camp. They are dressed almost similarly to our Rifles, and seem fine active little fellows. Their band came in playing "Rory O'More." About ten a.m. a troop of Dragoons came in, escorting ammunition and stores from Meerut, which is very acceptable at present, our shot having run short. Davenport accompanied them. He remains in charge of his regiment. Poor Moore became much worse this morning. He is in a very precarious state. Remained all quiet to-day, which is a great relief, for the Ghoorkhas will be rested and able to go in at them. All the wounded were sent in to Meerut this evening under the same troop of Dragoons, Duff going in in medical charge. Waterfield, our commissariat officer, being quite a tyro at his trade, did not provide them with any bread, so their departure was delayed until ten p.m. till it was provided. They will reach in about twelve hours. De Bourbel's fingers (three) were removed this morning by Dr. Mackinnon. I amputated Sergeant-Major Still's (of the 6th Dragoons) leg this morning. It was shattered to pieces by a round shot, but had sufficient sound flesh to get a covering by the circular operation. Doing well when put in doolie for Meerut.

June 2nd. Nothing to do this morning, all the sick having left. The Ghoorkhas having no huts have been plundering the thatching of the villages and have erected abodes for themselves. Tents are on their way from Meerut. No alarms to-day, which is wonderful. A good deal of firing in the direction of Delhi, heavy guns every now and then booming in the distance. It is said to arise from alarms of our approach, when immediately guns are fired in all directions. Poor Perkins' things were sold this morning. It is a most melancholy thing ; an officer whom you saw yesterday the picture of health, in the grave, and his goods being scattered to the winds. One of his chargers was bought by Major Tombs, he having lost both his own—one wounded, the other killed. The Rifles and some of the Ghoorkhas were out burning a village about three miles on the Delhi road this evening. It was the one they were entrenched in on the last day's fight. Cooler to-day. Strong hot wind blowing from the west.

June 3rd. The alarm bugles sounded about four a.m. A man had heard the sound of pickaxes near the village burned last night, and without approaching nearer to reconnoitre, he galloped in with the tidings. The approach of the Chief on the other side of the city will keep them fully occupied for the present. The rebels are erecting a battery at this side of the bridge of boats across the Jumna, but they will be disappointed at our not approaching it. Walked with Davenport to the river, which I had not yet seen. It is a slow muddy stream, in some places very deep. It is only about thirty yards across. The bridge across it is an iron suspension one, with a wood roadway. At the Delhi end we have erected a breastwork of sandbags and two heavy siege guns, one an 18-pounder commanding the road. The iron railing bears here and there marks of round shots which were fired at the Rifles while crossing. The clouds of dust in camp are most unpleasant, filling every corner, and at breakfast the quantities swallowed would astonish anyone at home. News has come in this afternoon that we are to remain until Harvey's Volunteer Corps comes in to take our place. The Chief has spies in Delhi. They report that in these two days' fighting the rebels lost about five hundred men. At Delhi, except some of the Meerut Sepoys and Sappers, all are in great alarm packing up their plunder, and ready to bolt on the first opportunity. One of Captain Hall's irregulars rode out to a village near Delhi and brought back word that the mutineers had left Delhi to attack the Chief. They will get nothing but hard knocks there. On the last day's fighting the Sepoys left in Delhi broke the bridge of boats, expecting that we would follow and enter with the enemy across the river. This accounts for the firing that evening.

June 4th. Firing of heavy guns again heard last night. Rode out with Davenport to where the fighting took place. The road is beautiful, and the cooing of pigeons contrasted greatly with the ravages done by men's hands. A village just beyond the toll-house is completely destroyed, and not a human being to be seen. Here and there a dead body was lying in the hollows with dogs tearing at it; clouds of vultures, and other unclean animals, hovering about. The smell in places was disgusting. Rode to the piquet, about a mile and a half from the bridge. The view from this ridge (where the enemy's guns were placed) is most beautiful. It extends all over the Doab and up to Delhi, which, however, was covered by mist. The country is well wooded, and everything appeared peaceful and still, as if it had never seen the ravages of war. A letter from Forsyth to-day. Poor Moore died the evening of the 2nd; great extravasation of blood was found, and extensive fissuring at base and opposite side from wound. De Bourbel getting on well. The Sergeant-Major not so well. The native doctor of the 11th N.I. was flogged for having his Sergeant-Major's property in his house; he ought to have been shot. We march this evening at six p.m. For more than two hours we remained on the ridge where the fighting was, until the baggage came up, and the bridge broken down by the Engineers. We turned off the Delhi road about half a mile beyond the bridge, striking across country by a hackery track. We arrived at the banks of the Eastern Jumna Canal about three a.m., and had again to wait until the baggage came up. Along the banks of this we marched about five miles.

June 5th. This canal is the work of the great Mogul, I believe. It must have been a great undertaking for those days; its remains would still attract notice, though small compared with our works. It is beautifully planted with trees on each side, and it is the prettiest road I have seen here. There was only water here and there in it. Even here the miscreants have been at work, and one beautiful house with gardens was in ruins. We came a most roundabout way, and after leaving the shade of the trees the march was tiresome in the extreme. We did not arrive at our camping ground till nine a.m., quite done up and fit for nothing. The heavy guns, with some of the hackeries, did not arrive until three p.m. The reason of this long march (about eighteen miles) was to join thirty elephants sent to carry our baggage. When we reached Kekra, we found that Captain Macandrew had left with them that morning for Bagh Pat. The Calcutta dâk was delivered to-day; the first for fourteen days. There had been a great panic there until the arrival of the 1st Madras Fusiliers, who are occupying the fort. The 53rd are at Allahabad; the 84th at Cawnpore. Troops have been ordered from Ceylon, and the China expedition being stopped will furnish four regiments. It is said the Governor-General has written home for fifteen thousand men. At Moradabad the 29th N.I. have revolted, as also the 44th at Bareilly. The former were attacked by the 8th Irregular Cavalry, and many cut to pieces. Had letters from Drs. Wilson and Moir. Started again at ten p.m., all rather stiff and tired.

June 6th. The roads last night were very bad, being narrow, sandy, with high banks on each side. This caused us to proceed very slowly, and, although only eight miles, we did not arrive at our destination until 3.30 a.m. Arrived at Bagh Pat about three a.m. Found the bridge of boats still entire, which on the part of the mutineers shows great carelessness. The Jumna here is a very rapid stream, with high clay banks on the left. It is on this side the village stands. The right bank is flat and sandy. We advanced about a mile, and our camp was pitched. The baggage and heavy guns had all arrived about seven a.m. Yesterday, at the village of our encampment, we heard of Assistant-Surgeon Bateson, of the 74th N.I. He had been kept there for ten days, and passed off as a fakir. He left with the elephants in the morning. The Brigadier started early this afternoon to join the Chief. We had a most violent dust storm at six p.m., followed, as usual, by deluges of rain, thunder, etc. We received orders to start at nine, but the rain descended with redoubled fury, and we had to wait until eleven. The night was cloudless, and nearly a full moon served to guide us on our way. Our march was across country; seven miles of hackery track, and five of the great trunk road. The first part was pleasant enough, except from the roads being so narrow. The lanes, with hedges on each side, reminded one of home. Our course often led through rice fields, which by the rain were made very stiff. Colonel M. Mackenzie commanded us.

June 7th. At daybreak we arrived at the high road, the one between Karnal and Delhi, about fourteen miles from the latter place. We met soon after some of the 3rd I.C., who were being sent back to Meerut. The Rajah's men were the first troops met. One of the first persons who came out to escort us in was Sir H. Barnard, acting Commander-in-Chief. He was accompanied by Colonel Curzon, his military secretary. After him, officers of all grades and men of all regiments met us on our arrival. We reached our position about seven a.m. Not a tent or hackery came up until nearly nine a.m., so we had to make the best of it beneath trees. The troops assembled here are the 9th Lancers, 1st and 3rd Bengal Fusiliers, H.M. 75th, H.M. 60th, 6th Dragoon Guards, etc., etc. The first brigade consists of the 2nd Bengal Fusiliers, H.M. 60th, and the Sirmoor battalion; the second, H.M. 75th, 1st Fusiliers; the cavalry brigade of the Lancers and Carabiniers. The artillery under Brigadier Wilson. The first brigade is commanded by Brigadier Showers; the second by Brigadier Graves; the cavalry by Brigadier Grant, 9th Lancers. The enemy have taken up an entrenched position, about five miles from this, on the road to Delhi. It is intended to drive them from it to-morrow morning. The only news to-day is that the 15th N.I. have mutinied at Nuseerabad; whether any officers have been killed is yet unknown. The place we are encamped in is called Allipore. The number of guns with us are twenty-two, heavy and light, so we should give a good account when we meet the enemy. Our force numbers 600 cavalry, 2,400 infantry.

June 8th. Marched at about two a.m., the vanguard consisting of a squadron of Lancers, Major Scott's battalion, the 75th, and 2nd Fusiliers, all under Brigadier Showers. The second column consisted of the 1st Fusiliers, H.M. 60th, and the Sirmoor battalion, with Captain Light's heavy guns. Just as day broke, when about the sixth mile from Delhi, we came upon a strong entrenchment commanding the road. Its vicinity was first discovered by an 18-pounder whizzing over our heads. The troops immediately deployed to the right and left, our guns advanced and took up a position. The storm of grape, round-shot and shell, was incessant for some time. The 2nd Fusiliers lay down until the enemy's fire was taken off them. Scott's battery advanced, pouring in shot, and Light's heavy pieces gave them 18-pound shot. Major Tombs' troop had been sent round some distance to come upon their flank The banks of the canal had been broken down by the rebels, so the country was flooded, and his advance delayed. When the firing commenced he hurried on with two guns, the other two having stuck in a ditch. On his arrival he opened with grape upon their flank. In the meantime, the

75th had been exposed to a severe fire. Some staff officers rode up, exclaiming, "Form square; the cavalry are down upon you." They did so, no enemy appeared, but they lost severely by it. Colonel Curzon now led them on, and with a loud cheer they charged the battery, having about three hundred yards of open rice fields to cross before reaching it, for the shot dealt death on all sides. The enemy did not wait for the bayonet, but leaving all their guns, rushed in a tumultuous body towards Delhi. Tombs' guns did not increase their courage. To the right of the battery, was a large serai—Badli-ki-Serai—with high walls rather in ruins, but still a strong post for determined men. In this several Sepoys were found armed. All were killed. One was a fakir, who was first wounded and then hung by the 75th. The enemy had tents and everything complete. Our loss was severe, considering the duration of the fight—about an hour. Very few of the enemy's killed or wounded were found, as they always carry them off. Our loss was Colonel C. Chester and Captain Russell, late 38th N.I., who were both killed by one round-shot. The former was Adjutant-General of the army. His loss will be deeply felt. The only other officer killed was Captain Harrison, 75th, shot through the head while charging the battery. Captain Light was wounded lightly in the head by a grape shot. The killed of the 5th in the rice fields were about twenty-four. The Horse Artillery and Lancers followed in pursuit; but both sides of the roads being lined by gardens, these had to be cleared before we advanced. We dressed the wounded in the fields, and brought them on in doolies. We found it the greatest trouble to get the bearers to advance, and with assistants who are afraid, it is no easy matter. The enemy retreated fast, but kept firing grape from an 18-pounder whenever we came in sight. Their cavalry also threatened to charge several times, but grape soon made them change their intention and gallop off. All houses were fired as we advanced, so our course was a melancholy sight. Bodies lying with frightful wounds, shot and shell strewing the ground, while horses, cattle, etc., killed, lay here and there; broken guns, carts, ammunition wagons, left by the enemy, and burning houses on each side, gave one a low opinion of the "circumstance of glorious war." Our advance was slow, the gardens being full of rebel Sepoys. One column was detached to the left, and advanced to cantonments up the Mall. Captain Money's troop was with them. The enemy had a battery at the flagstaff tower with four guns. A few shrapnel falling among them sent them off, leaving their guns. They spiked one, but they did not wait to do more. The last attempt at a stand made by the enemy was in a village, Subzee Mundi, about one mile from Delhi. They were soon driven out, leaving their 18-pounder in our hands. The houses were set on fire, and all the goods destroyed. Everything was as if the inhabitants had only retired on our approach. We turned off the Delhi road to the left, and proceeded along a road which runs behind the rocky ridge which overhangs Delhi. Behind this we were perfectly safe, the shot whistling harmlessly over our heads. Only one part of this road was exposed to a gun, at the Lahore gate, and whenever any body of men were seen a shot was

2

sure to reach them. Until the heavy guns crossed this place, we remained with a portion of the Carabiniers in a hollow. The range of this ridge at this point the rascals had to a nicety, and every shot struck somewhere near. Captain Light got one 18-pounder into position to reply, but he had no sooner done so than it was dismounted by the firing from the city. At this place we lost two men cut in two; over it we advanced as quickly as possible. I, being on foot, kept to a nullah on the left. At the summit of this road is what is called Hindoo Rao's house, two stories high, strongly built of stone. In here the Ghoorkhas had got quarters, looting everything. The enemy fired several shots into it, but without doing any damage. Near this house is an old mosque, which is commanded by a gun. The Carabiniers, while passing it, lost two men by one shot. The enemy's practice is wonderfully good, but it is accounted for by the continual practice. These were the guns we heard so often at Ghazi-u-din-nagar and other places. Near the mosque one of Major Scott's tumbrils was set on fire by a shot from the city. No one was killed, but poor Davidson had his clothes set on fire, and his face, hands and legs severely burned. It is only superficial, and although it will lay him up for long, he will recover without being marked. One or two native drivers were also slightly burnt. After waiting some time at Hindoo Rao's, went down to our encampment, which is on the parade ground close to the native lines, and about two miles from Delhi. The cantonments are all in ruins, having all been fired. Our camp is not beyond the reach of shot, but there is no gun bearing directly on it. That our movements were not directed in the best way, and that we wanted due activity is agreed to by all. Our greatest want is good cavalry, the heavy being of little use against such a foe. The number of guns captured was thirteen; one 24-pounder, two 18-pounders, one 8-inch howitzer, six 6-pounders, and three 9-pounders. Our heavy guns not having arrived with the siege train, we were doomed to remain in inactivity. The enemy disturbed us now and then by a round shot, whenever any body of men were seen on the ridge. These, however, did little harm to anyone. About four p.m., being curious to know what we were doing, and wishing to entice the Ghoorkhas to join, the enemy came out of the city in considerable numbers and advanced against the heights. The Ghoorkhas were the only troops up there, but they, with Major Scott's guns, were sufficient to keep them back until reinforcements arrived. They then returned to the city, having obtained what they desired, but probably not encouraged at seeing us encamping. During the evening they kept firing in all directions, and throwing out feelers to annoy us. They did not succeed in pitching any into our camp. The dressing of the wounded kept us employed all the afternoon. It is extraordinary that the Artillery lost no one all day, although exposed to all the firing. The savages of villagers, after the troops passed, came out and butchered all the wounded. Several of the Lancers were brought in hacked in pieces. After this, my first day of actual firing, I must confess it is a very disagreeable sensation being under fire. The uncertainty of your fate and your total inactivity—having none of the excitement of the officer to make you regardless of danger—gives you time to think. The medical man, although under fire, has to be cool and retain all his presence of mind, without which he can be of little use in performing his duties. With shot and shell falling around you it is no easy matter. After seeing the horrid wounds and gashes inflicted upon men full of health and spirit, now groaning in agony, I am of opinion that the pomp and circumstance of glorious war is only an idea emanating from a poet's brain, and that there is no Christian man who can look on it but with abhorrence. The present fighting is a necessity; we are not fighting alone to revenge our murdered brethren, but also for our own lives. From the enemy coming out this evening, the mutineers cannot be greatly depressed by their defeat, but show considerable pluck in coming out again. That the capture of Delhi will not be so easy, as supposed, is now the belief of all, and that our force is small enough for the work it has before it. The enemy stopped their firing during the night, but something kept them engaged on the other side of the city, shots being heard in that direction.

June 9th. Cholera has, I am sorry to say, appeared in camp. One man of ours died last evening. Two of the medical men of H.M. 75th have been seized with it—Surgeon Coglan and Assistant-Surgeon Whytock. The corps of Guides came in this morning under Captain Daly. Their arrival is very welcome at present. They consist of cavalry and infantry. Davidson is doing well; eyesight not injured. Our heavy guns are being placed in position, and will be ready to open fire about mid-day. The first shot from ours was about one p.m., so the siege of Delhi may be said to have commenced. About three p.m. the enemy began to come out to the number of about two thousand men. They advanced up the woody height to the right of Hindoo Rao's house. They called out to the Ghoorkhas to come over to them; the only reply was a volley. The Guides and Rifles, in spite of the rocky ground, drove them back into the city. The former followed them up to the Lahore gate. Whenever any group of rebels was seen our guns sent shot and shell among them. They brought out a nine-pounder gun, but after firing a few rounds, it was silenced by Major Scott's guns. Our loss was not severe, but several officers were wounded. Lieutenant Battye, second in command of Guides, was wounded mortally; Lieutenant Hayes, their adjutant, slightly wounded; one private was killed. None of the Rifles fell. One of the Sappers was killed in the battery. Our mortars are being erected; one is already in position. Our firing in the early part of the day was bad, but improved, and some good shots were taken by an 18-pounder. One shot entering in at the embrasure of a gun, a shell was dropped at the side of same. About eight p.m. a fire was seen near one of the gates, it was caused by a carcase; after burning for some time it flickered and went out.

June 10th. All quiet during the night. A spy was caught last evening near our right battery. Our guns are too far distant from the city to do much execution—1,500 yards. What is to be done no one seems to know. The warrant officers are showing cowardice; the Brigadier threatens to hang one or two. The troops at Jullundur have revolted, and gone off towards Peshawur. Surgeon Coglan, of the 75th, died last night; the Assistant-Surgeon still alive, and getting better. Lieutenant Battye died this afternoon, greatly regretted by his men. I went up in the morning to Hindoo Rao's house. The road up is rather dangerous, the round shot striking among the rocks. A piece of shell fell about ten yards off where I was. Our guns still firing with little effect. In the evening the mutineers again came up the woody heights, accompanied with two guns and some cavalry. The Ghoorkhas and guides kept them in check, but did not pursue, as the guns and cavalry were drawn up, expecting them to fall into the trap. We lost two artillerymen yesterday; they were in the act of drinking when a round shot came and killed them. The Ghoorkhas lost three men; one gunner and four or five guides were wounded. It appears that the rebels have always some men posted in the hollow immediately below the pass where we lost the men on the 8th. The ground at this place is so rough, thickly wooded, with large boulders, that, if they had a little courage, they could do us a great deal of harm. The remains of the murdered officers of the 54th N.I., five in number, were found last night near the flagstaff tower. The bodies had been sent up from the Cashmere gate in a cart. Colonel Ripley had gone with his regiment to stop the mutineers from Meerut. He, unfortunately, did not make his men load their muskets. When the rebels fired, the regiment, of course, ran off, leaving their officers to their fate. Good news from Calcutta—the arrival of six Queen's regiments; so in a little time we shall have the upper-hand again. The 75th, on the 8th, lost 25 killed and 54 wounded; the 9th Lancers, 15 killed and 10 wounded—total casualties, 51 killed, 132 wounded.

June 11th. This morning, soon after daylight, shells and round shot came dropping into the Carabiniers' lines at the extreme right of our encampment. Their tents were all removed before any damage was done. A false alarm about 11.30 p.m. last night. Cholera, I am sorry to say, is on the increase. Four of the artillery admitted, and one death to-day. They never come into hospital until collapsed, when medicine is useless. Very quiet all day. A European woman came into camp from Delhi. The inhabitants have all left this side of the city, and have gone, to escape the shot, to the other side. The woman tells us that they have only provisions for five days, but the country being open on the other side, they will have no difficulty in procuring supplies. Our guns kept silent almost all day, firing being found useless, and wasting our ammunition.

June 12th. We fire a great deal towards morning. About 5.30 a.m., continuous firing of musketry heard towards our right flank. It arose from the Guides, who are posted near the Subzee Mundi, set on fire by us on the 8th. It is on the high road to Delhi, and about one and a half miles from the Lahore gate. The firing increasing, the troops all turned out, and our batteries at Hindoo Rao's house began to throw shells into it. The enemy had come out in a very strong body and tried to turn our flank. The village was soon again on fire, and the Rifles and guides, supported by the 1st Fusiliers, drove them out of the gardens and houses in which they were. One party of thirty were caught in one place by the Rifles, and everyone killed. There were some irregular cavalry out, but a round shot from one of our guns sent them to the right about. The Guides' cavalry pursued them. After an hour's continuous roar of musketry there was a lull, but some of the 1st Europeans beating the gardens, came upon small parties who had been separated from the main body, and prevented from reaching Delhi by our troops intercepting them. Not a man escaped. The enemy's loss must have been severe. It is said that the inhabitants of the city are getting discontented at their houses being shelled, and insist on the mutineers going out and driving us away. This attack was intended for yesterday, but the rebels are not fond of fighting, having plenty of loot. Two of our guns had a narrow escape of being spiked at the flagstaff tower. The piquet of the 75th was being relieved, when the rebels were seen coming up a nullah to the left. Instead of our men lying down on the top of the ridge, they lay some distance on this side. The rebels consequently reached the top where the guns were. They advanced about fifteen paces further, when the 75th started up, fired a volley, and drove them down the hill with the bayonet. Captain Knox, commanding, was killed. One Sepoy was shot about two hundred yards from our powder magazine. The number of the enemy killed, according to the general dispatch, is three hundred. One party of the Rifles came upon forty-nine of them in a garden, where all were bayonetted without a casuality on our side. Our killed were four of the 75th, and eleven wounded; four of the Guides fell; none of the 60th. The conduct of the Guides was admirable; they bore the whole brunt of the fighting. Ever since their arrival they have always been on duty, although after a march of 580 miles in 22 days. Cholera still the same; three fresh admissions to-day; but it is solely confined to the battery, none of the troop being affected. This afternoon a shell fell to the right of our tent, about fifty yards; it buried itself and went out, which was lucky, as the place was surrounded by cattle, hackeries, etc. It was wrapped round with rags, and although and 8-inch one it had the fuse of a five. Towards evening the firing increased. They have now got a mortar erected, but their firing with it is bad. After sunset I sat watching the shells in their course. The parabola described is beautiful, but the beauty is forgotten by the explosion which immediately follows. To-night at mess it began to be whispered that an assault would take place early to-morrow morning. Of course it was not generally known, in case it might reach the rebels. Our guns kept firing continuously all night.

June 13th. On awakening this morning found everything quiet. The regiment had all paraded at one a.m., and some men marched off, but from some misunderstanding they did not know where to go, and the piquets not having orders to join, everything went amiss, and this golden opportunity was missed; when it will take place now is unknown. Several spies have been caught at Hindoo Rao's house, and immediately hanged. One man of the 38th N.I. returned to Delhi, but not having brought some desirable news, was sent back again, but being seized, was hanged. It appears that the fault this morning was owing to Brigadier Graves having neglected to give some orders. The Rifles and Guides were within four hundred yards of the gates, and no alarm was given. Our hope of capturing at present is over. Very quiet all day. Towards evening the alarm sounded and the troops turned out, but the enemy had been driven back by the piquets. Lieutenant Kennedy was dangerously wounded. Several of the Guides and Ghoorkhas were killed yesterday. A body of about one thousand men were seen crossing the bridge of boats, probably flying from the city. They were fired upon by their own comrades.

June 14th. How different from the quiet and sober Sabbath of Scotland ? How little we value it when there ? How many of us are fated never to see it again, is only known to a merciful Providence. The distant booming of guns every now and then recalls the dangerous work we are engaged in. Went to the flagstaff tower to see what was going on. Delhi and the surrounding country were under a haze, and the stillness of early morning was only broken by the roar of a cannon. What a dreadful thing that man alone should mar the beauties of such a scene ! News was brought in that the enemy were coming out in great force to attack us. To-day was dreadfully warm. One of the Sikh regiments is expected in to-day. The dâk is again stopped at Allygurh. Four Sepoys were shot this morning at this side of the ridge at Hindoo Rao's house. They had got over during the night, and remained in concealment expecting to fall in with some officer. Two of the Rifles discovered them, and two were shot with one bullet, the other two were also killed. News has been received that the mutineers, having no doctors, bury the wounded with the dead. This will have a great effect on their fighting. Everything was arranged for an assault this evening, but it was reported that four or five hundred Pandys were collected in some gardens on our right flank, so it was delayed. Two heavy guns have been mounted on the mound to the right of our camp.

June 15th. The enemy probably heard of our intended attack, as their firing became quite incessant about one a.m. Cholera has abated, and I hope no more cases may occur. About six a.m. this morning the alarm was sounded, firing of musketry began at the mosque where our left mortar battery is. It continued very sharply for about an hour. It was chiefly confined to the piquets. As soon as it had ceased in this quarter it commenced on the ridge below Hindoo Rao's house. Here a large body of the enemy had come, with a green flag among them. They kept at a respectful distance, but still firing. Our heavy guns on the mound fired two shots—one with shrapnel—when they retired. Another alarm sounded about ten a.m. Our men were all ready, but after a little firing of musketry near our batteries, the enemy retired. Colonel Chamberlain has been made adjutant-general, Colonel Nicholson, Brigadier commanding the Punjaub moveable column. Every symptom of the approaching rains—the horizon in the mornings and evenings being misty, with great heat during the day—we shall be in a bad way if the rain overtakes us before taking Delhi.

June 16th. Reinforcements are on their way down from the Punjaub—a wing of H.M. 8th and 61st, etc. The 4th

Sikh Infantry left Umballa on the 8th ult. Dr. S. Batson has been appointed field surgeon. Time is beginning to feel slow in its movements. Books are scarce and eagerly sought after. The firing last night stopped from nine p.m. until three a.m., when the enemy sent several shot and shell in quick succession, after which all again became silent. We are to wait until the European troops arrive, then throw up some parallels, form a breach, and take the city in this way. A battery is being thrown up in Sir T. Metcalf's compound. but unless well guarded the guns will be in great danger. The 18th N.I. have mutinied at Bareilly, and all the officers, except three, are said to have been murdered. It is said they came into Delhi to-day; if so, they will probably try their hands with us. The same regiment never comes out twice. One hundred recruits (Artillery) and forty of the Rifles are ordered from Meerut. Very quiet all day. The enemy try to throw mortar shells into our camp, but they always burst high in air.

June 17th. Hardly a gun was fired last night. The guns that bear on us are placed on the Lahore and Cash mere gates. There is an 18-pounder on the first which enfilades Hindoo Rao's house, causing us much damage. Their firing is best from a battery in front of the English church, near the Cashmere gate. A day or two ago, a sergeant of the 2nd Europeans found in the shot belt of a mutineer (a subadar of the 74th), a Government paper to the amount of 4,200 rupees. This is a proof that their rebellion arises from some cause affecting, or supposed to affect, their best interests. That a man, especially a Hindoo, should give up this amount, probably all his savings, and turn rebel with such uncertainties, can only be accounted for from some fanaticism. A round-shot to-day killed an officer, two Carabiniers, and two of the Ghoorkhas. The former, Ensign Wheatly, 54th N.I., was doing duty with the Ghoorkhas. He was asleep at the time. The shot struck the wall and broke into fragments. This evening eight hundred men were sent out with some light field pieces to destroy the battery the enemy were erecting on our right at the Ead serai. It met with perfect success, their entrenchments were destroyed, and one gun, a 9-pounder, was captured. Our men got into the centre of the enemy who were concealed in thick cover, and were exposed for some time to heavy fire. Major Tombs had two horses wounded under him, and got a graze from a bullet in arm. The greater part of the enemy were in a large serai (the Ead), from which they fled on the Rifles opening fire. They took shelter in another building too near the walls for us to follow. Our loss was trifling. A captain of the Fusiliers was severly wounded. About one hundred of the enemy are said to have fallen. The capture of this gun will prove rather disheartning to their courage, even now at a low ebb. They run whenever they catch sight of us, unless when in such broken ground that one man is as good as another. Major Tombs has had five horses killed and wounded under him since this commenced.

June 18th. Waterloo Day. This, the most glorious day in English history, finds us (the descendents of those heroes who bore the fate of Europe in their hands), fighting for the brightest gem in England's Crown—India. One hundred years have elapsed since Clive first commenced at Plassy, the glorious history of our Indian victories. Is it fated that we are to lose this bright empire? At present there are no warnings, and with the taking of Delhi the tranquility of India will be restored. This day I enter upon my twenty-fourth year—what a change from this day last year—little did I imagine then, in Scotland, to be campaigning at the next anniversary. Where shall I be next year on this day? This is only known to the Almighty. Rumour says, to-day at Cawnpore the rebels have risen, and the Europeans are fighting with them. At Bareilly, it is said, the magistrate, Mr. Robertson, and the civil surgeon, Dr. Hay, were hanged. At Shahjehanpore, the 28th N.I., rumour says, attacked the residents when in church, and murdered all. After such atrocities, what can be expected when Delhi is stormed but indiscriminate slaughter.

June 19th. The rains are still keeping off, but the mornings are still very cloudy and hazy. A good deal of firing last night, but no damage done. All remained quiet until four p.m., when word came from our batteries that the enemy were issuing from the Lahore gate in somewhat regular order, and in a large body. They went a long circuit, and came in upon our rear, about one and a half miles. A spy who came in told us there were two regiments of infantry, five hundred cavalry, and six guns. The infantry were some of those who had lately joined them, and on demanding a share of loot, were told they would get none until they went out and fought with us. Our troops immediately turned out, but, being sent to our right, they lost the opportunity of attacking the enemy on their flank movement. After an hour wasted in doing nothing, Major Tombs was ordered to take his guns, with some of the Guides' cavalry, and proceed down the road to our rear. Brigadier Grant was officer of the day. At a gallop they proceeded for more than a mile, when they suddenly came on their foes with all their guns. To retire was impossible without losing the guns, so a stand was made, relief being expected in a short time. The enemy kept firing grape and round shot, which flew harmlessly over the troops heads. We replied with the same, and with more effect. The Pandys, on seeing the guns unsupported, plucked up courage, and advanced after as near as forty yards, and picked off the gunners. Captain Daly tried to charge, but with only partial success. He was severely wounded in the shoulder. The Lancers also charged, but the road being lined by walls, they could not get at them. In about three quarters of an hour the Rifles arrived, but only advanced a few yards and began firing, instead of charging the guns. This is the evil of the Enfield rifle; the men prefer taking long shots when they are sheltered, to advancing. The 1st Fusiliers soon after came up, they passed the Rifles, but did not advance to the guns. One of the enemy's ammunition waggons was blown up by our fire. Darkness coming on, and our men beginning to fire at each other, we were obliged to retire; our loss was severe, but the firing was sharper than any day as yet. We lost Major Yule, 9th Lancers (missing); Lieutenant Alexander, 3rd N.I., killed; and Lieutenant Humphreys, wounded mortally. Tombs' troop alone lost one killed and five wounded. This was a dreadfully mismanaged affair, no one seeming to know anything, and orders being given and executed by whoever chose. Colonel Becher, the quartermaster-general, ordered out the troops on his own responsibility. He was wounded in the arm, and no one seems sorry at it. If infantry had been sent forward at once, we should have captured their guns and turned them out of the gardens where they were posted. Artillery and cavalry are almost useless in such a place; what their object in this daring movement was is uncertain. To seize our camels—in this they partly succeeded, making off with about one hundred (since recovered), or was it to attack our reinforcements, or take in with them some of their mutinous comrades on their way down? As to cutting off our supplies, they must know we would not tamely allow this, but turn them out at whatever cost.

June 20th. Everything remained quiet during the night. Twelve of our light guns with eight hundred infantry and most of the cavalry went out at daylight, but found the enemy had retreated from the gardens, leaving their dead. Major Yule's body was brought in dreadfully mangled. About two hundred of the enemies' dead were seen. We found one 9-pounder and two empty ammunition waggons. Some panic must have seized them. They are said to have taken up a position at a greater distance to our rear. Our troops had only arrived in camp when the enemy were seen approaching. The alarm sounded, and off our guns went. Our troops assembled at the other side of the canal; the guns of two troops in the centre, the cavalry on each flank, while the infantry lay down in the rear to escape the shot the enemy were firing. As soon as our guns advanced and opened fire the enemy retired, and whenever they attempted a stand our shot soon drove them off. Some panic seized them, probably thinking we were cutting them off from Delhi. From whatever cause they were seen rushing into the Lahore gate in a tumultuous body and in a great fright, which was not allayed by our 24-pounder playing upon them. One of the 1st Bombay Lancers was caught this morning wounded. He, with twelve others, had fled from Nuseerabad. He pretends to be very penitent and demands mercy. The Bagh Pat bridge has been broken down by the Goopirs, so that the recruits and stores from Meerut must now come *via* Karnal. It is said that the demonstration to our rear was to meet the Jullundur mutineers, which they did. Guns almost silent all day. Flies, for which Delhi is famous, are becoming most troublesome. They enter the tents in legions, and are the most persevering and active tribe I ever saw. Nothing daunted by attempts at their life, they return buzzing and will not be driven off, so that passive resistance is all one can do, until one more bold than his comrades begins frisking over some part more sensitive than the rest when your anger rises, and after a fruitless attempt you are content to return to your usual apathy.

June 21st. All our camels have been recaptured, so we have come off better than we deserve. Another Sunday, and still encamped as on last. The capture of Delhi being as far distant as on the 8th. Waiting for reinforcements which are expected about the 24th. Our small force not being sufficient to hold it if taken. The rebels are said to have occupied the same position at Bad-ki-Serai that cost us so many lives on the 8th. This requires confirmation. The recruits are not coming from Meerut, General Hewitt considering the roads too disturbed. The Jheend Rajah has been sent out to repair the Bagh Pat bridge. Lieutenant Daly is getting on better than at first expected. A false alarm about 2.30 p.m. The enemies' cavalry was seen crossing the bridge of boats. Six or seven cannon shots heard at the other side of Delhi, probably they are fighting among themselves. A new battery has been erected on our rear and armed with two 18-pounders.

June 22nd. Yesterday was the longest day—it is now light until about 7.30 p.m. All quiet. Days are very warm; they are generally so before the rain. The dâk from the N.W. comes in daily, none from the south for weeks. At Mussoorie there have been several alarms, bridges being broken down, etc., to prevent the approach of an imaginary enemy; the next day the servants are to murder them all; and on a third that the food is poisoned. We have it from good authority that in Delhi there is a scarcity of powder, and that they are manufacturing it at the rate of four maunds per day. The immense quantity in the powder magazine in cantonments was, as soon as the guard left, attacked by the Zemindars and Goopirs, and most of it removed to the neighbouring villages. Warned of a grand attack that was to be made on us at daylight to-morrow morning on our right flank and rear. Preparations are being made accordingly.

June 23rd. The first of our reinforcements came in this morning. The 1st troop, 1st brigade H.A. under Major

Olpherts, 120 men of the 75th, 250 of the 2nd Fusiliers, and a portion of the 4th Sikh Infantry. They brought in a large convoy of ammunition. Near this they were followed by some Sowars, but a few rounds from the guns, killing several, set them to flight. A continuous fire of shot and shell from Delhi all night. Our troops turned out at daylight. The enemy were as usual posted in the gardens and houses of the Subzee Mundi, on our right flank. The firing commenced about six a.m., and continued with little intermission all day. The object of their attack was the capture of our 24-pounder battery, and their shot killed and wounded fifteen men in this one alone. The fighting in the village was obstinate, every house being loop-holed and full of these rascals. From one to the other they were at last driven, but our men became so done up that they could not seize upon two guns which were about two hundred yards from them, and only required a rush to obtain. The day was cloudy, but oppressively warm. The rebels got into a large white house, two storied, where they kept our men long at bay. There was no entrance to be found into it, so they kept popping away at the windows. At last they were driven from this and from the entire village, retreating towards the large serai (the Ead) which we attacked on the 17th. Our men being now quite useless, having been out from five a.m. until five p.m., we did not advance, but remained in the village until sunset, when our men were brought in. Our loss must have been great with such difficulties to contend against. It is a pity that when these houses are in our possession they are not destroyed, as they are always reoccupied. Want of powder is the excuse. This is the centenary of the battle of Plassy. Oh! for another Clive at this crisis. The Pandys were told if we were not all killed to-day, we would conquer. The Rifles lost 4 killed and about 20 wounded; the 1st Fusiliers, 10 killed and 24 wounded; the 2nd Fusiliers, 4 killed, 8 wounded; the Guides, 10 killed and 9 wounded—total killed and wounded, about 150. The only officer killed was Lieutenant Jackson, 2nd Europeans. Captain Jones, H.M. 60th, wounded. News has come in that the whole Gwalior contingent have mutinied, and are on their way to attack Agra. No officers mentioned as killed with the troops there, and those on their way up; there should be little fear. These rascals have, however, a third-class siege train and three companies of artillery. The Bagh Pat bridge is repaired, and the Jheend force protecting it.

June 24th. Very quiet last night, except a fire of musketry that was kept up for three or four hours from the walls of Delhi. Their sentries proclaim "all's well" by firing their muskets. Last night they must have expected an assault. A reinforcement of forty-five artillerymen came in this morning. Went to the flagstaff tower and watched the firing. That of the enemy is excellent. Every shot from their battery near the Cashmere gate, striking the sand-bags of our left. They have erected a new battery at the end of the "bridge of boats," on a point of land jutting into the river called the Selim Ghar.

June 25th. Still continuing the same monotonous existence. Now and then the booming of a gun alone breaks the stillness and reminds us of the siege. The enemy are said to be coming out to-morrow morning. The Morey gate is beginning to look dilapidated; the 24-pounders in our battery keeping its fire down.

June 26th. All the troops were out at daylight, but although small bodies of men came out, they did not attack us. News from Umballa that 450 men of H.M. 61st, and Coke's Irregulars, in all about 1,500 men, had left there on the evening of the 24th. They ought to reach this about the 30th. H.M. 8th is in front, and is daily expected. Sir John Lawrence is assembling an army of 40,000 Sikhs in the Punjaub. The report of so many having fallen at at Bareilly was untrue, most of the officers having reached Nynee Tal. Until a gun was fired the Sepoys had remained true in appearance, and had even told their officers to recall their wives from the hills as they would be quite safe. This had luckily not been done. Such is the Sepoy who has been petted until, like a spoilt child, he resents. He has proved himself regardless of every oath and tie, forgetful of all the kindness bestowed upon him; of the salt he has for years been eating, and for the sake of a few rupees has risked his life and that of his family. What worse enormities could have been performed by mortals? And yet this is the quiet inoffensive Hindoo who it has been long the custom to pity and regard as an oppressed race. This ill-used race will soon find, when under no laws but that of the strongest, that their rising has been rash and ill-timed. When this crisis is over, he must be ruled as a servant, and kept in his place, not treated and supported as a pampered dependant.

June 27th. The attack expected yesterday, took place

this morning. Although not issuing in large bodies, they were still numerous. By five a.m. we were ready for them. They again attempted to take our right heavy battery, it being a great annoyance to them. They were as usual driven back. At our piquet, in front of Metcalf's compound, there was a great deal of firing, but with little loss on our side. The enemy lost about fifty here. The Pandys were driven back, but took shelter in the Ead Serai towards the Lahore gate, where they fought obstinately. They brought out three or four guns, which annoyed those in our batteries, but not causing loss. The firing continued until about two p.m. Major Scott's company lost one man killed and two wounded (one mortally); H.M. 60th, one killed and four wounded. The 2nd Fusiliers lost most, having borne the brunt of the fight. The rains commenced to-day about eleven a.m., and it kept pouring almost without intermission until five p.m. Our tent being on a high piece of ground remained dry, but many others were in a miserable plight. When we went out in the evening, the sight was singular. Between us and the hospital tents was a large pool of water, with a stream running into it. The tents looked like floating islands, being surrounded on all sides by water. We had to wade to reach them. Luckily the floors had all been raised in the morning, and the men being on charpoys, they were all dry. After getting men to work, the water was drained off to a tank in the rear. What will it be when the rain continues for days instead of hours.

June 28th. It rained a good deal during the night, but the camp looked dry in the morning. It began to clear up soon after daylight, but every appearance of a showery day. The wind was S.W. yesterday; to-day it has veered towards the west. H.M. 8th came in this morning, about six hundred men. There were also two guns belonging to the 5th troop 1st brigade. The gunners are natives. It is commanded by Lieutenant Renny. Lots of ammunition also came in. It is rumoured that the troops seen issuing from Delhi on the 26th, have occupied the bridge at Bagh Pat, and intend cutting off our communication with Meerut. Another Sunday and still before Delhi. By the *Lahore Chronicle* we find that nine European regiments have arrived in Calcutta. From Delhi the last news is that the King has issued a proclamation, ordering all the women to be massacred whenever our troops get within the walls.

June 29th. It rained for a short time last night. Met Hunter of the 2nd Europeans this morning. Except in being stouter and more set, he is not changed since leaving Edinburgh. Lieutenant Hodson, 1st Europeans, rode out to Bagh Pat. He found the bridge broken but no enemy. He brought away what boats remained. The Lieutenant-Governor, Mr. Colvin, the papers say, has been superseded by Sir H. Wheeler, on account of his proclamation offering pardon to all Sepoys who came in except those who had committed any atrocities. In Oude, when the 48th and 71st N.I. mutined, Brigadier Handscomb and three officers were killed; three wounded. Colonel Longfield, H.M. 8th, has succeeded Brigadier Graves, the latter being sent to the hills as useless. Yesterday and during the night scarcely a gun was fired.

June 30th. Fortune is indeed on our side. The greatest piece of luck that could have happened occurred last night. The bridge of boats at Delhi was partially carried away by the sudden rise of the Jumna, and several boats have been destroyed. Its repair will take some time. This was what everyone was anxious to see done, but no one could devise a plan. Guns have been erected to command it, and booms placed so as to prevent any burning vessel being sent down. "There is a divinity who shapes our ends, rough hew them how we will." Everything has gone well with us since the commencement of this campaign, yet we have shown no great ability, no daring. This morning the enemy came out with some guns; the firing continued some four or five hours; the Pandys were driven back as usual, but we lost severely—about fifty killed and wounded. Among the latter are two officers of the Sikh corps, Lieutenant Yorke (since dead), and Lieutenant Parke, who will probably recover. Our losses before Delhi have been greater than if we had assaulted it at first. The enemy began to take up a position in front of the Ead Serai, on the right. Towards evening about eight hundred men, under Brigadier Showers, were sent out to capture the guns. They, however, had been removed about two p.m. Our troops, after marching uphill, had just to march down again. Several houses were burnt, but no enemy was seen.

July 1st. From the flagstaff battery, saw the Bareilly mutineers crossing the Jumna. The bridge of boats has all been repaired, except at the left bank, where there is a space about one hundred yards without boats. Across this two large barges were ferrying; the current did not appear strong. These Pandys were in no order, but walked in parties of four and five. About three hundred men were waiting on the left bank for the boats. This morning our fire commenced in earnest, the guns all being laid pointing at the Morey bastion. It is expected that a breach can be made at a distance of 1,500 yards. Our firing was good, but two guns from the bastion were fired now and then in reply. Her Majesty's 61st, about 450 men, came in this morning—their band leading them in. Weather has become hot again without rain. This evening the wounded (166) were sent to Umballa under the care of Surgeon S. Batson.

July 2nd. The effect of our fire on the Morey bastion was to breach one side partly in pieces. Coke's Irregulars, the 1st Punjaub Infantry, came in this morning, numbering about 1,000 men. From Agra, we hear that two European regiments are expected there by the 4th; probably the 84th Queen's, and the Madras Fusiliers. At Cawnpore, there had been several days hard fighting, but Sir H. Wheeler had got the upper hand. Colonel M. Mackenzie was wounded this morning in the knee by a peice of shell, but not severely. He would be a very great loss at present; I hope he may be soon well again. The Bareilly force have, it is said, about three hundred rupees apiece. It has not come too soon, as we hear the King is badly off for pay. The Pandys get eight and the Sowars twelve annas a day. When their pay stops so will their allegiance. Jackson is assistant surgeon to Coke's corps. A company consisting of Poorbeas, belonging to the 4th Punjaub regiment, was disarmed this afternoon, the Subadar and Jemadar being hanged. They had tried to get the Ghoorkhas to go over. The 9th Irregular Cavalry are also suspected, and intended leaving for Delhi this morning at the cross roads, but Coke sent on some of his corps and prevented them.

July 3rd. Last night after an intensely hot day a violent thunder storm came on. The camp was soon flooded, and everything appeared very wretched except the interior of the tents, which were dry. The ground was dry by the morning, the soil being sandy and well drained. Everything was prepared for an assault last night, but at almost the last moment it was again countermanded. This was caused by a report of the enemy being in our rear and going to attack us. This, when reported in Delhi (as it will be without doubt immediately) will put them on their guard. Why publish it until everything is settled, or why assemble regiments and then send them back again? Someone is exceedingly to blame. An attack was expected this morning, but it was not until five p.m. that the alarm sounded. They were seen issuing from the Lahore gate, about three thousand in number, with one heavy gun and five light field pieces. With these were tents, elephants, doolies, etc., in fact, just what we would carry with us on a similar excursion. Their leader was mounted on an elephant with a large umbrella held over him. They took a long circuit; made a bridge across the canal, having brought out materials, and proceeded in a north-westerley direction. Their object, it is supposed, was to capture two lacs of rupees on their way here, with some artillerymen. Our troops went out but saw nothing of them. Weather is getting warmer and warmer daily, it being felt more now that the air is saturated with moisture.

July 4th. About twelve p.m. guns were heard at a long distance in our rear. At the same time a blue light was sent up, and immediately answered at the Cashmere and Ajmir gates. The enemy came out of the city and advanced half up the ridge at the right battery, when they retired. Soon after this some Sowars came into camp, and gave information that the Pandys had attacked Allipore, where Captain Younghusband and some two hundred Sowars were posted. They retired about two miles towards Raie. The village was looted and burnt, but nothing of ours was lost. Before daylight our troops were on the move to intercept them in their return. Captain Money's troop, Scott's battery, H.M. 61st, Coke's Rifles, some squadrons of the Lancers, and the Guides' cavalry were sent out. On coming within fourteen hundred yards we opened fire, but the enemy, after firing, weakly fled, and a running skirmish was kept up. The loss on either side was small, the Pandys thinking discretion the better part of valour. No guns captured, but an ammunition waggon and cart, both full. By whose fault our guns did not approach nearer is uncertain. Two of them stuck for a little in some marshy ground, and this intimidated them from proceeding. The enemy's guns were, some of them, drawn by bullocks, so surely our light field pieces and cavalry could have cut them off. Great mismanagement did occur, and we have lost a grand opportunity of destroying the whole party. When our troops came up they had passed through a village, and were on an open plain with no shelter for about two miles. How our cavalry could stand and see this going on is the fault of the officer in command. Our troops returned after following them some distance. The guns came back to camp, the soldiers remained in a village. While the action was going on about two thousand men came out of Delhi. These, approaching the village about twelve a.m., and seeing only some of the Lancers, expected to cut them to pieces, but Coke's Rifles were hid in a nullah, and the 61st behind a wall. When they had advanced close, the latter jumped up, fired a volley, and went in with the bayonet. The Pandys lost a considerable number. Our guns were again sent out, but before they reached this body had disappeared. The sun being very strong, and the day scarcely bearable, being the hottest we have had, and not a breath of wind, our men suffered exceedingly from the heat. Five men alone of Tomb's troops were brought in. All remained quiet in the rear after this. To show how things are managed, a good instance occurred to-night. Two bridges were said to allow the enemy to cross and re-cross the canal when they chose, and to be of no use to us. After they had been effectually blown up, an order came not to do so as they were found of great benefit to us. Alas! that there is no one of decision in camp. How different if Sir C. Napier had been here, or even if Brigadier Wilson had the command.

July 5th, Sunday. Heard service by Mr. Rotton this morning; he gave us a sermon on the uncertainty of life, which ought, at such a time as this, to be constantly before us. What a commentary on this, is what is occurring at headquarters. Yesterday morning I saw Sir H. Barnard on the flagstaff tower looking well, and watching the progress of the fight. Now he is dying. Early this morning he was seized with cholera. He has overworked himself with writing and anxiety. How radically decayed must the management of an English army be, when it requires its chief to toil to the death. Lord Raglan was one victim, here we have another. Such things never occur among Continental nations. He was chief of the staff in the Crimea, and came out here in place of Wyndham, of Redan celebrity. Although not a great general, being too fond of giving way to the opinions of others, yet he had endeared himself to all who came in contact with him, by his gentlemanly conduct and desire to please everyone when it lay in his power. Certainly, God's ways are not as our ways. Two chiefs of this force have already been struck down by the same dire disease, within a short period, and many less useful officers spared. The General died at three p.m. It seems that sixty of the Jheend Rajah's men were killed at Allipore yesterday. Whether this has disgusted him is likely, as he was faithfully promised assistance whenever in danger of being attacked. At any rate, he is off to his own country to raise more men, he says; probably to wait until affairs take some turn.

July 6th. Had a dreadful storm last night; sky as black as ink; lightning flashing continually, making everything as distinct as daylight. It rained as only tropical storms do, and our camp was soon like a lake, nothing visible but tents and "water, water everywhere." This morning everything, of course, soaking. Heavy clouds floating about give warning of more rain. The 4th Irregulars have bolted from Meerut. A volunteer corps has been raised there, who, with two guns on elephants, go about collecting the revenue. It is now rumoured that we are to await the arrival of Sir H. Wheeler, who is coming up with some European regiments. The rebels in the city are quarrelling again. Last night there was a great commotion, beating of tom-toms, etc. The Bareilly men are told that they ought to go out and fight, while the others remain at home smoking and enjoying themselves. Over this bone of contention they are, it is said, snarling. The treasure (two lacs) came in safely this afternoon, with eighty Artillerymen and a wing of the 17th Irregulars. The latter are not trustworthy, and are to be sent back to their homes. The funeral of Sir H. Barnard took place this morning in the churchyard; it was attended by a great many officers. Major-General T. Reed, C.B., who commanded at Peshawur, and now officiating as Commander-in-Chief, is to be the commander of the force here assembled. He does this to allow Brigadier N. Chamberlain, a capital soldier, to be the director of everything.

July 7th. Weather excessively warm. The flies still tormenting us in swarms. No relief from them, they are so active and persevering. From the city we hear that the King holds frequent durbars, at which the English are represented as monsters of cruelty. The Pandys have only seven lacs (700,000) percussion caps. This appears a large number, but on such an occasion, and with no prospect of getting more, it is small in reality.

July 8th. Rockets were again tried last night, but, as

usual, with only partial success. Two went into the city. The Bareilly force, disgusted with the other mutineers at their cowardice, have left the city, and are encamped outside the walls to the S.W. This morning a force under Brigadier Longfield was sent out to attack them. It consisted of H.M. 8th and 61st, one squadron of Lancers, one squadron of Carabiniers, the Guides' cavalry, 1st Punjaub Infantry, etc., and eighteen guns! Yet with this imposing force nothing was done except blowing up a bridge. Our troops seem perfectly useless in any movements. Of pluck there is no want, but to have it directed in the proper direction seems impossible with the officers we have. No one seems to have any ability when a combined movement is required. The Generals are too old, and want energy. A great deal of firing during the night, which for some time has been unusual.

July 9th. The firing of the enemy became almost incessant towards ten a.m.; about that time the alarm sounded, but, before the men could turn out, about one hundred Sowars of the 8th Irregulars made a charge on our right flank. They got up within charging distance unperceived, the gardens and trees concealing them. At that side we had two guns of Tombs' troop, under Lieutenant Hill; and twenty Carabiniers under Captain Stillman. Hill, to give his men time to load the guns with grape, charged them alone. He cut down two, but he and his horse were knocked down by the rush. The Carabiniers were drawn up, and, when ordered to charge, hesitated, turned and fled; Stillman only got one man to follow. He charged, but no one would come within reach of his sword. The Sowars galloped on, but, on approaching the tents, walked. They asked twice of Colonel Mackenzie's bearer if the sahib was in his tent. He luckily said no. Lieutenant Rudd, on seeing them pass, went out and asked them where they were going. Expecting to escape by attacking no one, they went to the native troops and told the men to follow them. They, however, remained staunch. Being thus disappointed in the object of their attack, they rode down to the churchyard, intending probably to cross at the bridge, and return by the other side of the canal. They were frustrated in this by meeting some of our troops, and returned hesitating. They killed a conductor (European) who was coming in with some ammunition from Umballa; then cut down several of our hospital patients who had run out of the tents on their approach. Two hundred of the Fusiliers were by this time drawn up along the graveyard wall, but some staff officer ordered them not to fire as they were our own men. Several shots from the other side of the wall, from those who were dismounted, opened their eyes. Volley after volley was sent after them as they retreated slowly along the canal, but only three or four fell. The others were pursued, and their leader, with fifteen men, were killed. The former belonged to the 1st Oude Cavalry. In the graveyard two were killed—one who had taken shelter up a tree, and the other hiding below some wood. In the pursuit, one man tried to cross the canal, but his horse fell. He immediately dismounted, took off his boots and uniform, and began washing his "cummer-bund" (waistcloth). This being seen, he was shot. Another party of their cavalry, about two hundred in number, appeared on the other side of the canal, threatening our near battery, but thirty of the Lancers kept firing and intimidated them. A few rounds of shot sent them to the right about. When Hill had picked himself up, he found two men in the act of charging him. One he shot with his pistol, the other Tombs did for. They were in the act of retreating to the mound on their right, when the latter Sowar rose and was making off with Hill's pistol. Tombs and he, on seeing this, went at him. The rascal said his father had been killed by the latter, and that his life would alone atone for it. He kept waving his sword, made a cut at Hill, then at Tombs; both were parried. Hill made a lunge, the fellow jumped aside, giving him a cut across the top of his head. Tombs then ran him through. The cut is not severe, although the outer table is injured in one place. This daring attack, and their slow retreat, is the admiration of everyone, so contrasted with the conduct of our Dragoons. One man immediately behind our tent dismounted from his horse, took that of the apothecary and left his own. Lieutenant Hodson, 1st Europeans, who had raised some Irregulars, came up with some of them. Not suspecting they were the enemy, he asked them where the Sowars were. They pointed in our direction which he took, while they retreated. With the cavalry, a large body of infantry had come out and advanced to our right flank. Brigadier Chamberlain sent one party to attack them, while he and the guns proceeded towards the Subzee Mundi to intercept them. This ruse succeeded, the enemy coming up within a short distance of the guns without seeing them. Grape was immediately poured into them, when they retreated into the walled gardens. From there they were successfully driven, and they at last sought shelter in the Ead-ghur Serai. This they had barricaded, and made quite impregnable, without guns. Scott's battery was brought forward, and the gates blown open. Out of this the Pandys rushed, but were exposed to the musketry of our men ready to receive them. We followed in pursuit, and it was not until the guns at the Lahore gate opened with grape that we retired. The Rifles and the Ghoorkhas had a very hard fight of it when the enemy came out about nine a.m. Their loss was consequently heavy. That of the Pandys must be very great. It kept raining from morning to night, and, although very disagreeable, it made it cool and good for fighting. The whole talk of the camp is the conduct of the Dragoons. Captain Stillman remonstrated with the men, and tried in vain to get them to charge. Only one man named Roberts would do so. The others rushed into camp, many without helmets. Where they went, or whether they reassembled, no one seems to know. Captain S. I saw with the Fusiliers, by himself. Colonel Custance, when he heard of it, put them all under arrest. That something ought to be done to these cowards there is little doubt, as a warning to others, but this remains with the Chief. There is scarcely a precedent in British history, of twenty dragoons on piquet, and entrusted with an important post, being put to flight by one hundred horsemen without firing a shot or making a charge. Alas! for India; if such conduct goes unpunished, our star will soon set. The 14th Dragoons bolted at Chillianwallah, but then they had showed good fight previously, having been well pounded, and like a man who has been well punished in a fight, could not come up to the scratch. The 6th Dragoon Guards had no such excuse, and that they may soon have an opportunity of washing out this stain on their fair name is what everyone wishes. Her Majesty's 8th had 8 killed and 11 wounded; the 61st, 2 killed; the 1st Europeans, only 3 wounded. The loss fell to the Rifles and Ghoorkhas. Total killed, 1 officer (Lieutenant Mountsteven) 8th Queen's, and 40 men; wounded, 180. Total *hors de combat*, 220.

July 10th. Rained almost incessantly last night. This morning fair, but very watery; a strong breeze from the north-east blowing. The enemy are computed to have lost one thousand men killed yesterday. The 14th N.I. have risen at Jhelum. Two companies of H.M. 24th were sent against them, but did not succeed in killing all by evening, although they had two guns with them. Colonel Ellice and an ensign were wounded. Twelve Europeans were killed, and sixty-six wounded. During the night three hundred tried to escape, but, being followed, were cut to pieces. One or two alone swam the Jhelum. Our gun, which they had captured, was found in the river. The enemy came out about four p.m., and attacked our sappers and coolies, destroying walls near the Subzee Mundi. After killing seven or eight of the latter, they retired into the city on the advance of our men. A committee is sitting upon the 9th Irregulars for yesterday's business. Although supported by Brigadier Chamberlain, their old officer, they are to be sent out of camp, and the 17th Irregulars from Allipore brought in.

July 11th. Rained all last night. Everyone preparing for it. Our encampment is said to be under water at this season. If this be the case, which is doubted by some, fever will be raging amongst us soon. News has arrived that the 46th N.I. have risen at Sealkote, and that everyone had been killed. The Punjaub movable column was on its way to disarm them, but the Pandys got word and took the initiative. The day before yesterday eight regiments came out and three remained in. Their commander is said to be a Subadar of the 28th N.I. Three cannon were carried about the city to-day, and a crier proclaimed them as having been taken from *us* at the last fight. This was to stimulate them to attack us again. The spy said it was arranged for to-morrow morning at four p.m. Eckford rode over from Meerut with Mr. Saunders, late judge of Muradabad. They met with no opposition, but everyone seemed anxious to assist them. The former is on the Quartermaster-General's department.

July 12th, Sunday. The enemy's cavalry tried last night to come into camp, past the piquet at Metcalf's house, but were driven back Hot and close this morning, like a green-house in England. Everything green is shooting up with a rapidity only seen in the tropics. Heavy showers occur three or four times a day. No attack this morning as expected. It is said that in the city the Pandys are beginning to open their eyes, and that they have no hope of beating us. Having implicated themselves so far, they are determined to fight to the last. The Hindoos are said to be quarrelling with the Mussulmen; the latter insisting on killing cattle for food. Firing has been heard all day towards the N.E. Some

Europeans, so the spies from the city say, are advancing up country, and that the men have gone out to blow up the Hindan bridge. No other authority is given for this rumour. The Native Troop in camp (the 5th of the 1st brigade) were disarmed this evening; not because they gave any symptoms of mutiny, but because the rest of it had been similarly treated in the moveable column. The 9th Irregulars, known to be ill-disposed, have retained their arms; while natives who had fought along with us, and were staunch, are disarmed. The men burst into tears when they heard what was to be done, and requested to be allowed to fight alongside the Europeans. They may have been crocodile tears; but why not act up to a principle, and disarm the whole native army?

July 13th. News from Agra of the 7th ultimo. On that day the Neemuch mutineers approached to attack. The 3rd Europeans, the 2nd company 5th battalion, under Captain Doyly, and the Kotah contingent went out to attack them. After some fighting the contingent went over to the enemy. One of our guns was taken, and Captain Doyly killed. We captured two of the contingents. Our troops retired in good order into the fort. The cantonments were all burned down. Colonel M. Mackenzie's Troop was at Neemuch, and was the one that came there. It is the 4th Troop, 1st Brigade Native. The King is said to have intercepted a letter for us, in which it says (so the spy says), that 1,600 Europeans are about Allygurh, and that at Benares about 7,000 are collected under Sir P. Grant. The first cannot be true, as at Agra, nothing has been heard of them; the latter is probably correct. One report says that Sir H. Wheeler is with the former, another, that he is holding his own at Cawnpore with 200 men, and some Sikhs, against all the Oude mutineers and the inhabitants. The regiments composing the 1,600 are even mentioned: the 35th and 47th, and 84th Queen's, and the Ceylon Rifles. A salute of one hundred guns was fired this morning at the other side of the city, probably on account of the Agra affair, which they will claim as a victory. From the moveable column we hear that a drummer of the 46th N.I. had been sent off on the breaking out of the mutiny at Sealkote. He acquaints us with few particulars, but that Brigadier Brind had been wounded, and Captain Bishop (46th) killed. The column was waiting to see where the mutineers were going, then follow and cut them off, as it is impossible for them to escape from the Doab. A letter came in from Sir J. Lawrence this evening, with the information from Lord Canning, that on the 11th June 4,200 Europeans had left Calcutta, and that 3,000 would follow towards the end of the month. He added that Sir H. Wheeler would be by this time, about Allygurh. This accounts for the native report, and for the Pandys seen crossing the bridge of boats.

July 14th. Another convoy of ammunition came in yesterday from Umballa with fifty Sikh Artillerymen. The enemy are beginning to fire badly, their gunners having been killed, it is said. Their shells rarely burst, as fuses are scarce, obliging them to use portfires. The enemy came out in a large body this morning. Our men were ordered to remain concealed, and waste as little ammunition as possible. From nine a.m. until three p.m. the firing of the

Pandys was continuous, yet, strange to say, not one of our men was killed. Their attack was on the Subzee Mundi, and our right battery. About 3.30 the enemy began to press onwards, emboldened by seeing no one. Reinforcements were sent out. The 1st Europeans advancing, came unawares upon a large body of the Pandys lying concealed, and were exposed for some time to a most deadly fire. This body and the others of the rebels soon retired, we pursuing them with Turner's Troop almost up to the walls. We advanced too far from ignorance of the ground, and came under fire of grape from their guns. This put Coke's Rifles into some disorder, and the enemy trying to take advantage of this, began to come out in pursuit with some cavalry, but our heavy guns began firing, and set them into confusion and retreat. Our loss in the latter part of the day was severe. Killed, 18; wounded, 153. Among the latter are Brigadier Chamberlain, shot through upper part of left arm; Lieutenant Thompson, Artillery, and Lieutenant Tulloch, 25th N.I.

July 15th. Although quite well when I awoke this morning, yet on my return from hospital from seeing some cholera patients, I was seized with some of the symptoms of that dreadful disease. My manner of living, regular and very temperate, so there was nothing to predispose me to it. The attack was luckily mild, and I being strong and healthy was able to struggle against it.

July 16th. About twelve p.m. I was almost pulseless, but from that hour began steadily improving. Left very weak.

July 17th. Another attack this morning on our right. Until they advanced near we did not attack them. This defensive plan is much more successful than the offensive. We cannot spare twenty or thirty men killed in each day's fight. The enemy know this, so they badger us to attack them. General Reed has gone to the hills in bad health, and Brigadier Wilson has now command of this force. Colonel Garbett commands the artillery division.

July 18th. Still the talk of troops coming up country. A report is current to-day that Sir H. Wheeler, with two hundred men, had been obliged to surrender with all the women and children. He made the agreement that they were to be allowed to go on board boats for Allahabad, but on coming out of the fort they were all murdered! There is no official report of this, so it probably originated in the city. The Subzee Mundi again attacked, and with the same result. Four men captured a woman dressed as a man leading on the Pandys. She was drunk with "bang," and fought desperately. Before being seized she killed two men of the 75th, and it was not until wounded in the face that she was caught. She, on being examined, affirmed she was a native of Delhi, but someone suspecting she might be the Afghan Prophetess, who has been preaching death to all the Feringhees, she has been detained in confinement.

July 19th. Weather dreadfully close and warm, and, in my weak state, almost unbearable. Rain greatly wanted. Cholera is killing many men now. Four officers died yesterday of it: Lieutenant Ellis, 6th Carabiniers; Ensign Walter, 45th N.I.; Captain Rivers, 75th Queen's; and Lieutenant

Ross, acting adjutant of the Ghoorkhas. Poor Ellis and I stood talking together the last day I was well; he was in good spirits, and looked as healthy a man as you could see. He was ill for only about eighteen hours, was getting better, and died suddenly of apoplexy.

July 20th. The enemy came out towards our right battery. Lieutenant Dickens was wounded through an embrasure by a musket shot, which will, I hear, probably prove mortal. They kept firing all day, but we kept quiet. In the evening we drove them back within the walls. We discovered a quantity of saltpetre in the Subzee Mundi, we removed it in carts into camp. A party of Sowars tried to intercept them, but they received such a volley from the 75th that they fled. The quantities of nitre in this village must have been immense, but how it accumulated there no one seems to know. Things are better already under Brigadier Wilson. Instead of piquets being placed with no one knowing who commands it, officers are posted to each, and have to make a report every morning.

July 21st. A melancholy case occurred last night. Captain Greensill, H.M. 24th, while on piquet at Metcalf's house, went out to reconnoitre, having made an agreement with his brother officer to whistle on his return. From some mistake he came in on a different side. The sentry demanded the parole three times, but no answer being given he fired, and poor G. fell shot through the body. After lingering some time he died. Haldane Stewart, of our service, was taken ill with cholera this morning. For some days he had been unwell, but felt so much better yesterday that he went to mess. During the night he was seized. He has been getting rapidly worse all day. Mackinnon has little hopes of him. From the Punjaub nine hundred Europeans and twelve hundred Sikhs are on their way down here. It is to be hoped the Sikhs will prove staunch when in such numbers here. From Agra an officer has received a letter, informing him that three Queen's regiments were expected there on the 20th ult.

July 22nd. Slight quantity of rain fell to-day, which will be of great use in purifying the air and driving away the cholera. Still very hot in the daytime. Just before daybreak, a deal of firing of guns and musketry heard. The assembly sounded in camp. It turned out to be the enemy firing grape, etc., from the walls, imagining we were approaching to assault. Stewart in a very precarious state all day; got a little better towards evening.

July 23rd. The Pandys being tired of attacking us on our right flank, came out on our left. Under cover of a heavy fire from their guns, they issued from the Cashmere gate about seven a.m., with several field-pieces. Their points of attack were the piquet at Metcalf's house, and our left battery at the mosque. At the flagstaff tower they threw shot and shell, but with little damage. Several guns were brought to bear on the mosque; but the shot passed over it, and came into our camp without hurting anyone. When they had advanced near enough, a party of our troops were sent out, and Turner and Money's guns. Our infantry were to take them in flank, while the guns and cavalry advanced. We got within a short distance of their pieces (which ought to have been captured), when our infantry got in front of our guns and prevented their using grape. This enabled the enemy to retire in great confusion, with all their pieces and with little loss. We lost a great many wounded, but only one officer killed—Lieutenant Law, 10th N.I., of Coke's Corps. Wounded, we had Colonel Drought, 60th N.I.; Colonel Seaton, Captains Turner and Money (severely) Artillery. This is another of the numerous day's bungling we have had. That several of their guns ought to have been taken everyone seems to think, but from the incapacity of the officer commanding we did nothing. No one that has gone out against the Pandys with all the responsibility on his shoulders has done anything.

July 24th. Very quiet day, scarcely a shot fired. It rained most of the day. The weather is cold and pleasant. Colonel Becher, Quartermaster-General, says that within fourteen days we shall have the European regiments and a siege train up from Agra. Jones, of the Engineers, wounded some days ago, died this morning. H. Stewart is gradually getting better, but is still not out of danger. Fever has appeared, but is not of a severe type.

July 25th. The Queen's 52nd had arrived at Umballa on the 22nd. The 2nd Punjaub Infantry and the Kemaon Battery of Ghoorkhas are also on their way to join us. By the 15th August, Brigadier Nicholson is to be here with four thousand men. Reinforcements from the south ought to be far up country by that time, but rumours are going about of the massacre of Sir H. Wheeler and all the Europeans at Cawnpore. His provisions having been exhausted, he entered into a capitulation which was broken, and all murdered. A force of about two thousand men have left Delhi, but where they have gone after crossing the river we are as yet ignorant. The Neemuch mutineers are daily expected to reach the city. Rain still falling.

July 26th. By a letter received from Mr. Colvin, at Agra, we are informed of an engagement at Futtypore between the Europeans on their way up, and the rebels. Our troops were commanded by Colonel Havelock, Adjutant-General Queen's forces. They consisted of sixteen hundred Europeans, and four hundred Sikhs. The mutineers, probably the Cawnpore and Oude Regiments, were defeated with great slaughter; twelve guns captured, and seven lacs of treasure. This ought to dishearten them in Delhi, and warn them of the approaching retribution. Where the rest of the troops are, under Sir P. Grant, we have not heard. A man belonging to the Commissariat came in to-day. He had been at Allygurh, where there is no one; from that he went to Agra, where all is quiet. Stewart is now out of danger. Colonel Mackenzie mending slowly. Lieutenant Dickens is sinking. The only shot almost fired from the city to-day killed two Ghoorkhas. Very warm this afternoon. Sunday.

July 27th. The Neemuch mutineers have got no ammunition with their guns, having fired all they had away at Agra. If ours had only not been finished, we would have captured all their guns. They are hesitating about coming into Delhi. The regiments at Indore have revolted, but as yet the Maharajah Holkar has remained staunch.

He is the descendant of a great Mahrattah chief, and consequently might give us a world of trouble. The 4th Irregulars were disarmed in camp yesterday. One half have been long mutinous, and killed their adjutant. At Peshawur the 64th N.I., who had been disarmed, tried to corrupt another regiment, promising them arms. They were found out in time, and John Lawrence will not spare them. Lieutenant Dickens, Artillery, died this afternoon, never having become sensible. The Pandys are keeping very quiet, scarcely a shot being fired.

July 28th. For some days there have been rumours of the Pandys trying to mend the bridge across the canal, broken by us on the 8th, and getting to our rear. A party was assembled early this morning to attack them, but word was brought that no one was there. Yesterday powder to the amount of two hundred and seventy barrels came in. Our supply had run short, so this will set us up for a month. We have expended about six hundred barrels since our arrival. A moveable column has been made to scour the country. It consists of Major Tombs' Troop, some of the 1st Europeans, and Coke's Rifles. Ireland goes in medical charge. They are to hold themselves in readiness to start at a moment's notice. Saharanpore is talked of as their first trip.

July 29th. The troops coming from the Punjaub consist of one thousand two hundred Europeans, two thousand eight hundred Sikhs, and three thousand of Goolab Singh's men. The 55th N.I. tried to escape to Cashmere, but they were stopped, and about seventy were shot. News of another fight between Colonel Havelock's force and the rebels at Cawnpore, has been brought in. The particulars have not been given, but what was left undone at Futtypore has been completed. The rebels have been defeated. Had a slight attack of intermittent fever this morning.

July 30th. The rebels are quarrelling in the city. A band of Musselmen fanatics have arrived from Tank, who say they will kill a cow before the Jumma Musjid; this the Hindoos refuse to allow: so before long, there will probably be a fight amongst themselves. It is rumoured that at Allahabad a great number of officers have fallen, principally young ensigns. The 6th and 47th N.I. were there. It is said seventeen officers were murdered in one mess-house. The direct road to Meerut is now open. Letters and goods had previously to go *via* Karnal. As the Goopirs stopped everything. We are getting stores for the mess. Surgeon O'Callaghan rode over to-day and reported all quiet. The Meerut Volunteer Horse have been fighting the Goopirs near the Hindan, and killed their chief.

July 31st. The alarm and assembly sounded about 6 a.m. The enemy were reported as coming out at the Cashmere and Lahore gates. They did not attack us, but proceeded towards the S.W. They are supposed to be coming to our rear to intercept a convoy with five hundred barrels of powder, now at Raie. They have taken out twelve guns and four regiments. Our moveable column has been ordered to proceed to Allipore this evening. It consists of four guns of Tombs' Troop, two of Money's; two hundred of the 1st Europeans, and four hundred of Coke's Rifles. A native from Cawnpore confirms the report of the massacre of all the Europeans there. From want of provisions they capitulated with the rebels, who allowed them to go into boats, when they killed all. Our troops are killing every male they come across. The regiments there were the 2nd L.C., the 1st, 53rd; 56th N.I.; the 1st company 6th battery Foot Artillery; 1st company 8th battery N. Foot Artillery. There were seven Europeans, who had been wounded when others were killed. They were taken and put in the jail. On the advance of our troops, they tried to communicate with them; were found out, and all murdered. It was seeing their bodies that roused the indignation of our soldiers, who broke through all restraint and slew every black face they came across. The Flying Brigade, with two hundred of H.M. 75th, instead of the 1st Europeans, started for Allipore in the evening. It rained in torrents all day, accompanied with thunder and lightning.

August 1st. This is the Hindoo feast of the "Bakrie Ead." A salute was fired in the city this morning about seven a.m. The King goes in state and kills a goat, after which the feasting commences. Our convoy came in this morning with the moveable column without seeing anything of the enemy. The rain probably sent them back into the city. The camp is quite flooded this morning, with no prospect of its clearing up. The Pandys have repaired the Bussy bridge, but have not been seen as yet. On the 5th July, at Agra, we lost forty-nine killed and ninety-two wounded. The bridge erected by the Pandys of planks and trees was carried away by the rain. After burning and looting the village of Bussy, they returned and attacked us about six p.m. They advanced against our right battery, and with six light guns kept up a continuous fire. They attacked the sammy house in front of it. The Guides and Ghoorkhas kept them off. Their bugles sounded the advance, but they only replied with shouts and firing of musketry at random. They kept throwing grenades, but remained in the valley with their guns throwing shot and shell at the battery.

August 2nd. About one a.m. there was a lull. The Neemuch Brigade, who had been fighting up to this time, retired to the city for prayers. Their place was soon taken by fresh troops, and the same popping recommenced. Lieutenant Travers, of Coke's corps, was the only officer hit. We scarcely lost six men all the time. For the last twenty-four hours musketry has never entirely stopped, and at present (ten a.m.) is going on as vigorously as ever. We are acting solely on the defensive. We hear that at Sitapore, in Oude, sixty-nine Europeans have been massacred; names not given. Received three English letters. They had not heard of the breaking out of the mutiny at Meerut. The date was the 8th June. Little did they think what I was doing at that date! About two p.m. the firing stopped. The enemy must have lost severely. Eighty were counted in one place, thirty in another. The *Lahore* informs us that the Rajah of Rampore has occupied Muradabad, and is keeping it quiet for us.

August 3rd. No attack last night. It is said that the enemy on the 1st advanced in regular order, stopped within a short distance of our batteries, when prayers were read and replied to by cheers. Lieutenant Travers was shot through the head, and died in the afternoon. Our loss only amounted to about ten killed and wounded. Several of the Kotah contingent were slain yesterday. The Sikh *cossid*, who had been sent with despatches from General Reid to Colonel Havelock, came in to-day. He brings in two letters, one dated the 16th, the other the 26th July. Colonel Havelock had defeated the enemy four different times, and on each occasion taken all their guns—total, 23. He had advanced to Cawnpore, where they found the reports of the massacre only too true, not a European having escaped. One boat full had escaped ten miles down the river, but were there attacked and put in the jail. The town had been burnt down, all the blacks being killed. All the women and children belonging to H.M. 32nd had been massacred. He passed through Cawnpore and attacked Bithoor, which he had burned to the ground. From there he had crossed the Ganges, erecting a *tête-du-pont*, and leaving a small European force to protect it. The second letter was dated twenty miles from Lucknow. Having strict orders to relieve it, he could not comply with General Reid's request and advance against Delhi. He mentions Sir P. Grant as coming up with large reinforcements, but as to his whereabouts he does not inform us. There had been several day's hard fighting at Lucknow, and, most melancholy to say, Sir Henry Lawrence had been killed; he was wounded on the 2nd and died on the 4th. His loss is the greatest that England could have sustained at the present moment. To fill his place there is no one.

5

August 4th. The disarmed 26th N.I. have broken out at Mean Meer, and after killing their officer, Major Spenser, fled. They have gone up the left bank of the Ravee, but cannot escape us. Dr. Spilsbury is dead, and Forsyth comes on the medical board. Senior Surgeon Barber was appointed Supt. Surgeon of Sealkote, but having wounded some of his servants with a sword, he has been recalled. Fugitives are crowding the roads to Delhi, fleeing from the vengeance of our troops. They will be rather a weakness than a strength to the mutineers in the city; procuring provisions for them will be a difficulty. Lieutenant Snell, 64th N.I., has been killed in Oude, so this will give my brother a step. No news to-day, all quiet in the city.

August 5th. Five hundred of the 26th have been caught and killed. The first part of the China force has arrived in Calcutta, as also the 5th Fusiliers (seven hundred strong) from the Mauritius. The 14th Irregulars have left Delhi in a body and have gone to their homes. A letter received this morning from Colonel Tytler, Quartermaster of Sir P. Grant's force, dated Cawnpore, July 26th, informs us that Brigadier Havelock left that place on the 25th, to relieve Lucknow, which was expected to be effected about the 31st ultimo; further, that Sir P. Grant was on his way up with between four and five thousand Europeans, and a large number of guns, and he expected to be with us shortly. No dates given. They will come *via* Meerut. It was not at Cawnpore, but at Bithoor, that our men killed all the natives. The Rajah of Bithoor, Nana Sahib, massacred all the women on the approach of our soldiers. Two attempts were made to-day to blow up the bridge of boats. A raft was constructed carrying a barrel containing eighty pounds of powder. The sides had feelers, which, on coming into contact with anything, drew a trigger, and ignited the powder. The first attempt signally failed, the explosion taking place opposite Metcalf's piquet. The second was also unsuccessful, for when about half a mile from the bridge, two Pandys on *mussocks* swam out and took it ashore. Why it did not then explode, is extraordinary. There being eighteen feet between the boats, its success if it had reached is doubtful.

August 6th. Another English mail in. No further news had been received of this outbreak. The Bill for the admission of Jews into Parliament has passed the Commons. The enemy attacked us this morning. Their attempt was again at the right battery. They did not advance near it, but kept firing at the embrasures, which are very wide. We lost three men killed in it. Captain Kennion, Artillery, and four men wounded. Two officers doing duty with the Kemaon Battery were killed: Lieutenant Browne, 35th N.I.; and Lieutenant Temple, 49th N.I. The enemy's light field pieces kept up a continuous fire, but did little execution. They have erected a battery of heavy guns in Kisnagunge, to the right of the Ead Serai, which enfilades the whole of the ridge. It will render our right untenable if we do not take it.

August 7th. A sharp fire of musketry near the mosque awoke us at two a.m. The alarm was sounded, but the firing soon after ceased. The weather is again very warm, not a breath of wind blowing. Showers now and then falling cools the air for a time. Yesterday morning the enemy's cavalry made a charge at Metcalf's piquet, but, being received by an unexpected volley, they fled, leaving two killed. A great deal of firing all day from this new battery erected by the Pandys, and by numerous light field pieces. It caused considerable damage to our right heavy gun battery. Theirs have two eighteen-pounders, ours have the same. We silenced theirs towards evening, destroying their rampart. No great loss on our side, although musketry continued all day. From the Pandys not aiming true, and remaining about four hundred yards distant, we escape. They began to throw rockets into camp about six p.m. One passed about three feet from us, passing through a *mussock*, it buried itself in the ground, doing no harm, but covering us with earth. It fell about twenty feet from our tent. Another alighted in the Park, but did no harm. An explosion occurred in the city this afternoon, not from any shell of ours, but from some accident. It is said to be their powder manufactory.

August 8th. A force was told off to attack the new battery at daylight, but when our guns were seen committing so much damage, it was countermanded. Our guns were ordered to continue firing all night to prevent them repairing it. About two hundred rounds were fired during the last twenty-four hours. Received a letter and several papers, which, from carelessness, had lain in the post office since the 9th June. The explosion yesterday is said to have killed five hundred men. The Pandys are beginning to suspect

Buckdar Khan, their leader, of being in league with us. Two regiments in the city tried to get into the Palace to loot yesterday, but the 60th N.I. shut the gates, and refused them admission. The enemy have repaired their battery, and have carried it more to the left. They have three heavy pieces in it. All yesterday, musketry and light field pieces kept popping at our light battery, but doing little damage to us. In the afternoon, as a cart was on its way to the batteries with one hundred 5½-inch shells, a rocket set them up, and eighty-six were destroyed, killing a native camp follower.

August 9th. Sunday. Very quiet last night. A few shots now and then fired by the Pandys, who are always in considerable numbers below the right battery, alone disturbed the stillness of the night. Two hundred men are daily working at fascines, etc., so that no delay may occur when Sir P. Grant arrives. Camp still remarkably healthy, although the days are excessively warm. Other attempts have been made to destroy the bridge of boats, but have all proved futile. The same firing continued all day. The Pandys have always seven or eight light field pieces. They attacked Metcalf's piquet, but did little harm. Towards evening they attempted to send some rockets into camp, but without success; almost all falling short. They come from some place below our right battery. We have got some mortars erected which commands them there. No news of any sort.

August 10th. The enemy have been keeping up the same straggling fire all day. They brought out several guns at the Cashmere gate, and attacked our piquet in the "cow house," in front of Metcalf's house. The fire became so severe that our men had to be withdrawn in the afternoon. We have placed three 5½-inch mortars at the mound behind this. The trees are so thick near this, that the enemy's position could not be ascertained with a certainty. All day and night the firing is continued from guns of all sizes. The musketry never stops, but does us little harm, the Pandys firing at random. The sammy house, the right battery, and the mosque, are the three places where it is kept up. The Pandys come out in four relays, but the King is often appealed to, and those in the city refuse to go out and relieve their comrades.

August 11th. The enemy had two heavy guns in front of the Cashmere gate this morning. They have also occupied a bungalow near Ludlow Castle; from which they fire at anything like a man moving at the Mound piquet. The disarmed regiments at Lahore have been trying to rise. Quantities of ammunition and arms were found concealed in the native lines. The death of the Maharajah Goolab Singh, ruler of Cashmere, is reported to-day. His loss will be severely felt at present, as he was sending troops to assist us. A letter received late this evening, from a staff officer attached to Colonel Neil's force, informed us that Lucknow had been relieved and the Pandys defeated in several actions, and thirty-three more guns captured. This makes in all fifty-six captured by them. No news of Sir P. Grant, nor any prospect of our receiving assistance from that quarter. A heavy fire of musketry at the mosque about nine p.m. Our men scarcely replied to it, and it gradually died away in about half an hour.

August 12. As fine a morning as ever greeted the longing eyes of the keenest sportsman. How many an anxious look has been turned to the east to see what were the prospects of the coming day? What a difference in our life at present from that of many a person among the hills of Scotland. They are enjoying themselves among scenes as beautiful as eye has ever seen. There, solitude is only broken by the cry of grouse or the shrill scream of the peewit or curlew, and replied to by the roar of the fowling-piece, echoing among many a quiet glen. With us, this morning, so eventful to the sportsman at home, began in a very different manner. The booming of cannon, the bursting of shells, and the roar of musketry, accompanied with a British cheer, told what deadly work was going on. The light guns outside the Cashmere gate causing us considerable annoyance, it was determined to capture them at day-break. Unknown to everyone in camp except those attacking, the column advanced from Metcalf's piquet as day began to dawn. Their approach was so unexpected that, as the Pandy sentry challenged, our men made a rush and got up to the guns. The horses were in one, but they had not time to remove it. A number of gunners were bayonetted at them. Our loss was not severe until after the guns were captured. Then, through some mistake, Coke's Rifles fired into our men, and the enemy opened a sharp fire. Our loss was Lieutenant Sheriff, 2nd Europeans, killed; Brigadier Showers, wounded slightly; Captain Greville, 2nd Europeans; wounded slightly; Major Coke, wounded slightly, etc. The guns taken were two 9-pounders, one 6-pounder, and one 24 lb. howitzer. Two ammunition wagons were also seized. They contained powder of their own manufacture, very coarse, in lumps, and leaving a stain when touched. The 6-pounder belonged to Colonel Mackenzie's troop (the 5th of the 1st Brigade) which was at Neemuch. The Golandauze (native gunners) killed are said to have belonged to the same. After burning some houses and huts near Ludlow Castle, our troops retired. The enemy advanced from the city, but were too late for anything. The battery at Kishnagunge is completely destroyed by our guns, as also their rocket-stands. They have, however, a number of light field pieces there, which require to be taken by a *coup de main*, as well planned as that of this morning. The total *hors de combat* on our side amounts to 10 killed and 109 wounded. Both sides remained comparatively quiet all day, but towards sunset a body of about three thousand men were paraded outside the Lahore gate, having several guns with them. The firing began on both sides with great fury, but ceased about seven p.m., the Pandys probably returning into the city. The two heavy guns in front of Metcalf's piquet were missed by us this morning. They were more to the left on the river's bank.

August 13th. A letter received yesterday by Mr. Greathed from Mr. Colvin, at Agra, acquaints us with another battle won by Havelock's force near Lucknow. It occurred on the 29th July. The fighting continued all day, and terminated with the capture of twenty more guns. In the action at

Futtypore we did not lose a man. Captain Mande's troop, Royal Artillery, did wonders. The letter further narrates, that Colonel Havelock expected to return to Cawnpore in twelve days from his departure, on about the 8th August; that he would then advance, *via* Agra, on this. About twelve p.m., sharp volleys of musketry suddenly broke out at Metcalf's piquet. Something had alarmed Pandy, and he had fired his muskets at random. His dreams are not of the calmest, it is probable; and he will now daily hear of more unpleasant things, which ought to be rather annoying to him. Another *cossid* came in from Agra this evening. The fight of the 29th seems to have been long and bloody. Colonel Havelock had been obliged to send to Cawnpore for reinforcements before advancing further. On the banks of the Gargeah, two thousand five hundred Ghoorkhas were encamped, preparing to join us on our advance on Lucknow.

August 14th. A similar attack to that of last night, took place at Metcalf's piquet. Very quiet, except the usual popping at the right battery. This morning H.M. 52nd, under Lieutenant-Colonel Dennis, seven hundred and fifty strong, came in; as also the remaining wing of H.M. 61st, four hundred and fifty men; the 3rd company 1st battalion Artillery, under Captain Bouchier; the 2nd Punjaub Infantry, under Captain Green; and five hundred Mooltanee horse. In all about three thousand fighting men. With them were three 24-pounders and two eighteens. The siege train left Ferozepore for this, on the 10th ult., but cannot reach here until the 1st September. The regiments at Dinapore, the 7th, 40th, and 65th N.I., who were left with their arms, have gone off without killing anyone. The Queen's 10th, and a battery of Fort Artillery, have proceeded in pursuit, expecting to come up with them before crossing the Soane. With the thirty steamers now running between Calcutta and Cawnpore, all armed, there is little chance of their being able to cross the Ganges. Had a violent storm of rain this evening. It made Pandy keep quiet, and for the first time since the first, we had a perfect cessation of musketry.

August 15th. From the arrival of these troops yesterday, a new arrangement of brigades has been made. They are as follows:—

I. Brigade—Brigadier Showers, 2nd Europeans. H.M. 75th; 2nd Europeans; Kemaon Battalion.

II. Brigade—Brigadier Longfield, H.M. 8th. H.M. 52nd; H.M. 60th; Sirmoor Battalion.

III. Brigade—Brigadier Jones, C.B., H.M. 61st. H.M. 8th; H.M. 61st; 4th Sikhs.

IV. Brigade—Brigadier-General Nicholson, 27th N.I. 1st Europeans; 1st Punjaub Infantry; 2nd Punjaub Infantry.

The effective rank and file is as follows:—Artillery, European, 548; Native, 477. Sappers and Miners, 673. Cavalry, European, 485; Native, 769. Infantry, European, 2,703; Native, 2,467. Total, 8,122.

A report brought in by a native this afternoon, of a body of Pandys being seen about twenty miles in on our rear. Lieutenant Hodson, with his Sowars, has been sent out to reconnoitre. The King has been holding a durbar, and abusing his "brave defenders" for losing their guns the other morning. They, it is said, are disgusted at this, and have removed into the city all the guns outside the Cashmere gate.

August 16th (Sunday). Not a shot was fired all night. Whether this arises from disgust, or from finding it impossible to drive us off (which they boastingly told the King they could do), remains to be proved. Five gun lascars in our batteries were found emptying the cartridges and filling them up with sand and gravel, etc. They have all been imprisoned until a Court is assembled. The powder, it is supposed, is sold to the Pandys; a large sum being offered for it. This afternoon, as Lieutenant Hodson, with his horse, was patrolling in our rear near a village, a Subadar of an Irregular Regiment came up to him, trying to get information. Lieutenant Hodson, after getting all he could from him, shot him. On advancing into the village twenty-seven Sowars were found in a house. From this they would not come, but remained abusing the Feringhees in general, and Lieutenant Hodson in particular. Fire being applied to the house, they soon rushed out and were cut down, two only escaping. A special service appointed by the Bishop was performed to-day. Its object was prayer and fasting, on account of the awful calamity which has befallen so many of our countrymen.

August 17th. It has been raining a good deal the last two days. Still the same cessation of firing on both sides. Pandy from despair; we waiting the arrival of the siege train. It is the individual styling himself Rajah of Mallaghur who stops our communication with Cawnpore. He has hanged two of our *cossids*. The spies inform us of an attack planned against our right flank. The last two nights we have been expecting it, but they both passed off in unusual quiet. Four cases of cholera occurred to-day, and strict orders for cleaning the camp of all litter have been issued.

August 18th. A letter from Agra, dated the 12th, came in to-day. Colonel Havelock on the 3rd was still outside Lucknow, not being able to advance until reinforcements arrived. They were hourly expected. The Pandys are making off from the city. Five hundred were seen about five days ago crossing the river at Gumukteser Ghaut without arms. There is still a body of them at Sonipat in our rear. They have two guns. They left Delhi under the pretext of collecting revenue for the King; but it is said they are looting the villages, so they will probably go to their homes.

August 19th. Except for a musket-shot now and then fired at the right battery, everything is quiet. From spies we hear that large bodys of Pandys leave the city nightly, and that if this continues a short time longer, we shall be able to walk in without opposition. A European woman, wife of a conductor, was brought from the city to-day by an Afghan. She had been concealed by him ever since the outbreak. A coolie brought in news that Lieutenant Hodson, with his cavalry, were shut up in Rohtuck. He had followed the body of Pandys that were at Sonipat, consisting of 1,500 men with two guns. By some means he was surrounded, and had taken shelter in the jail. A force under Brigadier-General Nicholson was immediately ordered off to release him. It consists of the fourth Brigade with Tombs' Troop, and two guns of Olphert's. Rohtuck is above forty miles from this, so they will not be back for three or four days.

August 20th. Two guns were sent down to the Metcalf piquet to destroy a house where Pandy had his piquet. All the batteries opened upon them, but what was the result we are as yet ignorant. Raining this morning. Days exceedingly hot and close. After proceeding as far as Allipore, it was found that the country was flooded, and quite impassible for guns. The column therefore returned. A letter was received from Lieutenant H., saying that he had never been surrounded, but was charging and cutting up stray parties of Pandys. A *cossid* arrived this morning from Cawnpore. He left on the 5th. Nothing new of Havelock's force, but on that day heavy firing had been heard in the direction of Lucknow. The Neemuch Brigade, it is said, has left the city, and intend coming to our rear, *via* Bagh Pat, proceeding up the left bank of the Jumna. From the city we hear that the heir-apparent has been deposed. Buckdar Khan has applied to the King for charge of the Rohilcund district, but his services cannot be dispensed with at present, so rumour says. Received a letter from home to-day. Mentions the firing of the bungalows at Meerut, but not the massacre. The news reached England on the 27th, so they would be in a nice state of mind until they got my letter.

August 21st. Brigadier-General Wilson has been made a Major-General. By this he will lose command of the Regiment of Artillery. Another *cossid* from Cawnpore. On the 29th ult., one officer was killed. General Mills thinks Havelock ought to have followed up the flying enemy to

Lucknow, instead of returning for reinforcements. He had received some guns, making nineteen with his force, and a company of H.M. 84th. With these he had again advanced. The Pandys have erected a heavy battery on the opposite bank to Metcalf's house. They have got heavy guns and mortars in it, but have done little mischief as yet. The King, we hear, has no money to pay his soldiers, so discontent is breaking out. The 12th and 14th N.I., it is said, have left the city with their wives and wounded for Jhansi.

August 22nd. An attack on our right flank was expected last night. The H.A. horses were harnessed and everyone ready to turn out, but the night passed quietly. This is the first day of the Mussulman Mohurrum, so something was expected. The Rifles (one hundred and fifty) are coming from Meerut with some artillery recruits, *via* Karnal, being sent that way to join the siege train. The 66th N.I. (Ghoorkhas) are to defend Meerut. Colonel Havelock, on the 10th, was still in the same position, not finding himself strong enough to advance. Two steamers with the Queen's 5th Fusiliers and the 90th had, however, arrived when the messenger left. With our siege train we are getting one thousand rounds per gun. That miscreant Nana Sahib has again turned up at Futtehgurh. His wives and eunuchs were drowned, while he escaped into Oude. He is collecting troops. The regiment from Saugar, either the 31st or 42nd N.I., has joined him. He has six guns. He intends attacking General Neill at Cawnpore, who had only five or six hundred Europeans with him by our last accounts. Troops, however, must be coming up fast.

August 23rd. The 10th L.C. have broken out at Ferozepore. They are being pursued by the Bombay Fusiliers and some Sikhs. No mail from England; it is overdue many days. Its despatch may have been delayed for some reason. Our first parallel was made yesterday in front of the sammy house. Fever of a mild character is very prevalent among the native part of our force. A letter was received to-day from Lieutenant Delafosse, of the 53rd N.I. He and three others are all that have escaped from Cawnpore. It was Captain Moore, of H.M. 32nd, who made the treaty with that miscreant the Rajah of Bithoor. When the ladies and everyone had entered the boats, after laying down their arms, several guns that had previously been concealed, opened fire on them. Only three boats got loose. Two were very soon sunk; the third after taking as many as it could hold got off. They were exposed to musketry from both banks, and soon many were killed and wounded. The boat now stuck on a sand-bank, and from this it could not be moved. Fourteen men were detailed to attack those firing at them. Among these were Lieutenant Delafosse and the three others. They chased the enemy away, but pursued too far, and being surrounded and cut off from the river, they ran a mile parallel to it, and sought shelter in a mosque. From this they were driven by its being set on fire. They charged out, and five reached the river, into which they plunged and swam about three miles down. One of the number was killed, having approached the bank while swimming on his back. The enemy now left them, and some villagers seeing them, shouted that they were friends of the English and would assist them. Into their hands they put themselves, and were taken to a neighbouring Rajah, who kept them a month, when he allowed them to go; and they on their first day's march to Allahabad, fell in with a detachment of H.M. 84th, with whom they returned to Cawnpore. General Wheeler and all the others were, we fear, massacred. The Rajah of Bithoor hates the English, because Lord Dalhousie deprived him, for some reason, of his pension. As long as the English hold India, and wherever the English language is spoken, Nana Sahib, with Suraj Dowlah, will be remembered as murderers of the deepest dye. Their treachery—unknown among western nations—and the cold-blooded massacres they ordered, will be talked of with horror by all nations. Two hundred and ten helpless women and children were by this monster slaughtered.

August 24th. English mail telegraphed this morning. Firing had almost entirely ceased on both sides. News was brought in from the city that five regiments with eighteen guns had left, intending to take up a position at Allipore, and prevent our siege train coming in. They intend making a circuit of about forty miles to get round the large jheel (lake), but there are great doubts of their ever being able to proceed, the roads being almost impracticable for guns. A large force was, however, ordered off from camp to start at daybreak. It consists of three troops of Horse Artillery, about two thousand Infantry with Cavalry. They are to remain out for four or five days. The only news as yet received is that fourteen thousand troops were to be sent *via* the Cape from England. This is surely incorrect.

Putting off time in the arrival of European troops will cause things to become more difficult of readjustment.

August 25th. Letters and papers arrived in camp to-day, bringing news to the 10th July. All officers at home, on sick certificate or on private affairs, have been ordered out immediately. Sir Colin Campbell has been appointed Commander-in-Chief. He is a passenger in the present mail. They do not seem to look on this affair in England in as serious a light as they ought. Rained all day.

August 26th. An officer came in this morning from the column under Brigadier Nicholson. They had fallen in with the enemy at four p.m.; completely defeated them and captured all their guns—thirteen in number. Our loss is light, but Lieutenant Lumsden of the 1st Punjaub Infantry, and Lieutenant Gabett, H.M. 61st, are mentioned as killed; Lieutenant Elkington and Assistant-Surgeon W. Ireland, severely wounded. Horses and camels were sent from camp to bring in the guns, etc. The column, with all their spoils, arrived here about six p.m. Their proceedings were as follows. After leaving camp they turned to the left, and followed a road which leads to the large jheel from which the canal gets its supply of water. At eleven a.m. they had only advanced about ten miles. Here they halted for about an hour, while Brigadier Nicholson was trying to find out from villagers the whereabouts of the enemy. They denied that any troops had left Delhi—at least to their knowledge. However, from fires lighted in all directions as they advanced, it was evident that they were signals of our approach. On the column's return this village was found barricaded. The headman was therefore taken and shot. The roads here were in an awful state; the country was one large swamp, and whenever the path entered a hollow, the water took men up to the waist. Four guns stuck completely in one place, and it was not until they were unlimbered, and the 61st gave assistance, that they could be moved. After proceeding in this way for about eight miles they came upon the enemy's position. Their outposts (consisting of Sowars) retired without showing any fight. To give time to our rear-guard to come up, the men were halted. Brigadier Nicholson and Major Tombs went forward to reconnoitre. The enemy were drawn up upon rising ground by the side of the large jheel, called the Nusuffghur; their left flank was protected by a large serai, and in the centre by the ruins of some houses. Our Infantry were arranged behind a ridge. The serai being the key of their position, our attack was directed against it. The Infantry, with four guns on each flank, and the remainder in reserve, with the Lancers and Mooltanee Horse, moved in close column against the building. Our fire was concentrated upon it. One man was conspicuous on its top directing and stimulating the men. They, however, did not seem inspired by his words, but fled on our approach. Three guns were taken in it. Our troops now turned to the right, but the Pandys fled immediately, making for their camp, which was in the rear. They, however, did not stop long there, our guns firing upon them, but rushed in a tumultuous mass towards a causeway which crossed the marsh, and terminated in a bridge across a nullah. Into this mass our guns kept pouring shot and shell with great execution. This was almost the only place where they gave us the chance of killing any of them. Here they abandoned their guns, waggons, camels, and all their camp equipage. Our guns followed up to the bridge, and here, from two pieces, made some good practise. The first shot killed three horses and a man. A gun laid by Lieutenant Wilson, however, blew up one of their waggons, which seemed to frighten them, as they fled shouting. In rear of their camp was a walled village, in which some three hundred Pandys sought shelter. Coke's Rifles, which were in pursuit, were ordered to hold it, and prevent the captured guns being retaken. After firing for some time they ran short of ammunition, and none could be sent them. They were obliged to act on the defensive, but they lost severely. It was here Lieutenant Lumsden and Gabett were killed—the latter by a bayonet wound. They held the village till morning, but the Pandys had taken advantage of the darkness and fled. Night having fallen on the scene, after blowing up the bridge, everyone sought a dry place to rest in, after marching fourteen hours. Our trophies were considerable—thirteen guns, above seventy ammunition waggons all full, camels, bullocks, a few teams of horses, and all their camp equipage. The guns were as follows:—One 24-pounder howitzer, two 9-pounders, five 6-pounders, four 3-pounders, and one 8-inch howitzer. All Colonel Mackenzie's guns have been recaptured—one on the 12th, four on this occasion, besides one of his spare carriages with a howitzer from the Delhi magazine. The 3-pounders are said to be the property of the King of Delhi, but the conductor here, who was in the city, said they belonged to some Rajah. Buckdar Khan's buggy was captured This individual from his rank could not demean himself by walking. The destination of this force, so ignominiously driven back, was probably Jhansi, where General Van Cortlandt, with several thousand Irregulars, is doing good service. Not having bullocks, or any draught animals, the waggons, all full of ammunition, had to be blown up, which is the more to be regretted as they are our own. This victory was attained without any of the bungling which had previously occurred, and the credit is due to Brigadier Nicholson for making the decisive arrangements. The troops, after a march of eighteen miles over such a country, and at such a season, deserve every praise. We, in camp, after about a fortnight's quiet, were aroused about one p.m. by the alarm sounding. The fugitives, to account for their defeat, had said, that all our fighting men were out, and that the batteries could be taken, but the infantry came surrounded by cavalry, and well primed with "bang." They advanced up the heights, but our guns opening with grape, made them hesitate. The Sowars tried to make them advance, but, after losing about fifty killed, they had to retire. What Buckdar Khan will say to the King concerning this defeat is doubtful. He cannot claim a victory. He had been sent out in command as doubts of his loyalty were arising. This will not tend to allay their fear.

August 27th. Lucknow still unrelieved. Colonel Havelock had returned to Cawnpore, having crossed the

Ganges. Fears are beginning to be entertained of its fate. Sir H. Lawrence, two days before his death, wrote to his brother saying that if the women and children were not with him he would move out and occupy a stronger position, thus showing he did not feel quite at ease even then. The enemy have been receiving reinforcements ever since, we none. May God deliver our people from the hands of such miscreants. The delay in sending reinforcements up has arisen from the mutiny at Dinapore. These rascals have been cut up, so no further delay ought to occur. They have four Queen's Regiments there, the 5th, 10th, 37th, and 90th. Lord Elgin has arrived in Calcutta. He ought, by his advice, to be of great use just at present. The account of our victory in the city is as follows: that we with all our troups came out, defeated them, and took thirteen guns, but, on our return, the Zemindars, with ten thousand men, defeated us, recapturing all their guns, with four of ours. Such is the account given to quiet those who remained in the city.

August 28th. A *cossid* from Agra brings news to the 22nd. A native report was in circulation there, that Havelock had again defeated the enemy at Bithoor, and captured their guns. A man had come into Meerut, having left Lucknow on the 8th. When he left they were fighting. This unfortunate fellow, who was servant to some commissariat contractor, had been seized, probably by Nana Sahib, had both his eyes put out, and otherwise tortured. Last night Pandy made an attack on the breastwork in front of the "sammy" house. He remained at a safe distance, and kept firing musketry at random. His guns poured in grape, but without doing any injury to our men. His purpose was probably only to alarm us.

August 29th. Five hundred hackeries with ammunition stores came in this morning from Karnal. The siege train had been delayed a day or two in crossing a river. A disarmed regiment at Umballa has been mutinous—eighty of them fled. One hundred and thirty were taken to the jail, but when they reached it they became insubordinate, and one hundred and ten of them were shot down by H.M. 8th. The Bagh Pat road is again closed. Last night about 8.30 p.m., a body of men were sent up to capture the enemy's breastwork, in front of the "sammy" house. The Pandys were driven out, and it was occupied. This was done to allow our approaches to be made. We lost very few. This place is only some six hundred yards from the Morey Bastion, so good protection will be required.

August 30th. H.M. 33rd, five hundred strong, have arrived at Bombay from the Cape. The Naval Brigade which was destined for China, is coming up the Ganges under Captain Peel, and are to occupy the Fort at Allahabad. Some gunboats are with them, so they will be able to move about and keep the district quiet. Lieutenant Warrand, of the Engineers, lost his arm in our advance parallel by a shell. Pandy sent in this evening offering to surrender. The ringleaders would be given up and all arms, if the regiments who had not fired on their officers were spared. This will not be agreed to. They are mutineers, and our law for such is death. Sunday.

August 31st. The Hindoos are leaving the city. The Mussulmen are crowding in, to defend their religion. The former have been the cat's paw of the latter. Religion, there is little doubt, has been at the bottom of this outbreak. The followers of the Prophet are longing for the glory which formerly belonged to them, and the rule which they so cruelly abused. A report from the N.W. has come in, that Lucknow has been relieved by the Ghoorkhas and that Sir H. Lawrence is still alive. If this news be true, we shall soon set things aright again. Fever of a remittent character is beginning to prevail to a great extent in camp. It attacked the natives first, but now it is spreading among the Europeans. The wind, when from the west, which is the usual direction at this season, blows over one continuous marsh from Karnal. The Nusuffghur Jheel lies also in that quarter. Few deaths occur from it. Assistant-Surgeon Woodward is the only case I have heard of yet. It was not Pandy who sent in for terms, but the mother of the young king. The old man is not now recognised as the "Great Mogul," but one of his sons has been raised to this post by the Pandys. The three Queen's regiments that were at Dinapore, have been detained by some new disturbance in that quarter, but of our small force to-day there are two thousand three hundred and sixty-eight in hospital.

September 1st. It rained all day yesterday. To-day it is damp and very warm. Very different from the fine autumn weather at home, with its partridge shooting, and stubble fields, etc. The 51st N.I., although disarmed, have risen, and attempted to seize the arms of a Sikh corps, but were prevented in time. An example will be made of them. No other regiment at Peshawur has followed them. A shell, yesterday, fell among the men of Metcalf's piquet. It killed two of the 61st, one of the Lancers, and wounded six other men. Another, in our new battery, killed one Sapper, and wounded two others. This battery is to be armed with light guns, to prevent an attack on our right flank.

September 2nd. Shells, etc., are being prepared for the final bombardment. Where our batteries are to be is a secret only entrusted to the General, Chief Engineer, and a few others. The curtain between the Morey and Cashmere gates is generally supposed to be the spot by the knowing ones. The Governor-General has issued a general order that no terms are to be listened to with the mutineers. Lieutenant-Colonel Hogg, Artillery, has arrived from Meerut. He is to be commander of ordnance here. Captain Young continuing as deputy-commander. Out of 830 of the 51st N.I., 750 have been "accounted for." No news of any description to-day. I am to be attached to the 3rd brigade H.A. Except in increase of pay and having Europeans to treat, the advantages are not great.

September 3rd. One of the most curious things during this outbreak, is the news from Saugar. The 31st N.I., although deserted by their officers, attacked the 42nd N.I. and some cavalry, who were proceeding to pillage the treasury. Oude is to be entered by two columns. One advancing from Benares by Fyzabad on Lucknow; the other from Cawnpore. Pandy remains very quiet now, only one or two men are out firing. He is said to be making off from the doomed city. Some, however, will remain, and these are probably preparing, inside the city, barricades, etc., against our assault. No news from any quarter. Fever still on the increase; one hundred a day are admitted into hospital. The 61st have lost a great many by cholera; one day fourteen died. They had been moved to the other side of the canal, to very marshy ground, and where the litter of camp was at first thrown.

September 4th. The siege train came in this morning, about twenty heavy guns. Six 24-pounders, eight or nine 18-pounders, and several 8-inch mortars. The remainder have not arrived yet. Two 13-inch mortars have been ordered, but it is doubtful whether they will arrive in time. A wing of the Beloochee battalion came in as guard. They are a fine looking body of men, but I fear no great fighters, if Sir C Napier's deeds among them are remembered. Their dress is picturesque. A fez with blue "pugrie" wound round it; a dark green tunic with red facings; the pants of a light blue colour. The men themselves are not so dark as the Hindoos, but their hair is jet black, glossy, and arranged in ringlets, which hang down over the shoulders. They wear beards and mustaches. Two hundred and fifty of H.M. 8th, some of H.M. 61st, and convalescents to various regiments came in. Colonel Gaitskell has arrived and taken command of the Foot Artillery. The 12th Irregular Cavalry have mutinied at Segowli, killing Major Holmes, their commandant, and Dr. Garner, the assistant-surgeon, with their wives. A telegram from England has arrived with news to the 15th July. It is not the usual mail, but it came by an Australian steamer to Aden, and from there was brought to Bombay by a chance vessel. Six additional regiments and eight companies of Royal Artillery have been ordered out. Lord Ellenborough seems the only one who looks upon it in a serious light. The Jews' Bill has been thrown out by the Lords by a majority of thirty-four.

September 5th. We have thirty-two heavy guns in camp, which within a week will be in position. It is generally rumoured that breaching will not be easy. The wall is faced by brick on both sides, while the centre is filled with mud, stones, etc. Scaling will probably be the way in which we shall gain admission. The Infantry are being drilled in this exercise every morning. Cawnpore news has arrived. Havelock's force had, by cholera and fighting, been reduced to one thousand men. Reinforcements were expected the following day. Lucknow was reported as holding out, in good spirits, on the 25th August, and that they had provisions for many days. Three officers were buried this evening, a thing very unusual for some time back. Lieutenant Elkington, H.M. 61st, died of wounds received on the 25th; Second-Lieutenant Somerville, Artillery, of fever; and Lieutenant Wandly, 36th N.I., doing duty with 1st Europeans, of cholera. Terms, it is said, have again been offered by the Pandys. Sixty lacs they are willing to pay. Everything is going on steadily and quietly. Little firing on either side. Of Pandys there are only eight thousand in the city, and four thousand more armed men, or rather rabble.

September (6th Sunday). Began my duties with the 3rd Brigade. Surgeon Brown is ill, so I have sole charge of two troops. The Rifles, two hundred in number, and one hundred Artillery recruits, under Major Campbell, came in this morning from Meerut. The battery made in front of the "sammy house," was armed with light pieces last night. Two breaches are to be made if possible, and a scaling party is to go in at another place. This being Sunday, all work was stopped. To-morrow night, however, the first battery, somewhere near Ludlow Castle, will be opened. It is reported that a party of H.M. 10th were led into an ambuscade near Dinapore, and only sixty, out of two hundred and fifty, escaped. The story is, that they were proceeding up in a steamer, when, by some means, a man delivered a letter to them, purporting to come from the magistrate. They landed, and were proceeding as directed, when this catastrophe occurred.

September 7th. Our new battery was armed with six 9-pounders last night. Pandy has got up three heavy guns in Beharipore, which play on our right battery. Our guns have been firing all morning, so they will soon be silenced. Captain Remmington with the 1st Company, 1st Brigade has charge of it. No medical arrangements made. Our Assistant-Surgeon, belonging to the Artillery, goes to some place near the trenches. Smith goes to-night. One hundred and sixteen men of the 3rd Brigade are ordered up at 12.30 p.m., to work in the breaching battery.

September 8th. Very quiet all night. Pandy was not apparently aware of our intentions. Only one man was wounded in making the battery. Ten guns were expected to be in position this morning, but the difficulties of getting them over the rough ground delayed them. The battery is a little over six hundred yards from the Morey, and twelve hundred from the Cashmere gate. Pandy, at daylight, began firing, and ours replied. Those on the ridge trying to silence the Morey. Our loss must be great, as the battery is not complete. As yet, Lieutenant Hildebrand, Artillery, has been killed, and Lieutenant Budd, wounded. Only six guns are in play. The top of the Cashmere gate can alone be seen from this battery, a rising ground intervening. Pandy brought out some light guns from the Lahore gate, and kept firing into the battery from the rear. None of our guns could touch them, not even the light battery in front of the "sammy" house, although erected for that purpose. The enemy's cavalry came out, but being met by grape, returned to the Lahore gate, which was shut on them. They then sought shelter in some nullah for the remainder of the day. Our battery was strengthened during the day, and no casualties occurred in the afternoon. The Morey towards evening became a heap of ruins, the guns rarely firing as the place became too hot for Pandy. Towards evening the enemy began firing rockets from Kishnagunge, and, although well directed, they did no harm. The Artillery lost four killed and some twenty-five wounded. The Quartermaster of the Beloochees was killed, Lieutenant Bannerman.

The battery now erected, or No. I., consists of two—one at each side of the road which goes from the mosque.

That on the left is the most advanced; it consists of six 18-pounders, and four 24-pounders; it is commanded by Major T. Brind.

No. II. Battery, or breaching battery, is to be made near Ludlow Castle—Major Campbell commands. Its guns consist of nine 24-pounders, two 18-pounders, seven 8-inch howitzers, four 10-inch mortars, and six 8-inch mortars—total, twenty-eighty pieces.

No. III., also a breaching battery, is commanded by Major Scott. It is to consist of eight 18-pounders, and twelve 5½-inch mortars—total, twenty pieces.

September 9th. Firing almost entirely ceased during the night. This morning all the guns in No. I. were firing. No. II. is not finished. The mortar battery, which is in rear of the heavy pieces, is ready, but it will not open until all the others are made. Sir T. Lawrence has killed five thousand Pandys in the Punjaub. There are twelve thousand still remaining unarmed, but with few Europeans to keep them down. Yesterday about two p.m. there was great excitement in camp; an explosion had occurred in the magazine, and pieces of shell were flying all about the tents. At first all sorts of rumours were current. Some Pandy in disguise had attempted to blow us all up! When, however, it was seen that none but natives were killed, it became evident that the explosion was accidental. Three natives were killed, and several wounded. The cause of it was as follows:—A hackery with seven live shells was being moved, when, by some accident, the cart shifted, the shells rolled out, striking against each other and stones. The shells, of course, exploded. This is the account given by one of the wounded men. Goolab Singh's men, with four 6-pounders, came in yesterday morning. The gunners wear the peculiar Sikh helmet—a round brass pot, with a spike and horse-hair rising from the top. A "purda" of chain armour hangs from this over the neck. They number some three thousand men. They are posted between the mound on our right and the Subzee Mundie. They furnish the piquet for the former place. The Morey was very much knocked about to-day. The guns were all silenced. Now and then a light piece was run out from its rear and fired, but they did not wait to lay it. The Cashmere bastion was also very ruinous, but the guns still kept firing. The battery No. II. will not be ready to-morrow morning as expected. Few casualties to-day, but many were struck down by the sun, the day being oppressively warm.

September 10th. No. II. Battery is complete, the platforms placed, but the guns will not be in position until to-night. It has been divided into two with ten guns in each. Scott's is to be made to-night, when it is expected we shall have some fifty guns firing. Received orders to go down to the trenches in the evening. Left at sunset, the firing generally ceasing about that time. The left battery of No. I. caught fire, and although every exertion was used to put it out, it was found impossible. This was caused by the rapid firing, not from the enemy. The guns and magazines were removed in safety. Although this was unfortunate, yet the guns had been ordered to the new battery No. II. On my approaching the nullah, where the doolies are, musket balls came whistling about, a few rockets also passed harmlessly over my head, and Brind's battery firing salvos at the Morey, and the glare of the burning battery gave one a vivid impression of what was going on. Reaching the nullah, I found the officers from the battery sitting down to dinner. They were all in good spirits, their battery having knocked the Morey to pieces. For an hospital, under such circumstances, no place could have been better situated. About one hundred yards in rear of the battery it is safe from shot and shell. Until ten p.m. everything remained quiet, the darkness being taken advantage of by us to repair any damage to the breastwork. At that hour Pandy made an attack; few came into the open, but from the walls volleys of musketry came. After about half an hour they were driven back with but little loss on either side. Six hundred Infantry were what we had there to protect the batteries. They consisted of Rifles, H.M. 8th, 2nd Punjaub Infantry, and the 4th Sikhs. Was astonished at meeting young Davidson commanding the Punjaubees. After leaving Calcutta, he had joined the 26th N.I., but it having mutinied, he was sent down as a volunteer. This nullah contained the guns and magazines of the burnt battery. They were removed during the night to No. II. battery. There are always one hundred men to defend the nullah.

September 11th. This day, 1803, Lord Lake took Delhi. It was not such a strong place then, nor had he the persevering foe we have to contend with. No. II. battery opened about eight a.m. with salvos. This is the breaching one.

It silenced the guns of the Cashmere bastion in a very short time. The enemy came out again about five a.m., but were soon driven back. The guns which annoy us most are some light ones about Kishnagunge, which cannot be got at by us. Major Brind got two down to answer their fire, but he did not succeed in silencing them. The nullah is about thirty feet; it runs parallel with the curtain. The shot, shell, and musket balls pass over it. Most of the last strike the opposite bank. The continued shower of missiles passing over is wonderful, but one soon gets accustomed to the noise. The enemy's Sowars came out and advanced on No. II. battery, but they were received so warmly with grape that they retired. They always advance in single file, with about ten paces between each horse. This makes shot have little effect. Scott's battery, No. III., is not ready.

The plan of attack will be seen from this sketch.

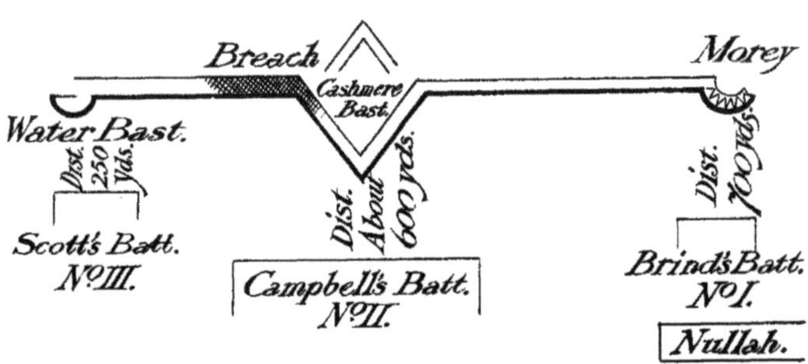

No. II. is the breaching battery. No. III. is first to destroy the water bastion, and then assist in knocking down the houses, or any obstacle behind in the rear of breach.

Pandy had some light guns firing from the Water bastion, which annoyed us in the forenoon. They struck our howitzer in No. II. three times without injuring anyone. They sent two 9-pounders' shot into the nullah, as also a ten-inch shell, which luckily did not burst. Pandy is digging a trench at an angle with No. I. It is full of men who keep up a continual fire at the embrasures. It is difficult to turn them out, as our men would be exposed to grape. They can be taken in flank, so they will probably be destroyed in this way. Brind, in the afternoon, gave up firing at the Morey (a large breach being made and all guns silenced), and turned the guns on the Cashmere. The centre battery on the ridge was sending salvos at the former. Pandy is making a bridge across the canal, to get round to our rear. Yesterday a number of Sowars crossed over and cut up several grasscutters. They were unsuccessful in carrying off the camels. The Guides' Cavalry went out after them, and cut up twenty-seven, besides wounding many more. The Jheend Rajah's men received news that they intend attacking us in rear, so Goolab Sing's guns have been moved to the site of our old rear battery. I was relieved at dusk. When I left the trenches the enemy were firing no guns. Campbell's battery still continued the salvos to prevent them repairing the damage done.

September 12th. Scott's battery still unfinished. Major Campbell received a grape shot wound of leg, so he will be incapacitated from further work. Scott's battery opened in course of day. It was masked by the wall of the custom house. When this was thrown down, it was found that only one gun would bear on the water bastion, to demolish which was the purpose of the battery. Very creditable to the Bengal Engineers! The Sowars from Delhi attacked a piquet of Punjaub Cavalry in our rear, and set them off. They are still prowling about, and the extraordinary thing is we allow the bridge to remain. When the assault takes place they will attempt an attack, but we have six guns and all our Cavalry to meet them, so we ought to give a good account of them. Went to the flagstaff in the afternoon. Heavy musketry fire about out batteries. The Cashmere and Morey were silenced; both very ruinous. The latter is a mound of rubbish. The Water bastion and the Selim Ghur batteries were firing. No. II. was sending salvos into the Cashmere, and the mortars threw the shells beautifully into the palace, where we watched them burst. The bridge of boats was crowded with hackeries bringing in fascines, etc., so Pandy intends making a stand in the city. We are bringing up our boats to Metcalf's house. This appeared to give Pandy uneasiness, for they slung round the gun which is on the river's bank, and fired at them without doing any damage. About fifty Sowars also left the city, came down the left bank, and tried to cross the river. In this, it is said, they were successful, and carried off five boats. At least, such is the rumour. In the evening we made a demonstration with Cavalry towards the river, as if we intended crossing. This was done with the intention of making them withdraw the gun, but this they would not do. We suffered an irreparable loss in Captain Fagan, Artillery, to-day. He was in Scott's battery, and exposing himself, as he always did, not knowing what fear was, when a bullet struck him on the temple—entering brain. He lived some hours, but, of course, quite insensible. He was universally liked and admired as an active brave officer. He leaves a wife and seven children to lament his loss. He was appointed prize agent for the East India Company's officers, and the General and field officers, instead of electing one for themselves, unanimously gave their votes for Fagan. The other appointed by H.M. officers is Sir Edward Campbell, H.M. 60th. It is intended to destroy the bridge of boats, and it is probable, if this is found impossible, that a body of men will cross the river and cut off all fugitives. Our mortars fired at the bridge to-night, but as yet without success.

September 13th (Sunday). Brind's embrasures were changed from pointing to the Morey (which was a heap of ruins) to the Cashmere. Scott's battery is now in working order. Pandy brought out yesterday two 18-pounders in the Kishnagunge direction, which, as they enfilade us, cause great annoyance. They are sheltered from any guns we can use. The only remedy is to capture them, and this can be done by none but Infantry. They would, however, be exposed to grape from the Lahore gate. Goolab Sing's men, with some Europeans, ought to seize and hold Kishnagunge. Scott's battery opened with all its guns this morning. He silenced the Water gate after it had fired three rounds. In the afternoon the only guns Pandy fired were those at Selim Ghur, two light pieces behind the Morey, and the heavy gun on the opposite bank of the river. A gun was also mounted on the post office. This, it is said, the Pandys made the budmashes erect. Our mortars were well placed. At this gun, and all about the palace, shells were dropped. The Jumma Musjid has been spared on account of the number of Mussulmen in our force. The Morey and Cashmere bastions were a mass of rubbish. From the half-moon between the two, some light pieces were firing, and it was covered by Pandy potting at us. Pandy was doing us little harm to-day, and we were giving them hard knocks. Twenty-five men were buried to-day, partly from casualties, but a number of H.M. 8th and 61st from cholera. The breach was declared practicable this forenoon, and it was generally believed the storming would take place in the morning.

September 14th. At two a.m. orders were issued to the troops to assemble at three a.m. The H.A. came up from the trenches being relieved by the F.A. The former were to man their own guns; some to assist in the attack, others to defend the camp. About an hour before daylight the troops moved off. The attack on Kishnagunge was to take place first, and as soon as progress was made there, the assault on the left was to begin. Goolab Singh's men, with the two battalions of Ghoorkhas, all under Major C. Reid, were ordered to seize and hold Kishnagunge. On going up to the flagstaff at daybreak, our batteries were all firing; our mortars at the bridge of boats, the palace, and the post office. The Morey, Lahore, and Selim Ghur still kept up their fire. About five-thirty a.m. the attack on the right commenced, and no sooner had the column appeared than the assembly sounded, and thousands of Pandys flocked out of the city. This attack was expected. We advanced some distance, Goolab Singh's men unlimbered the guns, and began firing. The shots beginning to fly about them, the drivers went off with the horses, leaving the guns to their fate. They ultimately all fell into Pandy's hands. At first we succeeded, but Major Reid, and Lieutenant Eckford, of the Ghoorkhas, being wounded, the corps became dispirited, and did not fight with their usual gallantry. Before we retired, two guns of the enemy were spiked. To cover our retreat, light guns on the ridge kept up a continuous fire, which prevented Pandy following up. In the meantime the attack on the Cashmere was delayed; that at the Morey was also. So ignorant was Pandy of our intention, that the foot of the walls and the trenches were filled with their riflemen. Our Rifles were thrown out in skirmishing order, these men retiring into the Water gate. Our Engineers advanced and blew open the Cashmere gate. This was no easy matter. In front was a rampart of earth, behind it a deep trench, and on the other side an 18-pounder. The explosion was, however, so sudden, that six or eight Pandys behind the gate were blown to pieces. This was the signal for the storming parties. The walls were cleared previously by 5½-inch mortars. Forward rushed our column, scrambling up the breach and the Morey, or using scaling ladders when required. The Cashmere gate was soon won —Pandy not waiting for the "could stale." The scaling party suffered severely. Five men in quick succession were killed. The regiments however passed on, although exposed to a heavy musketry fire. The breach column advanced towards the palace, but the magazine had been strongly entrenched, and a thick wall surrounding it, our advance was stopped. The Morey escalades advanced along the walls towards the Lahore, but here, being raked by a heavy fire of grape, retired. By great misfortune our soldiers came upon great quantities of champagne and beer. Over this they stopped, making beasts of themselves, and instead of pressing on, we were obliged to remain inactive. It is supposed Pandy, knowing the weakness of our men for drink, had left it as a bait. At last the goods from the other shops were all removed. Our men straggled behind, and could not be got on. At this place our advance stopped, and two heavy guns, 18-pounders, were ordered in to form a breach in the wall. One party of men advanced to the Jumma Musjid without loss, but the gate being shut, and having no gun to blow it open, they had to retire. In every street as we proceeded, the enemy had a gun, which poured grape on our men. From the Lahore bastion our troops were driven back by overwhelming numbers. Only about one hundred men remained together here. At night, therefore, this was the state of affairs: We held the Cashmere, Morey and Water bastions, with all their guns. Pandy had the Lahore, Selim Ghur, the magazine, and the palace. They had also a gun on the other side of the bridge of boats, which kept firing at the Water gate. On it we had pieces replying to Selim Ghur. Several hundreds crossed the bridge, whom we attacked, and large bodies were seen going off in the direction of Kootub. The King, it is said, has gone there on an elephant. Through over-confidence we expected to capture the whole city, but things are very favourable; and although it may not be entirely in our hands for some days, yet its fall is certain. Our army is too small for such an undertaking. Our field hospital was in a large yellow building beyond the racquet-court. About nine a.m. I went there, and of all the awful sights I ever saw, this was certainly the worst. Hundreds of wounded men were brought in, also many killed. The 8th Queen's and the 1st Europeans lost most. Amputations were going on in all directions. The noise was incessant. Strong men groaning in their agony; men with mortal wounds shouting for water; and the grating of the saw, as some poor fellows limb was removed, gave one no bad idea of a hell. In a small outhouse some thitty bodies were lying. To see a dead house during an epidemic, as of cholera, is bad enough, but nothing to this. Here were the strong and the healthy, who left in high spirits a few hours before, lying mangled and disfigured corpses. By three p.m. the wounded stopped coming in, and were all sent to their various hospitals. One of the most heartrending sights was the meeting of Brigadier Nicholson and his brother. The former was dangerously wounded, the latter had lost his right arm. Some officious person told them of their both being wounded, and when they met it was a most affecting scene. The Brigadier lying faint and pale, surrounded by natives, who appeared greatly moved—one I saw crying like a child. His brother, on seeing him, burst into tears, while the Brigadier did not seem able to turn his head and look upon him. Our loss has been very great, especially among officers. The Engineers had one killed and eight wounded. The 8th Queen's and 1st Europeans had six or seven officers wounded each. Few Pandys were killed, on firing a round per gun they bolted. We had to charge their guns, none of our Artillery being within the walls.

OFFICERS KILLED AND WOUNDED:—

H.M. 6th Dragoon Guards—Captain Roper (wounded mortally), since dead.

H.M. 9th Lancers—

H.M. 8th Foot—Major Baynes (severely), leg amputated, etc.

H.M. 52nd—Killed, Lieutenant Bradshaw; wounded, Colonel Campbell (hand), Captain Bayly, Lieutenant Atkinson.

H.M. 60th—Captain Waters (wounded severely), Lieutenant Curtis (slightly).

H.M. 61st—

H.M. 75th—Killed, Captain FitzGerald; wounded, Lieutenant Armstrong.

Staff—Brigadier-General Nicholson (mortally), Hon. A. Anson, H.M. 84th (severely).

Engineers—Killed, Lieutenant Tandy; wounded, Lieutenant Greathed (slightly), Lieutenant Saltkeld (dangerously, arm amputated), Lieutenant Chesney (severely), Lieutenant Howe (dangerously), Lieutenant Maunsell (slightly).

1st European Fusiliers—Major O. Jacob (leg amputated), Captain Greville (severely), Lieutenant Spike, doing duty (severely, since dead), Lieutenant Alex. Owen (severely), Captain Lambert.

2nd Europeans—Wounded, Ensign Gambier, doing duty (severely, since dead).

60th N.I.—Captain Hay (severely).

42nd N.I.—Killed, Lieutenant Murrray.

46th N.I.—Captain Caulfield (wounded).

1st Punjaub Infantry—Wounded, Lieutenant Nicholson (severely, arm amputated).

2nd Punjaub Infantry—Killed, Lieutenant Davidson, 26th N.I.

4th Punjaub Infantry—Killed, Lieutenant Homfray, 17th N.I.

Sirmoon Battalion—Major C. Reid (severely).

Kumaon Battalion—Lieutenant H. Boisragon, 1st Europeans (severely).

Guides—Lieutenant Shebbeare, 66th N.I.; Lieutenant Cuppage, 6th L.C.

The 1st Brigade H.A. suffered severely from heavy grape from the Lahore, when we attacked Kishnagunge, four killed and twenty-seven wounded.

Total—Killed, 8 officers and 162 men; wounded, 53 officers and 1,016 men, being nearly *one third* of the whole number engaged.

September 15th. Major Jacob died during the night from the effects of the amputation. Still in *statu quo* in the city. We are bringing up our guns, collecting the men, and getting them sober. The General and Staff have taken up their abode in the city. A few Pandys got in between our men and the Cashmere gate, potting at any one passing. We had to turn them out during the night. We drove the enemy from several houses, and kept shelling the magazine all day. There was an alarm in camp of cavalry approaching, but, as often proved, it was unfounded. We are, however, ready, day and night, to turn out at a moment's notice. Captain Roper, H.M. 6th Dragoon Guards, died to-day. He was orderly officer to Brigadier Grant, and while in advance with him, was struck by a ball which lodged in brain. Lieutenant M. Elliott was wounded in the city while advancing with a gun. We captured yesterday thirty-six guns of all calibres. The blowing up of the Cashmere gate was a gallant affair. Four or five Engineer officers being wounded and one killed. Lieutenant Salkeld was carrying a bag of powder when a ball broke his right arm ; he still went on, until he was wounded in the leg. Four men were killed in laying the bags, the fifth set the fuse, lighted it, and escaped unhurt. Pandy kept firing through a wicket in the gate. In the space behind the bastion, a European was found with his throat cut, tied to a stake, and his extremities burnt. When they saw our batteries, he had been brought out and murdered. The General has intimated that he will try any man found searching for liquor or drunk, and will hang him if he is condemned. We have now four heavy guns playing on Selim Ghur, and ten or twelve mortars shelling the city. Our casualties to-day were very few.

September 16th. The magazine was attacked this morning and taken, with the loss of only three wounded. About twenty Pandys, principally of the 30th N.I., were found in it, and of course all killed. There was not a musket in it, but thousands of bayonets. A great many guns, carronades, etc. (some say one hundred) were captured. No powder or caps. Two lacs of caps were found in the Water bastion on the 14th. Women and children are coming into camp, our men sparing them, but no man they come across escapes. Kishnagunge was evacuated by Pandy to-day. He left behind two 18-pounders, both damaged by shots, and several mortars. They have been brought in by us, and the place is being held by the Ghoorkhas. Our progress in the city is slow. On entering a merchant's house, a great quantity of liquor was found. In a room two of the Rifles and two of the 52nd were found hacked to pieces. They had gone in on the 14th, got drunk, and in this state were butchered. This store was immediately seized by the Europeans, and above one thousand were drunk as beasts. It is that which delays our progress. A severe example must be shown, or this will continue. The General has taken up his abode in Skinner's house. Every place is in a most beastly state of filth; bugs, mosquitoes, etc., swarming. A Mussulman was caught to-day. He had on him a lac of rupees, and fifty thousand of Government paper, belonging to Mr. Taylor, Principal of the College. A messenger from Agra. Mr. Colvin, the Lieutenant-Governor, was reported dead of cholera. Colonel Havelock still at Cawnpore. Three Queen's Regiments were expected on the 15th. Lucknow still holding out. Whenever the Lahore gate is captured, we will probably move our camp to some place near the walls.

September 17th. Pandy is said to be making off for Gwalior, but it is doubtful whether they will be welcomed there. At that place there is a second-class siege train. English mail, bringing news to August 10th, came in this morning. Great alarm at home. Regiments still being ordered off. Some three or four thousand Pandys are said to be in the city covering the retreat, and that they will soon follow their comrades. We are firing at Selim Ghur, and shelling the palace. The Bareilly Brigade have sent off their baggage, and are preparing to follow. The King has sent his zenana to the Kootub. It is the budmashes chiefly who give us annoyance. Selim Ghur scarcely fired to-day. A breaching battery is erected to breach the palace wall. Ensign Phillips, 11th N.I., doing duty with Rifles, was shot dead to-day, while repelling an attack made by some thousands of the city people. They tried to capture one of our light field pieces, but being charged with the bayonet they bolted. Little loot as yet found; except what natives care for—old silks, ghee, lotas, etc.

September 18th. Heavy firing during the night. We attacked the Lahore bastion, but our men bolted when just at the guns. Lieutenant Briscoe, H.M. 75th, was killed. The only Europeans worth anything are the Rifles, and right good work do they do. The 52nd are the disgrace of the army. They make a point of running away, and it is said the officers show them the example. It is rumoured they are to be sent up to camp in disgrace. A nice state for one of Her Majesty's regiments to be in at this present moment, when so much depends on British pluck. It is a very anomalous state we are in at present. One-half the city in our possession, and yet we cannot advance on account of our men getting drunk. Hanging is the order of the day in the city. Two fakirs were thus got rid of this morning. A number of women and children have passed through our camp. They are not allowed to remain. They are chiefly of the lowest class women of the bazaar. A beautiful eclipse of the sun this morning, about three-quarters of the surface being overshadowed. It occurred about nine a.m., and was at its greatest magnitude about 9-45. Lieutenant Speke, doing duty with 1st Europeans, and belonging to the 46th N.I., died last night of his wounds; as also Lieutenant Pogson, H.M. 8th. Got English letters yesterday. The attack on the Lahore bastion was a very disgraceful affair. On turning a corner, a gun fired a volley of grape, which killed the officer of the 75th. Although the gun was empty, and only five or six men about the bastion, the 8th, 75th, and Kemaon Battalion refused to advance. Everything is now to be done by the Artillery. The Engineers are knocking down houses to allow the guns to be brought against the gorge of the bastion. It is really lamentable the state of affairs. Few Pandys are remaining, yet we cannot advance on account of the drunkenness of our men. If the enemy had remained, there is little doubt we should have been driven out with loss. All quiet in the Punjaub. Three regiments crossed the bridge of boats on the 14th, and are making, probably, for Nana Sahib's headquarters.

September 19th. Weather much cooler now. A great deal of rain last night. All our Cavalry were out last night making a demonstration on our right. Nothing done by them. Things in *statu quo* in the city. The sudden change from a dry hot atmosphere to a cold moist one has produced cholera. It is a curious circumstance, it having attacked so many distinguished men. Mr. Greathed, Commissioner for the Governor-General, was in the city this morning, was seized in the forenoon, and died at twelve p.m. Sir Theophilus Metcalf, Captain Rothney, commanding 4th Sikhs, and Captain Nicoll, Brigade Major, were all attacked, but are going on favourably. A sergeant of the H.A. came in at two p.m., and died about seven p.m. Our advance in the city was some two hundred yards.

September 20th (Sunday). By burrowing through houses, our men were enabled to pick off the Pandys in the bastion at the Lahore gate. It was taken possession of by us during the night. This commands the "Chandnee Chowk," which is the principal street in Delhi, and leads to the palace. Our cavalry went out this morning to beyond the Ead Serai. They found the enemy's camp outside the Ajmir gate deserted. The powder in it was blown up by Pandy before retiring. They reported that Delhi is deserted, and that there are no Pandys to be seen at the Ajmir gate. The palace, it is said, was looted yesterday, and everyone has left but a few budmashes. Some two hundred men went over the bridge last night with a boat supposed to contain loot. Pandy is said to be making chiefly for Gwalior, but some for Muttra. Five light guns are said to be all their armament. The three light guns near the palace, which kept firing into the magazine, are left without any men. We are within fifty yards of them. The whole city was occupied by us this forenoon. All the gates, the palace, and Selim Ghur are in our possession. This forenoon the palace gates were blown open, but it was found looted and deserted. Outside the gate two guns were found ready loaded for our approach. In the first court, pointing to the entrance, were six guns, some 18-pounders, loaded with grape, drawn up in a semi-circle. If they had held the palace we could not have taken it without great loss. It is surrounded by a very strong wall and a very deep ditch. In the palace itself some twelve wounded men were found, who were all inhumanly murdered. The King's throne and howdah set with gold were almost all the contents. The building has been very little damaged by our shells. Out of a population of some 100,000, scarcely one remained except some old men and women. They dreaded a fate as at Bithoor. Everyone seems rejoiced at the evacuation, and the easy capture of a city which would have detained us for months, and been only taken with great loss. Some sudden panic had seized them, for although the city is well cleared out, their encampments have been left in a great hurry. In Selim Ghur was a very large camp; one half was burnt, probably by our shells. Their charpoys, cooking apparatus, etc., were as if the owners had just quitted them. An iron gun, a 68-pounder, which used to fire into our camp, was found in Selim Ghur burst. It was some native piece long buried. The English church, inside the Cashmere gate, is not much damaged, but Pandy has been using the brass ball on the top as a mark. A great many dead bodies are to be seen, but all the wounded have been removed. Hodson's Horse, the Carabiniers, etc., took possession of the camp outside the Ajmir gate this evening. About seventy sick and wounded men were in it; they were all butchered in their beds. It is said the General ordered no wounded men to be spared, but it is surely the duty of the Provost Marshal, not of a British soldier. This camp contained quantities of percussion caps (which they lately received from Cawnpore), a few muskets, plenty of easy-chairs, tables, etc., etc. Pandy will find little time to roll about in chairs now. All the plate of the mess of the 38th N.I. was found, the colours of the 26th N.I., and the poles of the 60th N.I. Crowds of villagers are passing through our camp and trying to get into the city to loot, but our guard at the Cashmere gate stops them all. Everyone is searched on passing out. The Guides were ordered across the bridge of boats, but from some accident one caught fire. It was luckily extinguished, but passage was stopped.

September 21st. A royal salute was fired this morning; it consisted of twenty-one guns. Pandy left with the intention of going towards Lucknow, but his course would depend on the intelligence he received on this march. If Lucknow was relieved, Gwalior would be the place—at least this is what the wounded men say. Went down to the city this morning. The road to the Cashmere gate was crowded with hundreds of women, children and old men. The poor creatures have lost everything, and are being fed by our commissariat in rear of our camp. The Cashmere bastion has been terribly knocked about, and is a mass of ruins. The marks of our shot are visible on every tree, house, and wall in the neighbourhood. The breach was a little to the left. The ladders are still against the wall, and everything as when the deadly struggle occurred. The gate is crowded with natives loaded with loot, trying to pass the sentries. The row and bustle is extraordinary—elephants, camels, carts, etc., etc., passing in and out continually through a narrow archway, the ground strewn with plunder of all kinds. The walls, riddled by shot, gives one a good idea of what one may expect in the city itself. The first place of note is the English church, in a large open space; its walls are marked by shot. What a change it has seen! Almost all who joined in the song of praise on Sunday, May 10th, were inhumanly butchered with their pastor, Mr. Jennings, on the 11th. Since then its interior has been polluted by the miscreants, its walls marked by shot, its brass ball and cross used as a target. On continuing our course towards the palace, the total desolation reigning everywhere strikes the beholder most. The houses have had all their valuables removed, nothing remains but rubbish, with dead bodies here and there. The magazine, which we took on the 15th, still contains mountains of shot and shell. The supply appears inexhaustible. Little impression seems made on the high pyramids. The number of guns is also immense—some 125. Further on is the college, now the headquarters of artillery. The gateway is knocked to pieces, and the ground covered with bullets. The portico was lined with sandbags, and everything arranged for a vigorous defence. Pandy must have become disunited after our assault, or we should have had hard work to turn them out. Outside this gateway is a battery erected by us. Pandy made his only fight in this quarter. Still further on is another battery erected by us to breach the palace. The first appearance of the palace is grand. The high walls, about one hundred feet, built of red sandstone, the deep ditch at the bottom and the massive gates, are well worthy of the residence of the Great Mogul. The gates were blown open by us, but although a large quantity of powder was used, it only lifted it off its hinges. The gate itself is studded with iron knobs and spikes. The guns still stand in the interior as placed by Pandy, to receive us. The road passes under immense archways, with galleries and shops. The height is immense, and as cool in mid-day as in other places at night. The walls are done over with native paintings, etc. Advancing, you pass through various courtyards overgrown with weeds and full of filth. Pandy has had an encampment here. In one of these is the Hall of Justice, Dewan Kas, consisting of numerous arches and pillars. In the centre, projecting from the wall, is the King's throne, formed of white marble. The carving is good, but the principal attractions are the mosaics and inlaid stones. They represent chiefly parrots, peacocks, etc. The one at the top is like an Italian work. It represents a man playing on a flute. Everything is dirty and full of rubbish. The hall is now the head quarters of H.M. 60th. Further on is an archway which leads into the *sanctum sanctorum*, Dewan Am. Its entrance is closed by an immense curtain. Opposite this is an open room with white marble steps leading up. The floor and walls are all of the same material. It looks out on the river, being built on its edge. This appears to have been the King's state chamber. It is now our head-quarters. To the right is the harem. The chief room consists of a raised platform in a recess, where the fair daughters of Cashmere spent their time. The floor was covered with guitars, bangles, etc., and from the roof hung a swing, the great amusement of the damsels of the zanana. From this apartment there projects a balcony with marble lattice work surrounding it. It overhangs a garden which is washed by the river Jumna. The view is extensive and the air cooled by passing over the water, must have made it a pleasant residence. Passing on parallel to the river you enter several chambers, redolent of sandal wood, but full of dust, filth, etc. One has a fountain in the centre, and appears to have been a bath-room. Pandy has been revelling here also, and wherever he has been, has turned it into a den of filth. Nothing of value remains, old clothes, bottles of medicines (!), perfumes, etc., are what are left behind. I went from this to the palace gardens, but these are destroyed. The orange trees, flowers, etc., still flourish luxuriantly, but no hand has been there to destroy the profuse growth of noxious weeds. Pieces of shell are lying strewn about. These came from our batteries. The only relic I got was a Persian book in the palace. Everything worth having had been carried off. When leaving the palace I saw a doolie entering, surrounded by some Sowars and several natives on foot. Its occupant was an old man with an anxious expression on his thin face. He appeared about sixty-five years of age, while he is in reality eighty-five. His countenance gave no signs of cruelty, but appeared mild. This was the representative of the Great Mogul, the Emperor of Hindostan! Lieutenant Hodson, with his horse, had gone out in the direction of the Kootub, having heard that he was anxious to come in. The King was surrounded by Sowars. These attacked Hodson's party, cutting down four men. Our Sowars charged, cut up sixteen, and rescued the King. His life was guaranteed by order of the Governor-General, but no terms are to be given to the royal family. This evening received orders to accompany the column proceeding to Agra. It is under the command of Colonel Greathed, H.M. 8th. The column is to consist of—1st troop 1st brigade (Captain Remmington), 2nd troop 3rd brigade H.A. (Captain Blunt), three companies 1st battalion F.A. (Captain Bourchier), H.M. 8th, H.M. 75th, 1st and 2nd Punjaub Infantry, H.M. 9th Lancers, 1st, 2nd, and 5th Punjaub Cavalry, half of Lieutenant Hodson's Horse. It encamps outside the Delhi gate to-morrow, and starts the following morning.

September 22nd. After having everything ready, was told I must remain behind, as the headquarters of the 3rd brigade were going, so Surgeon C. Brown would go, while I remained with the 3rd troop 3rd brigade and the sick. Major F. Turner goes in command of H.A. Dr. Mackinnon accompanies the force, intending to take up his appointment as Supt. Surgeon of the Agra circle. His loss will be severely felt in the 1st brigade. Lieutenant Hodson, with his Sowars, went out in the same direction as yesterday, and, at "Humayoon's tomb," fell in with the Shahzada and two other princes. He shot them with his own hand, and brought their bodies into the city. Two of them were sons of the King, the third a grandson. With them was a

European, dressed as a native. He turns out to be the Quartermaster-Sergeant of the 28th N.I. We were told at the time that the rebels had taken him by force with them, but it seems extraordinary his remaining with the princes when nothing prevented his returning. It is generally believed he has been a traitor, and assisted them in their fighting. If this is true, hanging is too good a death. No word of our moving our camp yet, which is disgraceful, as it is most filthy, and, since the removal of headquarters to the city, no care is given to keep it clean. The churchyard is in a revolting state. The graves are so crowded that they have to dig close to old ones, so the smell is most sickening; it is wonderful we keep our health so well. The hospital ought to be removed at once, as change of air is what the men alone want.

September 23rd. The column was to have marched early this morning, but it has not as yet struck its tents. It is found that the camels are so thin and weak that they cannot carry their usual burden, so they are obliged to have an extra number. The Mooltanee Horse have refused to march; they came here, they say, expecting loot, and they have got none. A great many Pandys, budmashes, and other miscreants were killed to-day in the city. They had concealed themselves on our advancing, but hunger had driven them out. The quantity of loot found has been considerable. Green's corps are said to have sold twenty thousand rupees' worth of plunder in the Sudder Bazaar. Things are being arranged, and quarters allotted to the troops, but it is done slowly. It is curious the effect the sudden change from the constant firing of musketry, cannon, etc., has upon one. The stillness is unpleasant. For three months we have been accustomed, day and night, to hear shots at all hours; now nothing breaks the stillness but the neighing of horses, voices of natives, etc. A seal with the King's name upon it has been found. It bears the date of the last Mohurrum, the commencement of their new year. The original stamp was seized early in May, and it was affixed by the rebels to all proclamations, letters, etc. At Ghazi-u-din-nagar the *Tessildar* of the village showed us a letter supposed to come from the King with this stamp affixed. The King has been removed from the palace, and placed in a building near the Lahore gate. His establishment consists of a moonshie, two eunuchs, some domestics, etc. Two queens are with him, and some fifteen female attendants. Brigadier-General Nicholson died this afternoon of wounds received on the 14th. He is a very great loss, being one of the best officers in India.

September 24th. The column under Colonel Greathed crossed the bridge of boats at four a.m. this morning. Their destination has been changed. They go first to Allygurh, then, perhaps, to Agra and neighbouring places. Their movements will depend upon who there is with any force stopping up the communication. The Nana Sahib may have a visit. It is full time that this arch-miscreant was swept away from the earth. It is reported that about five hundred miscreants, chiefly Mussulmen of the Chandnee Chowk, were killed yesterday. The Horse Artillery are to encamp outside the Lahore gate, and, as there is no house near fit for an hospital, the sick will still be in tents. Four days have come and gone and still no order for moving. Cholera still attacking individuals here and there. Lieutenant Cairns, 1st Europeans, died to-day.

September 25th. The column's progress has again been delayed from deficiency of carriage. They are encamped at Ghazi-u-din-nagar on the Hindan. Things are changed since we were there in June! Then, nothing was heard but of regiments mutinying; now the march of Europeans, and their victories, are terrifying the natives again into subjection. The cloud that overshadowed our glory is fading away, and it is to be hoped that our star will long shine with unblemished ray. The Jheend Rajah, who has been in camp some time, left suddenly, without acquainting the European officers with him. Some say it is one of his strange freaks which he delights in; others that the General refused something he wanted. If the latter, it is unfortunate, as the Rajah has done us good service all through this. The 9th Irregular Cavalry, who behaved so badly while in camp here, about the 9th July, have broken out. They were sent up to the Punjaub, and upon reaching the Indus, made off towards Scinde, where some disturbance has taken place. Lucknow still holding bravely out. About the 2nd ult. a mine was sprung below a large building from which the enemy annoyed the garrison. About two hundred rebels were killed. A sally was made at the same time, and one gun spiked.

September 26th. The Rajah of Bullubghur, who raised his standard for us some time back, is still holding out in his mud fort. It is only twenty miles from Delhi. A column leaves this afternoon under Brigadier Showers, 2nd Europeans, to enter his territory, relieve him, and assist him in raising troops. It is to consist of two hundred of the 52nd L.I., two hundred and fifty Guides' Infantry, one hundred nd fifty Guides' Cavalry, Lieutenant Bishop with four guns of 3rd battery 3rd brigade. The news from Cawnpore is improving. On the 5th ult. Colonel Havelock (Sir J. Outram having declined taking the command from him) will have a force of two thousand Europeans, three hundred Sikhs, and eighteen guns, so a good account will be given of the rebels. The latter have erected a battery, and intend disputing the passage. The *on dit* is that Nana Sahib offered to cross over into Oude, but he was politely informed that, having allowed himself to be beaten, his aid was not required. This miscreant has circulated a proclamation that the English had intended to coerce the whole of India into Christianity, and, to accomplish this, thirty thousand men were being sent out *via* Egypt. The Pasha having heard of the intention, collected his redoubtable Mussulmen legions, attacked this army while in their ships at Alexandria, and sunk all the vessels with the soldiers! Colonel Greathed's column is to attack the Mallaghur Rajah, who has so long annoyed us by killing our messengers. It is said, however, that he has bolted on hearing of the fall of the imperial city.

September 27th (Sunday). No news from either of the columns. Things are gradually disappearing from camp; every bullock, camel, etc., is employed conveying the pack-tents, etc., to within the walls. Weather fine and cool;

strong breeze from the south-east blowing all day. At eight a.m. the temperature was only 71°. Saw Major Campbell, Artillery, at general hospital; wound sloughing, and not showing any symptoms of healing.

September 28th. All the sick and wounded belonging to the 1st and 3rd Brigade H.A. were removed this morning from camp into Skinner's house, immediately in rear of the Cashmere bastion. It is a fine two-storied building, with large verandahs on all sides. The rooms are rather dark, but very cool. Mactier and I reside there also, in a marble verandah on the north side. Although considerably damaged by shot, yet the white stone gives it a cool appearance. Beneath it are marble bath-rooms, the zenana, etc., etc. Several books of the "Cr." and "Dr." belonging to the Delhi Bank were found to-day; the greater number, however, are destroyed. Twenty-five elephants have been captured in the direction of the Kootub. Their value is about 1,000 rupees each. Brigadier Showers column have found money and jewels to the amount of 40,000 rupees. They belong principally to the King, and consist of gold, trinkets, etc. Two more of His Majesty's sons have been found; they are still alive. The country in the neighbourhood of Mooltan is disturbed. At Googana the English mail from Bombay was destroyed. The officials here not having received the wishes of Government regarding what was to be done with this city, have written to the Governor-General for information. It is the current opinion that the walls will be destroyed, and a fortified magazine, guarded by Europeans alone, mark what was formerly a large cantonment. Dined at the Artillery headquarters' mess in "Darair Gunge," *i.e.*, River's Bank. It is the old cantonment, and was formerly the lines of the Sappers and Miners. It is on the south of the palace, and immediately beyond the Delhi gate of that building, but separated from it by a hollow. The officers' quarters overhang the river, and the view from the top of the house is beautiful in the extreme, ranging up and down the sinuous Jumna, with the stately palace wall on one side. The river is fast becoming smaller, and its banks are not improved by the refuse of this large city. The more one sees of the exterior of the palace, the more one must admire it. The lofty walls, with the deep ditch at their base, and surmounted here and there with turrets, gives one a very elevated idea of the race that planned and built such a royal abode. It is entirely built of a hard red sandstone, from which it derives its name of the "Lal Keila," or Red Fort. The walls are not solid, but, like so many things connected with the Mussulmen, the exterior looks well and solid, while the heart is composed of rubbish.

September 29th. News arrived to-day of an engagement between the column under Colonel Greathed and the Rajah of Mallaghur. He had taken up a strong position in the civil lines at Bolundshur, and had five or six guns with him. Our men behaved well, took the position with little loss on our side, killing about two hundred of the enemy. Two guns were captured. Some of the fugitives crossed the river by a neighbouring ghaut, others proceeded to the south. The fort of Mallaghur was reported empty, and Colonel Greathed had sent on the cavalry to reconnoitre, while the infantry were to advance in the morning. The officers wounded are Major Drysdale, commanding 9th Lancers; Lieutenant Sarel and Lieutenant Blair, of same corps; and Lieutenant Edgersalt, H.M. 8th Foot. Our cavalry distinguished themselves. Treasure to the amount of 60,000 rupees was found in the Chandnee Chowk to-day. It had been buried, but was shown us by some spy. Went over the Jumma Musjid this evening. It is certainly a fine pile of buildings. It is situated on the highest ground in the city, and can be reached only by a lofty stair. It is built of the same red sandstone as the palace. On entering the gateway the large court opens, with the dome and the two minarets on each side. The former is built of white marble, like all the other mosques in this city. In the centre of the court is a small tank full of fish. On each side are open verandahs with a gateway in the centre. The view through these embraces the whole city and valley of the Jumna. It is the barrack of the 1st Punjaub Infantry at present. The men were at drill while I was there. They wore no shoes, the place being too holy. Their band was playing, and I had the pleasure of hearing the "Highland Laddie" performed by Sikhs, in one of the holiest Mussulmen temples in India. The sick and wounded leave to-morrow night for Meerut.

September 30th. Brigadier Showers' column came in this morning. They only advanced a few miles beyond the Kootub. At Humayoon's tomb they found the King's zenana, consisting of over four hundred females. They were all sent in here. No enemy met with. Treasure still being found in considerable quantity. One lac was dug up to-day. Went over the Cashmere and Water bastions. Both have been terribly knocked about. The guns are still there, all broken and dismantled. They are both very strong, and the wide ditch at their foot, when filled with water, would effectually prevent any enemy from crossing. Passed the Morey in the evening. Its breach appears to have been much the most practicable, but then the fire was continued six days. The H.A. have removed their camp to the glacis, between the Morey and the Cabul gate.

October 1st. Another column leaves to-morrow morning under Brigadier Showers. It is to consist of H.M. 6th Dragoon Guards, Hodson's Horse, 2nd Fusiliers, 1st Punjaub Infantry (three hundred strong), Kemaon battalion. They will be away fourteen days. Their destination is Bullubghur. The latest news from Cawnpore is to the 16th ultimo. Colonel Havelock was then crossing the river. It is reported that there is a body of one thousand eight hundred Sowars at Bullubghur. The above column is to be sent against a native who is collecting troops in the district. When Buckdar Khan was made commander of the rebel army, the King bestowed upon him the suzerainty of twenty villages near here. He, as a wise man, offered them for sale at twenty thousand rupees. This native paid him the sum, and, since we have got possession, is desirous of turning us out by force. Colonel Greathed has written for more Infantry and some heavy guns. Numbers of Pandys are said to be still in the city—lurking in the large drains which pass below the city. Starvation will soon make them come out. A native, the son of a large shawl merchant, was taken prisoner lately. He became very talkative, and let out that his "papa" had buried fifteen lacs in the city. He was immediately taken to the prize agents, who will be able to make him show the place. No dâk from Lahore or Mooltan for many days. Some crisis must have occurred there. Road to Meerut quite safe. Wounded officers and men go nightly.

October 2nd. A Sowar came in from Brigadier Showers' force, acquainting us that a party of rebels, with guns, were in their front. They were to be attacked in the morning, and Hodson immediately started with his horse to join. The fort of Mallaghur has been evacuated. One gun was found on the walls. It has been blown up. An accident occurred in doing so, which resulted in the death of Lieutenant Howe, of Engineers, who distinguished himself in blowing up the Cashmere gate, for which he was recommended for the Victoria Cross. A village beyond the fort was supposed to be occupied by the enemy, but, on advancing, it was found in the hands of a party of Europeans from Meerut. The total amount of treasure found up to this date is said to be five lacs. The Mooltan road is now stated to be open. If the fall of Delhi had been delayed a few days longer, the whole of the Punjaub would have been up. A reinforcement of one hundred and eleven men of the 75th leave this on the morning of the fourth to join Colonel Greathed's column at Allyghur. Either Smith or I accompany them.

October 3rd. The only surviving son of the King, not in

our hands, has fled to the Rajah of Puttiala. He will probably escape punishment. Received orders to proceed to Allygurh. The troops going are one hundred and eleven of H.M. 75th, seventy-eight of H.M. 8th, ten Artillerymen, and a detachment of the 4th Irregular Cavalry under Captain Hall. A train of ammunition and guns also accompany us. We start on Monday morning. A Sowar from Cawnpore brings news of another victory of General Havelock. He had crossed the river without opposition, and met the enemy in an entrenched position. He drove them from their fort, capturing five guns, with the loss of only three or four men. This occurred about the 22nd. He would probably be at Lucknow about the 24th. The stock of beer and rum was running short there, but in other respects they were well. No news from either column. Colonel Greathed is stationed somewhere between Mallaghur and Allygurh. The enemy have taken the fort of Allygurh, and intend waiting our arrival. The Bombay letters do not come direct, but by some circuitous route. The villages in the Mooltan district still stopping the communications.

October 4th (Sunday). About ten thousand Pandys, the spies say, are at Muttra, only five marches from Agra. They have sixteen light guns with them. The only two they carried away from here of any size they could not cross some place with, so they were left on the road. They are stated to be in a great fix as to where they ought to go. Lucknow, they have heard, will be soon relieved. Gwalior is occupied by the Maharajah, and the fort guarded by Mahrattas. The Rajah of Bhurtpore is friendly to us.

Muttra is one of their sacred places, so they may remain there; but, with their failing fortune, numbers will go home. Buckdar Khan, with some followers, is stated to have joined the Rajah of Mallaghur in Allygurh. Drove, in the evening, outside the walls, past the Lahore, Ajmir, and Delhi gates. From there we went through the remains of old Delhi, towards the old fort and Humayoon's tomb. Scarcely any houses are, or have been, inhabited here for years. Our jail is the only place not a ruin. The ruins chiefly consist of mosques, castellated buildings, etc.—the remains of former greatness. The country is flat, but much broken up with mounds, beneath which, probably, lie the abodes of men who flourished centuries ago. It was not considered safe to proceed beyond two miles from the walls, the whole party being unarmed. The Pandy camp, outside the Ajmir gate, extends about a mile on each side of the road. Its whole extent is covered with broken pots, beds, and all sorts of native utensils. Major-General Wilson left last night for the hills, in bad health. Brigadier Chamberlain takes command until General Penny arrives from Meerut. The sick and wounded of the H.A. left this evening in carts for Meerut.

October 5th. Walked over Kishnagunge and up the ridge to Hindoo Rao. Our position there is very strong. The fire, often so severe and so long continued, has left undeniable marks on all things in the vicinity. Trees cut in two, rocks splintered to pieces by round shot, will give to the wanderer for many years to come a vivid picture of our position, and the dangers our brave men underwent during the three months we held the heights. The right and middle batteries are now quite deserted. Their only inmates being dogs, which prowl about in such myriads all over our camp. The cooing of pigeons and the cry of the grey partridge, are the only noises heard in the spot where our men so nobly bled and fought. Havelock has had another fight close to Lucknow. The enemy were again beaten and driven like chaff across a nullah into which they threw their muskets, guns, etc. He had fired a royal salute to let the devoted garrison at Lucknow know he was at last at hand to relieve them. Received orders to be ready to start about two a.m.

October 6th. Left the Lahore gate a little after two a.m. The column is commanded by Captain Cumberland, H.M. 70th. We marched steadily and reached Ghazi-u-din-nagar about 8.30 a.m. We are encamped about a mile beyond our old site of the 1st June on the Allygurh road, about twelve miles from Delhi. The battle field of the Hindan retains few traces of the deadly struggle four months since. The trees, it is true, bear their broken branches, injured by the grape and bullet. They are now clothed in a new garb, which conceals from the passer-by the injury sustained. The river still winds its solitary way, larger but with as sluggish a stream. Its banks are greatly changed. The plough and the harrow are busy. The husbandman is sowing his grain with the hope that he may reap it. The change from the rolling of guns and tramp of armed men, and the loud crash of the cannons' roar to the sound of peaceful times, reminds me of a still more famous river, immortalized by the great wizard:—

> "Sweet Teviot! on thy silver tide
> The glaring bale-fires blaze no more;
> No longer steel-clad warriors ride
> Along thy wild and willowed shore.
> Where'er thou wind'st, by dale or hill,
> All, all is peaceful, all is still,
> As if thy waves since time was born,
> Since first they rolled upon the Tweed,
> Had only heard the shepherd's reed,
> Nor started at the bugle horn."

The village of Ghazi-u-din-nagar was looted and burned by Colonel Greathead, but from some unaccountable reason, the high walls surrounding it and the strong gates are standing uninjured. English mail telegraphed no news of any importance. Twenty-seven thousand men are on their way to reconquer India.

October 7th. Left our encamping ground about three a.m., and marched with a beautiful moon overhead. Had only two stoppages, the night being cool and the sickly men being carried in carts. Reached Dadree about eight a.m. This was about eleven miles, or twenty-two from Delhi. Weather now very cool and pleasant. Out for two or three hours shooting with Lieutenant Gully, Artillery. He is a very bad shot and killed nothing. We saw four or five hares and plenty of pigeons. Got nothing but one small dove. Dadree has been burnt by our men. No inhabitants remain. What miseries some of these poor wretches must be undergoing without a house or anything to procure the necessaries of life,

October 8th. Started at 3.30 a.m., and reached our encamping ground beyond Secundrabad about 8.30 a.m. This is exactly thirty-four miles from Delhi. The *Tessildar* of the village showed us a letter from the magistrate of the district informing him that the roads between this and Agra were quite open. The Pandys have failed in crossing the Ganges at Muttra, and are said to be dispersing. Greathed is at present at Hattrass, beyond Allygurh. The village of Secundrabad must have been once a very important place. The remains of old mosques, houses, etc., extend for about a mile along the road. The immense mango trees show it is of no modern date. The present village is to the south-east of the old. It was completely burned and looted by the rebels some months ago. The houses are being re-erected, but desolation reigns over the largest part. This, the "city of Alexander," reminds me of old events, the invasion of the son of Philip and defeat of Porus. It is more probable that the great name he had gave rise to calling cities after him, than that either he or any of his Macedonian followers penetrated thus far into the interior of an enemy's land.

October 9th. Started at two a.m., passed Choola about 5.30 a.m. The distance is about fifteen miles, or fifty from Delhi. The Kotwal of the village informed us that Colonel Greathed was one march beyond Allygurh, going most probably towards Rohilcund. Pandy, he says, has left Muttra, after looting everything, especially the gold plating from a large Hindoo Temple, erected by Luckshad Chund, the great banker. This shows what the Mussulmen are after; rousing the Hindoos and using them as a catspaw, they plunder them when affairs are looking black. Pandy is making for Rohilcund. We are encamped at the junction of the Delhi and Meerut roads, going towards Allygurh.

October 10th. Started at two a.m. and marched thirteen miles to Somnagunge, sixty-four miles from Delhi. Colonel Greathead has had another fight at a place called Akrabad, beyond Allygurh. It terminated in the complete defeat of the enemy. After this he again returned to Allygurh, intending to go to Agra. The Beloochees, from Bolundshahur, attacked a place fifteen miles from Konjah, called the "Churuk." It is a strong mud fort. It was defended by heavy guns and our men had to retire, having with them only light field pieces. Our party was to have been sent for by Mr. Sap, C.S., but in the meantime it was evacuated and all the guns left behind. The Jhansi Brigade of Pandys, with whom Colonel Greathed had the fight at Bolundshahur, have made off to Futtehgurh, so they will be turned out by some troops from Cawnpore.

October 11th. Left our encamping ground at two a.m. and marched until 7.30 a.m., when we reached Allyghur. This was about fifteen miles, or twenty-nine from Delhi. A small party has been left in the fort about two miles from the town, but the column has proceeded by forced marches on Agra. The Neemuch and Bareilly Brigade of Pandys are about forty miles from it, and purpose attacking the fort. This has put the inmates into a great state of suspense, and, to relieve the place, the column has gone on. If Pandy does approach, there is sure to be a hard fight somewhere in the neighbourhood. Orders were left us to follow their course as rapidly as possible, so we shall probably start this evening. It is about fifty miles from here. The *Tessildar* tells us the Pandys, in great numbers, are crossing at Dholpore and proceeding towards Gwalior. Every day a new rumour. Each village tries to ingratiate itself by some news, regardless of its authenticity. On our encamping ground were two peculiar guns. They are made out of the sheath into which the telegraph posts are sunk. They bind it round with bars of iron, drill a touch-hole and the 6-pounder is complete. These original weapons were used at Bolundshahur and at several places in the district. The Meerut party in one of their incursions took six or seven from the walls of some mud fort. News reached us of the relief of Lucknow. Havelock had a fight outside the city, defeated the mutineers, joined with the garrison, and when the *cossid* left was taking the town itself. This is the best news we could have heard of. It breaks the neck of the mutiny completely. Colonel Greathed has had another fight at the other side of Agra the day before yesterday, taking seven guns and five hundred horses. The enemy have crossed the Chambal.

October 12th. Left Allygurh at one a.m., and made a forced march to Hattrass, which we reached at ten a.m. The distance to Agra is fifty miles, of which we came twenty-five to-day. The country almost all the way is beautifully cultivated, and the gardens on the roadside, which are very numerous, ornamented with immense trees. Hattrass is a very large town, once of great importance. A battle was fought here about fifty years ago. The old town is surrounded by a high mud wall and a very wide ditch, even now showing a very good front. The ramparts have houses built on them, which gives a very picturesque appearance to what would otherwise be a very ugly place. This is the same as what occurs in the old European fortresses, and is a very ancient thing in the East—witness the walls of Jericho. The *Tessildar* informs us that Pandy left Muttra, crossed country, and passed through Hattrass three days before Colonel Greathed's arrival. He says there were ten thousand Sepoys and forty thousand of a rabble. They had twenty-four light guns. Except taking grain, bullocks, etc., they did no harm. They are proceeding towards Cawnpore.

October 13th. Struck our tents at twelve p.m., and marched seventeen miles towards Kanowlie, which is only eight miles from Agra. About half-way passed through a very old-looking village called Shahabad. It had numerous mud towers about thirty feet high, which, with the narrow streets, would cause great loss to the enemy, if defended by determined men. Arrived at our encamping ground about seven a.m. The nights are becoming intensely cold, especially towards daybreak. Received orders in the evening not to enter Agra, but to march to the place where the Cawnpore road branches off, and wait there until the arrival of Colonel Greathed's column.

October 14th. Started at three a.m., and reached the cross-roads at six p.m., having come about eight miles. After waiting there about an hour, the advanced guard passed. We fell in, and proceeded about three miles on the Cawnpore road, where we encamped with the column. The affair on the 10th, at Agra, was a very gallant fight. After marching about twenty-seven miles, while in the act of camping, Pandy attacked them. They were the Muttra mutineers. They took us by surprise, but they were rather astonished at finding fifteen guns open upon them, instead of having no opposition but the 3rd Europeans. Their Sowars, who were dressed in their Sepoy uniform, charged a square of the 75th twice. They killed Captain French, of H.M. 9th Lancers, and wounded Lieutenant Blair in nineteen places. All their guns, twelve in number, were taken, and a great many men were killed. We pursued them eleven miles, when they were flying in every direction, not even seeking shelter in small parties. Among the guns two immense brass eighteen-pounders were taken; they are said to have originally belonged to Holkar. The Rajah of Bhurtpore is cutting up the fugitives and sending in some prisoners. Colonel Havelock has written for a strong brigade to advance down country to Cawnpore, and open up the communication. He has left H.M. 90th and 32nd in Lucknow, and intends coming up to Futtehgurh to meet us. The fort there, which is very strong, is occupied by Pandy. Colonel Greathed proceeds there. Passed this morning a detachment, consisting of three guns and two hundred of the 3rd Europeans, proceeding to reinforce the garrison at Allygurh. It was not until late in the evening that the baggage all came up. The crossing the bridge of boats was a very slow affair. The encamping ground was very bad—intersected by nullahs and steep sandhills. Received orders in the morning to return with Captain Hall to Delhi, but in the afternoon that we were both to remain. I am to accompany the column in charge of Hall's Sowars and one hundred and fifty Sappers. This, from a pecuniary point of view, is a dead loss. It was very provoking, arriving within sight of Agra and not being allowed to see it. The "Taj Mahal," or tomb of Nour-mahal, is distant from our camp some four miles. This is said to be the finest building in India, and travellers come from all places to see it. Some future day, if God spares me, I may have time to visit it. At Mynpoorie there are some Pandys, but they will probably fly on our approach. At Futtehgurh, where there is a fort, a fight is expected; but we are not strong enough to take it by ourselves. We will, therefore, probably encamp somewhere in its neighbourhood, and await the arrival of troops. The people of Agra are almost dying of pure fright. After being four months within the walls, they take a morbid pleasure in exaggerating their danger.

October 15th. Started at four a.m. with the advanced guard. Proceeded to the 12th milestone from Agra. Took up our position in the regular ground. Beside it is a large tank with a mosque in the centre, approached by a viaduct. It is in a ruinous state, and now the abode of cattle. Two others are placed on its banks, being the tombs of some heroes of bygone days. Heard this morning that the young Rajah of Mynpoorie passed this about a week ago, not believing the news of the fall of Delhi. He had remained staunch until then. He had three lacs given him to keep for us, which he has probably spent. Hearing of the total defeat of Pandy on the 10th, he returned this way with four guns and some cavalry; so we may fall in with him. Plenty of deer, antelope, etc., hereabout. A continued fusilade all day long has been going on, but with little success.

October 16th. With rear-guard, and did not start until five a.m., although the column left at two a.m. Did not reach the encamping ground until eleven a.m. This is distant twenty-six miles from Agra. All the villages up to this have been friendly to us, having Thanadars of our own appointment; now we are entering the Rajah of Mynpoorie's territory, and will probably come across many Pandys, etc. I was again appointed to the 3rd Brigade Horse Artillery. Nothing doing at present. A force left camp about two p.m., consisting of two guns of Captain Bourchier's battery, three hundred Sikhs, and some Irregular Horse, to surround a village about five miles from this, which is full of miscreants. It contains a small mud fort, into which some three hundred armed budmashes have thrown themselves, and, having some small pieces, intend fighting to the death. The party returned at sunset, after burning two villages. They were both deserted, except by a few old men and women. Everything of any value was removed. The news from Lucknow is that Havelock is still in the city, hemmed in, or rather, unable with his small force to retire on Cawnpore with all the women and children. We shall therefore probably march into Oude with a reinforcement from down country.

October 17th. Left Ferozabad at three a.m., supposing we had only eleven miles to march. However, we reached the 40th milestone from Agra, having come fourteen miles without finding ground to encamp on. It is close to a large village called Shekohabad, through which the road winds for about a mile. This is the last place containing a Thana (police station) of our choosing. The day we encamped near Agra (the 14th), the 28th N.I. marched within three miles of us in a strong body. They were on their way to join the heroes who were to capture Agra; but hearing of their total defeat they turned off and proceeded towards Futtehgurh. The Gwalior troops have advanced to Jhansi, and it is said they are making for Oude *via* Cawnpore. Two more of the King of Delhi's sons have been captured and shot. The King himself is to be tried by a Commission. The inhabitants of the villages burned by us on the 16th are in front of us, with four guns and some cavalry. They are making for Mynpoorie.

October 18th. Started at four a.m., and only marched eight miles. At six a.m. a sudden halt was made, our advanced guard having come across a vidette of cavalry. In the darkness the party, consisting of twenty-six Sowars, escaped. We moved on slowly, but no body of the enemy were met or heard of. They are probably only watching our movements and falling back on Mynpoorie, some twenty miles distant. Brigadier H. Grant, 9th Lancers, arrived this morning from Delhi to take command of the column. His travelling by himself in a "gharee" (carriage) shows the good effect we have produced marching through a country which has been for five months in the mutineers' hands. A party of the Dholpore Pandys, several hundred in number, have passed from Muttra *via* Hattrass down country. Jehaleedad, with the remains of his Malagurh force and of the Jhansi Brigade, is said to have fled to Bareilly. From Delhi we hear that Brigadier Showers' column found Rewaree deserted. Rao Toolaram evacuated his fort, although (notwithstanding his friendship for us) he had twelve guns and a mortar on the ramparts, all loaded. He had also a gun foundry, in which two new brass guns, just made, were found. General Outram still at Lucknow. A force of four hundred men at Alumbagh keeps open his communication with Cawnpore. Oude and Rohilcund will be the two districts where the cold weather campaign will take place. The former is entirely hostile to us, the people fighting like fanatics. Except for the Pandys in the latter district, the inhabitants are friendly to us.

October 19th. Left our camp at two a.m. Our march was very slow, from being obliged to reconnoitre every short distance. A party of sowars were seen on our left, after whom Lieutenant Probyn and the 2nd Punjaub Cavalry galloped, but without seeing anything. On approaching Mynpoorie the delays were incessant. A fight was expected, and when a halt was ordered about a mile and a-half from the fort, the anxiety was great, a roundshot being expected every moment. Time drew on, and a white flag being seen waved from a high building, it became evident that the place was evacuated. Mr. Cox, C.S., on advancing with the advanced guard, found that the Rajah had fled at twelve p.m. He had, however, left the treasure, amounting to two and a-half lacs, behind. He has crossed the Jumna, and is about twenty-five miles from this. He will probably return soon. Having treated some of our poor women and refugees kindly, his life will be spared. Mynpoorie is a very pretty station, well wooded, with trees of an enormous size. The work of destruction has not been so complete here. The kutcherry, church, etc., are scarcely touched. The civilians' property has been spared, but all their bungalows burned. We did not reach our encamping ground until 11-30 a.m., having marched twenty-four miles, to the 70th milestone from Agra. It is reported that two infantry regiments and one of cavalry, with eight guns, from Futtehgurh, have been joined by numerous stragglers and have taken up a position seventeen miles from this. This is our next march, so we shall have to knock them out of the entrenched position they are said to occupy. We are encamped on the parade ground. The lines at the time of the outbreak were occupied by the 9th N.I. The Rajah has left behind some guns—one brass 6-pounder, which we have taken, and three or four small iron pieces, which we have burst. The magazine contains about one thousand maunds of powder, with which it is intended to blow up the fort. No loot was found, but the civilians' property (Cox and Power, C.S.) is safe. This, and the kindness of the Rajah to the refugees, will probably save his life.

October 20th. The enemy at Baiwah have retired to Futtehgurh. Went over the church this morning. The exterior is still entire, but the interior has been stripped of all its woodwork. The font is smashed in two. The seats, window-sashes, etc., have been carried off. This was all done by villagers, not by the Pandys. The fort is to be blown up to-day. Captain Bourchier is removing the little it contains. A cheetah, which was shot this morning, a few turkeys, geese, etc., were all the inmates. The city people are said to be delighted at our return, finding that more money (the natives' god) is to be got under British than under Pandy rule. This day year I embarked at Southampton, little thinking of spending such a twelve months. God, in His great mercy, has spared me and all my relations since then, in many dangers. Great quantities of loot were found in the fort, but by far the greatest part fell into other hands than those of the prize-agents. Only some silver vessels, tumblers, and glasses fell into our hands. The mine for blowing up the place was not ready to-day, so the Sappers have been left behind to finish the work, and follow us. The young Rajah is to be deposed, and his place filled by his uncle, who has all along been on our side. Lieutenant Gough, with the ammunition, having arrived from Agra to-day, there was nothing to keep us here longer.

October 21st. Left Mynpoorie at two a.m. Reached Bowgong, where this road joins the grand trunk road, about five a.m. This place is strong, many houses being built of stone. A large serai, with towers at the four corners, had embrasures knocked out for guns. This was the only hostile preparation seen. Reached Baiwah about 8.30 a.m. It is here the road to Futtehgurh branches off. At the side of our encampment is a large mango tope, where a large party of Pandys had been lately encamped; some remains of fires still smoking. They tell us here that they bolted for Futtehgurh the day before yesterday. In the village we hear that a large force, consisting of the Bareilly and Neemuch

Brigades, proceeded to attack Cawnpore. Our people hearing of their approach, advanced ten or fifteen miles to meet them. There they threw up a battery. Pandy ran his head against this unconsciously, and received a proper drubbing. Our force is said only to have been seven hundred men. We took, so the natives say, eight or ten guns. This report requires confirmation. The rebels are said to be fleeing from Futtehgurh, and all crowding towards Bareilly, where Buckdar Khan is said to be. We are picking up stray Pandys here and there, who are summarily dealt with. We got a letter yesterday addressed to Brigadier Chamberlain. It was from Colonel Nichol at Cawnpore, and was dated the 11th. He sends a telegraphic message received from Sir C. Campbell, who is still in Calcutta, but who was to leave on the 15th. The Commander-in-Chief orders the headquarter staff—who rush to Simla, as if that was the centre of operations—immediately to start for Cawnpore. English mail arrived to-day with news to the 10th September. Great excitement over the news of the Cawnpore massacre. The frightened garrison of Agra have got a report that thirty thousand rebels have crossed the Jumna at the Gumukteser Ghaut, and were making for Agra to attack it. To avoid receiving any letter advising us to return, we marched at eight p.m. Brigadier Grant is anxious to reach Cawnpore and relieve General Havelock.

October 22nd. Our progress was very slow until early this morning. The elephants for conveying the Infantry causing delay. Did not arrive at our encamping ground at Gorrygunge until nine a.m. We marched twenty-nine miles leaving only sixty-five between us and Cawnpore. No confirmation of the battle of which we heard yesterday. There must be some truth in it, as several guns are said to be a march in front of us, which the rebels left in their flight. The rebels are bolting everywhere. From Futtehgurh they are crossing the bridge of boats into Rohilcund. The Nawab of Futtehgurh in vain orders them to fight, as this is the only chance remaining to them. They, however, are desirous of reaching their homes with their ill-gotten loot. It is the enemy's Sowars who stop up Havelock's communication. Unless under a strong escort nothing can be procured in safety. Brigadier Showers' column is doing good service already. He has sent twelve guns to Delhi, and a great many prisoners to be tried by the military commission. In Assam to-day we heard of an outbreak. The 1st Assam Infantry showing the example. It consists chiefly of Poorbeas. The landed proprietors in that district still recognise the King of Delhi as their sovereign, having received the title deeds of their estates from him. The tea plantations are said to be all burned, and the planters seeking safety in numbers. Two hundred sailors have started with guns to their assistance. The rebels have broken down the suspension bridge on the road to Futtehgurh. Twelve or fourteen Pandys were cut up by our cavalry in the village this morning.

October 23rd. Started at two a.m. Marched thirteen miles to Meeran Ka Serai. The force who went to attack Cawnpore were here a few days ago. Our cavalry were sent out to bring in the four guns left behind by the rebels. The villagers told us they were about a *coss* off the road. On approaching the place, which turned out to be Kanouge, the ancient capital of the Rajpoot kings, the enemy with four guns opened upon them. Two of our pieces were hurried to the front. They came up with the enemy after they had crossed a nullah. A few round shot and grape sent them off, leaving all the guns behind. Our cavalry went in pursuit, killing about one hundred and fifty. The enemy were Pandys from Futtehgurh, who had been sent out to bring in the guns left behind by the Bareilly Brigade. Their information must have been bad as we took them by surprise. The captured ordnance consists of one 24-pound howitzer, one 6-pounder gun, and two native pieces of 3 or 4-pound. Numbers tried in vain to hide themselves in the maize fields, but the Sowars killed them all. We had only four or five wounded. A *cossid* from Cawnpore came in this morning. Havelock is completely hemmed in at Lucknow. They have supplies only until the 10th November. Our force is to proceed as rapidly as possible and relieve them. It is a curious thing the Delhi army reoccupying Lucknow. In July, Havelock was writing to us, "I shall be with you in a few days." We may now write in similar terms. The troops also, which arrived from England, are with him. He has parts of H.M. 64th, 78th, 90th, and 1st Madras Fusiliers. The Delhi force has done good service. It has captured the rebels' stronghold, relieved Agra, and is now proceeding to do the same at Lucknow. Started at twelve p.m., having a forced march to make.

October 24th. Reached our encamping ground at Poorah

at eight a.m., having come twenty-three miles. This leaves twenty-nine miles to Cawnpore. This we are to do in two marches. Another *cossid* from Colonel Wilson, sending an order from the Chief for us to press on. These letters are written in English, on small pieces of paper. The important parts are always written in the Greek character. Except the residency palace and a few buildings, the city of Lucknow is in the hands of the rebels. It is the want of cavalry that hampers Havelock's communication so much. He has none, while the enemy have great numbers. The Gwalior force has been heard of, proceeding in the direction of Jhansi. The country through which we pass is everywhere under cultivation. The crops are of the finest quality. Ploughing and sowing is going on in all parts. This shows how erroneous the idea of Disraeli and others is—that this is a national outbreak. Except for the ruined chokees, the broken telegraph, and burnt dâk bungalows, the grand trunk road would bear its usual peaceful appearance. Heard on our arrival of a Zemindar, in a neighbouring village, who had four hundred muskets and quantities of powder. The Irregular Cavalry went there, brought away the former, and blew up the latter. Seven or eight Pandys were captured in it. About eight p.m. firing commenced at one of our piquets. They were firing on a native whom they wounded. He turned out to be an unfortunate man in our service who had fallen into the hands of that monster Nana Sahib. This brute had cut off his nose and one arm, a punishment he proposes to inflict on all individuals in our service.

October 25th. Marched at three a.m. Reached Chowbeepore, thirteen miles distant, by 7.30 a.m. This is only fifteen miles from Cawnpore. A *cossid* came in this morning with a letter. Colonel Wilson, H.M. 64th, commanding at Cawnpore, tells us that he has fifteen hundred British bayonets with him. The road is stated still to be unsafe for single persons, as numbers of armed budmashes are on the way. The Nana Sahib is said to be only six *coss* from here, somewhere about Bithoor. He is on his way to join the Gwalior force on the other side of the Jumna, said to be advancing in this direction. He is said to have one thousand men and two guns. The Gwalior force is moving in two bodies. The siege train is with the rear division. The dâk between this and Agra is stopped near Baiwir by Pandys from Futtehgurh, who have brought up great guns. Sunday. The days and weeks pass so rapidly that nothing but the dates are remembered.

October 26th. Started at three a.m. Marched about fourteen miles, and encamped on the parade ground about eight a.m. It is very melancholy entering Cawnpore after the awful tragedy that occurred here a few months ago. Every place and bungalow strikes you as if it might have beheld some massacre more or less cruel. The avenging force is, however, rapidly assembling, when it is to be hoped a bloody revenge will be taken. News from Lucknow bad. The garrison are on three-quarter rations. The city is crowded with armed men who have numerous pieces of cannon. Havelock lost eleven hundred men killed and wounded in trying to take the city. He took fifty pieces, and with five hundred additional men would have captured the whole city. About five hundred men left this a few days ago with supplies, but they are to halt at the Alumbagh until our arrival. This place is held by one thousand bayonets. The number of the enemy is fearfully exaggerated, and for the most part consist of the inhabitants armed with matchlocks. The Naval Brigade with four 24-pounders are on their way here from Allahabad. Three hundred and ninety of H.M. 93rd and some Royal Artillery are expected here to-morrow or next day. Between this and Allahabad there are a thousand men marching up. The Gwalior force is at Kalpee, on this side of the Ganges. They have with them all the guns, ammunition, etc., of the magazine. Eight hundred hackeries are said to accompany them. Their force only amounts, including all, to some seven thousand men. We shall probably go against them before advancing on Lucknow. In the Bolundshureen district forty-seven guns have been dug up. There seems no limit to the number of pieces in the rebels' hands. Brigadier Showers has captured the Rajah of Juggur and some other small chiefs. He has also got twenty-seven cannon. Orders have been received to destroy all the walls and fortifications of Delhi. The city is still to exist. The King is to be tried by a Commission, and whatever sentence is awarded is to be carried into effect. The Rajah of Futtehgurh is offering fifty rupees for the capture of any native in our employ. No news to-day from Lucknow, nor of the progress of the convoy. The Chief telegraphs to-day that he will leave Calcutta to-morrow, and expects to be with us on the 1st. The column is to march to Alumbagh and await his arrival. A troop of

Horse Artillery and a squadron of Lancers remain here to escort him.

October 27th. Went out early this morning to see the 93rd Highlanders come in. They arrived, however, before daybreak. Rode to the entrenched position in which General Wheeler and the Europeans took shelter and so gallantly defended. It is surrounded by a low earthwork about four feet high—a poor protection from the storm of shot and shell. The house was an old barrack, and was chosen from being at a distance from any other building and on a plain. The building was burned, and the wounded, with the women and children, huddled into a ditch without protection from the fierce sun of an Indian June. The house is riddled with shot. Its being built of brick saved it from being knocked down. Not a yard of wall but has several cannon shots through it. The exterior is a melancholy sight. It is strewn with remains of books, bottles, clothes, baskets, etc. Here and there on the walls are marks of blood. No place was there in which to seek for shelter, shot and shell passed through and through the house. To bring water must have been a dangerous errand. The well is situated in rear of the building, exposed on all sides. No tongue can tell the scenes of anguish that occurred there. The daughters killed at their father's side, the mother at the son's; Lieutenant Wheeler was lying wounded, when a round shot came carrying off his head. The wall at this spot is covered with blood and hair. The exterior contains pieces of the human frame. I picked up the frontal bone of a child apparently ten or twelve years old. Awful as were the scenes that occurred here, they were nothing to what happened to the women and children afterwards. Behind the Assembly Rooms (in which they were kept for some time), the house is seen where the awful tragedy occurred. It is a small native dwelling-house, with a courtyard in the centre. The rooms ran one into the other round the yard. They were small and dark. Here our poor countrywomen stripped naked, and after being publicly exposed and brutally used, were brought. The Sowars went in and fired at every one living. The children were removed. Butchers were sent to finish this horrible massacre. On the river side of the house the gallows is still erected on which the innocent children were hanged. Some had their brains dashed out against the walls. These marks are still distinct. On the approach of our troops the mangled remains were cast into a well in the next compound. This has been covered in with earth, and it is intended to erect a monument over it. Near to this a small entrenched place has been made. One side is on the river's bank, the remainder defended by a deep ditch. It has several heavy guns and will prove a formidable place against Pandy. Saw five or six of the pieces taken from the Nana. One a long 6-pounder carronade, the rest are three or four 4-pounders on carriages. One returns from such places sad, and praying to God that he may soon give us ample revenge. Suraj Dowlah was merciful compared to this arch-monster. The scenes enacted under his orders have never been paralleled. The red Indians are the only race that comes near them. The blood of fifty thousand of the rebel Sepoys will not be too much. An awful example must be made. No mercy shown to any prisoners. Death to all who have arms.

October 28th. No further news from Lucknow. The Gwalior force at Kalpee has dwindled down to a few hundreds. The remainder are no one knows where. We are waiting the arrival of the rest of H.M. 93rd and one hundred and fifty of the Naval Brigade under Captain Peel, V.C. They left Futtehgurh last night, and come in here to-morrow morning. The weather here is very hot even at night. The mosquitoes are also very troublesome. No cold mornings as we had about Delhi. Our advance is delayed by orders from Sir Colin. He says the movable column equires rest after all their labours. The Ramgurh Battalion with four guns, was met by H.M. 53rd somewhere near Raneegunge. All their guns were captured, and a great many killed. The dâk from Calcutta comes in daily. That from the north-west is stopped, and will not be again open until the Futtehgurh Rajah is driven out of his stronghold.

October 29th. The convoy proceeding to Alumbagh has arrived safely without meeting with any opposition. No news from Lucknow itself. A party of Royal Artillery, consisting of four officers and sixty-five men, arrived this morning. Went over the magazine here this morning. It was being abolished when the mutiny commenced. The rebels, however, got one hundred and forty guns from it. On the arrival of General Havelock the mutineers blew it up. There were sixty thousand barrels of powder in it. The buildings are complete ruins—merely heaps of stones. A few shells, shot, etc., are lying about, as well as empty cartridge boxes, tins for containing caps, and barrels. One large house still stands, but its walls are cracked from the top to the bottom. The magazine is situated on the river's bank. A petition, numerously signed, has been sent home from Calcutta, praying for the recall of Lord Canning. He is too undecided and changeable, and too merciful towards the rebels. Everyone is hoping that Sir John Lawrence may be his successor. The Gwalior force has recrossed the Jumna at Kalpee, having heard that we were advancing against them. The bridge of boats they were making is still unfinished.

October 30th. Marched at seven a.m. Crossed the bridge of boats that we have made immediately in front of the intrenchment. The road lies along a sandy deposit left during the rains. Encamped about three miles from Cawnpore, at a place called Oonao. This is a large marshy plain. It was here General Havelock had a fight. The enemy's battery still stands, commanding the road about half a mile beyond camp. Days are increasing in warmth. It was 95° about mid-day in a tent. A *cossid* came in from General Outram, saying that they were holding their own with ease, and that numbers were leaving the city. Their opponents were chiefly armed budmashes and the old soldiers of the King, who were disbanded on our taking the country. He had heard of the Gwalior force advancing, and said we ought to go and attack them first, as he could hold out till the end of November. The additional Infantry that we have received at Cawnpore, consists of three hundred and ninety of H.M. 93rd, one hundred and fifty of H.M. 53rd, fifty of H.M. 5th

Fusiliers, and sixty-five of the Royal Artillery. The whole of the Infantry is commanded Colonel Grey, H.M. 5th. The Highlanders are the admiration of everyone in camp, especially of the Sikhs. The latter cannot understand them, especially whether their calves are real or not. They still wear the same immense plumed hat, but with a puggree round the edge. Instead of a red coat they have got a fawn-coloured one with red facings. The men are splendid, of immense size, and of powerful build. Lieutenant-Colonel Hope commands them. The Sikhs admire the bagpipes immensely, saying it is the finest music we have. What a curious thing, the plains of Oude re-echoing with the wild airs of a nation previously unheard of by them, but well-known among western lands. The Highland Celt, in his native garb, coming thousands of miles to subdue the Mussulman. What a page of history does that open; in fact, the history of England during two centuries, with its virtues and great crimes.

October 31st. Started at two a.m. Marched fourteen miles. The whole country is marshy, and in some places large stagnant pools occur. This plentiful supply of water betokens a rich country. All houses and villages are completely destroyed by General Havelock. No inhabitants are on the roadside to salaam to you on passing. Cultivation is going on, but very sparingly when compared with the right bank of the river. Passed a large village, Buperutgunge, about 6.30 a.m. Havelock had a fight here. The town is surrounded by a large ditch full of water. A battery had been erected across the road at the entrance gate. The neighbouring houses bore marks of cannon shot. The road passes along the chief street. The houses are arched, and give it a pleasing appearance. A gate with two turrets at the other end of the village. About three hundred yards beyond this is a broad swamp with a sluggish river running through. It would have proved a strong position if properly defended. News from Lucknow to-day by natives. It is said most of the Sepoys are leaving. Maun Singh, a large Hindoo Zemindar in Oude, commands all the forces at Lucknow. Two expeditions went out to-day. The first produced nothing. The second was to a village seven miles distant, where three hundred Pandys are said to be. Whatever truth was in this rumour, only six were killed, everyone else having made off. One Sikh was shot dead by a Sepoy in a house. The Highlanders had their first day's work. They are all armed with the Enfield rifle, and will, no doubt, use it well. An indiscriminate slaughter of pigs, geese, chickens, wound up the day's forage.

November 1st. Marched at three a.m. Reached our encamping ground at Bunniabad, fifteen miles distant, at 7.30 a.m. About half a mile from camp our progress was arrested. A bridge over the river had been broken. The centre arch was cut away for about twenty feet. We were obliged to ford the river above. It was luckily only about three and a half feet deep. The hackeries were delayed some time. Distinctly heard the booming of heavy guns from Lucknow, about fifteen miles from this. There was one every five minutes or so. About ten a.m. they stopped, and were not heard again during the day. Sunday. Everything quiet to-day.

November 2nd. The march which was ordered for four a.m. was during the night delayed until seven. No one could give any reason, but it was supposed it arose from orders from the Chief to await his arrival, without advancing on Alumbagh. It turned out a very fortunate thing. We had only got about a mile from camp when musketry was heard at the advanced guard. The quartermasters had ridden on to mark out the camp about one mile further on, when they found themselves surrounded and obliged to run amuck through the Pandys. They all escaped unhurt. Two of Captain Blunt's guns soon after opened on the village. The 75th and some Sikhs were pushed on. Most of the artillery moved to the right to prevent any cavalry from coming up. The fire from the *Ghurrie,* or mud fort, for some time was very hot. They had no guns in it. No entrance could be found into the village for long, and when our troops got in, everyone had sought refuge in houses where they had bolted the door. A square tower long resisted all efforts to gain admission. In it were a lot of men armed with matchlocks, who kept up an incessant fire. At last one of the 18-pounders commanded by Captain Travers of the Royal Artillery came up, and after firing three rounds an opening was made, into which our troops entered and killed every man. The total number killed there was about fifty. Our loss was one Highlander, two Sappers, and one or two Sikhs killed, and ten or twelve wounded. A Captain McKenzie, of the 78th Highlanders, was shot through the thigh. These rascals were not Pandys, but probably the King of Oude's soldiers, as none had muskets, only matchlocks. The name of this village is Buntra. While this was going on the Horse Artillery advanced to the right, to a place from whence loud shouts were heard issuing. These turned out to be some three or four hundred men trying to make off across a large plain. About two hundred were Sowars. The guns advanced, unlimbered, fired a few rounds and again proceeded. This was kept up for about six miles, but Pandy had such good legs there is no getting up with him. The high sugarcane fields gave protection to most of those on foot. The pursuit was across a large maidan, only broken here and there by topes of trees and small mud villages. Several hackeries were run down containing women and children. They foolishly covered themselves over with clothes, so when our men came up they thrust their swords into them. One cart contained two women and six children; everyone of whom was more or less wounded. Even an infant, a month old, was cut in the chin, its mother being shot in the thigh. Beside another cart sat a women chanting a requiem over the body of her husband, newly slain. Such are the sad sights met with during war. After halting here for about half an hour we returned, expecting that our day's work was over. At the other side of the plain beneath a clump of trees a large body of infantry and cavalry were seen. Our guns and cavalry immediately advanced. When they were about six hundred yards from the enemy, the rebels sent a volley of grape, then a round shot, but without touching anyone. Everyone was expecting them to stand, but no sooner had a round shot been sent amongst them than off they went, dragging their guns. The cavalry did the same, at first trotting, then at a furious gallop as shot began to reach them. One Sowar was killed here. He was a Ressaldar. We advanced towards a village, outside of which a waggon was found full of ammunition, and at the entrance to the place a 9-pounder gun. The limber contained hammered round shot and powder, both of their own manufacture. This looks well, their supply must be running short. At this place we were only four miles from Alumbagh. After burning all the villages about, we returned four miles back, and reached camp at 1.30 p.m. What the motive of these rascals was is evident. They only arrived during the night, and, expecting that we would march before daybreak, they thought it would be a good opportunity of capturing our baggage. By allowing the column to pass they might have cut up a great number of the camp followers, and in the darkness make off with the camels. The receipt of the letter from the Chief prevented this disgrace. He wrote from Allahabad saying he would reach Cawnpore the morning of the 3rd, and ordering us, supposing we were still there, to cross the river and take up a strong position. Three Pandys of the 60th N.I., that fought so well at Delhi, were killed to-day.

November 3rd. Went over the village of Buntra this morning. A great part was still unburned, but we finished the rest. Saw only nineteen dead bodies. In the mud tower five were lying. These native villages are very strong, the passages between the houses are so narrow, and no direct communication through the place. From the tower, if they had been good shots, our loss would have been great. They commanded the approach completely. No loot was to be found, plenty of togs, baskets, and rubbish. Parties have been sent out to burn the villages around this. Everyone contains twenty or thirty matchlockmen. The whole population is against us. Yesterday the wounded family were in great terror we would murder them all, evidently having been told so. The Lancers were bringing them water and pouring it on their wounds; in fact, acting the "Good Samaritan." When such things are heard of it will allay the ferocity of the Mussulmen. Nothing but burning villages has been doing to-day. Fourteen in this neighbourhood were destroyed. No armed men were met with in any of them. A little firing heard early this morning at Lucknow, but none during the day. The Naval Brigade and the rest of the Highlanders have arrived at Cawnpore, and will probably join us. No news of the Commander-in-Chief.

November 4th. Went over the village of Buntra again. Swarms of vultures, dogs, and other unclean animals are prowling about. Most of the bodies are half devoured. It is a disgusting sight to see the human form lately in the pride of health now the food for dogs. There is a curious circumstance connected with the wound of Captain McKenzie, H.M. 78th, received on the 2nd ult. It is the *third* time he has been shot through the same thigh, while trying to reach Lucknow. A *cossid* came in from Cawnpore. The Chief is there. He had a narrow escape below Benares. The *gharrie* in which he was, was suddenly brought to a stand-still by some villagers. On his getting out, a party of the 32nd N.I. were seen in front. He has sent orders for one convoy to be sent in immediately to Alumbagh, its stores to be left behind, and the troops to escort it and the previous convoy back to Cawnpore. This is to enable fresh men to be sent out to join us. He sent us news of a fight at Futtypore on the 1st. The troops there, five hundred strong, chiefly consisting of H.M. 53rd, marched out to attack the rebels they heard were approaching. The rebels were the 7th, 19th (?), 50th, and 30th N.I., and numbered some three thousand. We had some of the Naval Brigade. The result was the complete rout of the enemy, with the loss of all their guns and three hundred killed. Our casualties were thirty killed and sixty wounded. Colonel Powell, C.B., H.M. 53rd, killed, and seven officers wounded. The mutineers were probably on their way to join the Gwalior force still at Kalpee.

November 5th. The convoy started about five a.m., escorted by Captain Bourchier's battery, a squadron of H.M. Lancers, 2nd and 5th Punjaub Cavalry, H.M. 5th Fusiliers, H.M. 53rd, H.M. 93rd, and one Sikh Infantry Corps. With such an escort there is little to fear on this side of Lucknow. Firing at Lucknow much more frequent this morning. The convoy arrived quite safe. Bodies of cavalry were seen all day watching their movements, but keeping at a safe distance. At one place they brought out a 4-pounder gun and fired a shot or two, but the first fired by us sent them to the right about. The garrison of Alumbagh consists of one thousand available men. It is commanded by Colonel McIntosh, H.M. 78th. He was in want of ammunition, and had received strict orders to act only on the defensive. Pandy taking advantage of this, has two light guns in position, and keeps firing every now and then. A few men could take it at any time. They had no news from Lucknow. They hear the rebels are mining the road. The Fort of Jellalabad to the south of Lucknow, is defended by two regiments. By all accounts the fighting is child's play compared with that at Delhi. The convoy arrived in camp after sunset. The elephants, bullocks, etc., are in very bad condition. No one was allowed beyond the walls, so fodder was scarce. About seventy sick were brought away, the large majority being wounded.

November 6th. Last night it was remarkably cold, quite a frosty feeling in the morning. It is the cold weather commencing at last. The empty carts, camels, and wounded started for Cawnpore about ten a.m. They proceed about fifteen miles, and expect an escort to be sent out for them. The guard from this consists of the 1st Punjaub Cavalry and Hodson's Horse, under Lieutenant Watson and Lieutenant Gough, 3rd L.C. Orders came from the Chief to have tents pitched for him immediately, as he would be here in two or three days. No news of any description.

November 7th. A letter from Alumbagh asking for reinforcements, as the rebels were making approaches towards them; as if a thousand Europeans were not sufficient to protect themselves against any number of Pandys. This request has not been complied with. About twelve a.m. our reinforcement came in, consisting of one hundred men of the Naval Brigade, with four 24-pounders, two hundred and fifty of H.M. 53rd, and about three hundred of H.M.

93rd, under Colonel Leith Hay. The sailors are splendid fellows; they all belong to Captain W. Peel's ship, the "Shannon." Their commander is on his way here with six more guns. Pandy will have little chance against such men. The sailors and the Highlanders divide the admiration of the Sikhs between them. The latter are called the *Piharrie Pulten*, or the *Gogra Wallahs* (the petticoat regiment). The sailors are prodigies to them. They say "*Itna burra wallah*," with their hands marking four or five feet, as the breadth of their shoulders. The people of Oude say the Highlanders are the ghosts of the women massacred at Cawnpore.

November 8th (Sunday). No news to-day. The Chief is daily expected. With the Naval Brigade we have two lords —Lord W. Kerr, brother of the Marquis of Lothian, and Lord Clinton. They are both middies; the former a tall strapping fellow, the latter a beardless boy of about fourteen. Lord Seymour accompanies them in search of new scenes, probably for information regarding India and its people. This country will for the future occupy the minds of statesmen more than it has done since the days of Warren Hastings.

November 9th. Shifted our camp about half a mile further on, to escape the filth that had collected during the last week. Colonel Biddulph, 45th N.I., arrived to-day. He has come as head of the Intelligence Department. It is to be hoped that he will obtain more certain news of the enemy than has been done as yet. The Commander-in-Chief, Sir Colin Campbell, with his Staff, came in about four p.m. He had ridden the whole way from Cawnpore, about thirty miles. His Staff consists of Major-General Mansfield, Chief of the Staff; Major Alison, Military Secretary; Sir David Baird, Captain Alison, aide-de-camp. Major-General Windham, of Redan celebrity, commands at Cawnpore.

November 10th. A European, Mr. Cavanagh, belonging to the Customs, came in disguised as a native from Lucknow. He states that they are all well in the Residency, and that there are only twelve thousand armed men in the city. The last part is not to be depended on, as at Delhi we always found calculations were in the end incorrect. Two guns under Lieutenant Macleod, with a squadron of Lancers, went into Alumbagh to-day with orders. Colonel Russell, H.M. 84th, goes in to take command. The remainder of the Naval Brigade, under Captain W. Peel, came in this afternoon. They brought two 24-pounders, two 8-inch mortars, and two 5½-inch. The remainder of H.M. 93rd and 53rd, with headquarters, came in at the same time. The latter are commanded by Major Clarke.

November 11th. A great deal of firing towards Alumbagh, supposed to be our soldiers going out to attack the guns that annoyed them. No news has come in. Received letters. The enemy's Sowars attacked our grasscutters to-day, killing one and wounding another. These rascals came out of Jellalabad, and cut up the unarmed followers. Had a parade of the whole force, to be inspected by Sir Colin Campbell. We were drawn up in a long line. The Horse Artillery, Cavalry, and Infantry stationed from right to left. He rode down the whole line at a gallop with his Staff, then walked back examining all, and returned, addressing some words to each regiment. He was enthusiastically cheered by all. The Chief looks well, and does not appear weighed down by the load of nearly seventy years. Had all the Naval Brigade dining with us. Captain W. Peel (son of the great Sir Robert) looks very young, about twenty-five. It was he who distinguished himself so much before Sebastopol, and got the V.C. for throwing a live shell over the parapet of a battery. The Military Train, sixty in number, came in to-day. They are mounted, and do duty as dragoons. They were horsed from the 8th Madras Cavalry that mutinied. Some Royal Engineers came in this evening. They number about one hundred and fifty. Major Goodwyn, R. E., commands the whole of the pack.

November 12th. Started at seven a.m. We proceeded to within a mile of Alumbagh without seeing anything of the enemy. On the advanced guard proceeding opposite Jellalabad, several guns from a battery, erected under a tope of trees, opened on them. The shot hit the road, passed across it, but did no harm. Two guns of the 2nd troop were ordered out and Captain Bourchier's battery. On seeing this Pandy, with bullocks, tried to drag away the guns. Our pieces, however, opening on them, they unharnessed the guns and bolted, leaving them to their fate. On our cavalry advancing, they were found to be two native pieces of 3 or 4-pound calibre. It was Lieutenant Gough, with Hodson's Horse, who captured them. The Irregulars continued the pursuit, and cut up about forty Pandys who were bolting.

Jellalabad was reconnoitred by the Chief. Armed men were seen on the walls, but no gun was seen or fired. While this was going on we advanced to Alumbagh, which was then, as it generally is, playing at long bowls with a battery of the enemy about twelve hundred yards away. They luckily have no shells, but fire one 24-pound shot out of a 24-pound howitzer. It is in front of a large yellow house, and is a capital mark for our gunners. Several of our shrapnell burst beautifully over it. One of their guns was silenced by us in the morning. While we were waiting for the marking out of our camp, bodies of Sowars and infantry were seen advancing, as if trying to get in our rear to cut off the baggage. The Lancers and three guns went out, followed by the infantry, under Colonel Hope. After firing a few shots the rebels fled, and so fast that the cavalry cut up none. After pursuing some distance, two guns from a tope of trees opened, so we retired, having orders only to protect the camp. Our tents are pitched about eight hundred yards on the Cawnpore side of the Bagh, so as to be beyond the reach of shot from the battery. It was not until nearly three p.m. that we got under shelter. The Alumbagh is a large square, about four hundred and fifty yards on each side. It is surrounded by a brick wall. Since our arrival we have thrown up earthworks all round. At the four corners are earthen bastions armed with guns. The place is safe from any number of infantry. In the centre of the garden is a large white building with four towers and a flat roof. On this roof we have erected a semaphore, which telegraphs with General Havelock. The Bailie Guard at the Residency can be distinctly seen. A salvo was to have announced our arrival, but a telegraph sign was made that they were aware of our presence. Messages are going and coming communicating our movements and giving information from Lucknow. The force now with us is divided into four brigades. The whole is commanded by Brigadier Grant, of course under the Commander-in-Chief's orders.

The 1st Brigade is the Cavalry. It consists of H.M. 9th Lancers, commanded by Lieutenant-Colonel Little; 3rd Punjaub Cavalry, under Lieutenant Watson, Bombay Army; 2nd Punjaub Cavalry, under Lieutenant Probyn, 6th L.C.; 5th Punjaub Cavalry, under Lieutenant Younghusband, Bombay Army; Hodson's Horse, under Lieutenant Gough, 3rd L.C.; Military Train, Brigade-Major Captain Hamilton, 9th Lancers.

II. Brigade. Artillery, Major F. Turner; Brigade Major, Captain Hammond, Artillery. Naval Brigade, commanded by Captain W. Peel, C.B.; Detachment of Royal Artillery, Captain Travers; 1st Troop 1st Brigade H.A., Captain Remmington; 2nd Troop 3rd Brigade H.A., Captain Blunt; 17th Light Field Battery, Captain Bourchier.

III. Infantry Brigade, commanded by Colonel Greathed, H.M. 8th; Brigade Major, Captain Bannatyne, H.M. 8th. H.M. 8th, Major Hinde; H.M. 75th, Major Gordon; 2nd Punjaub Infantry, Captain Green, 2nd Europeans.

IV. Infantry Brigade, commanded by Colonel the Hon. Adrian Hope, 93rd; Brigade-Major, Captain Cox, H.M. 75th. H.M. 53rd, Major Clarke; H.M. 93rd, Colonel Leith Hay; 4th Punjaub Infantry, Lieutenant Paul, 7th N.I.

The enemy's heavy gun did not fire at all after twelve a.m. They have probably removed it.

November 13th. Except a few musket shots at the piquet on our left front, everything was quiet during the night. A force started at 8.30 a.m., consisting of the two 18-pounders and one 8-inch howitzer, under Captain Travers, R.A.; four 9-pounders of Captain Bourchier's battery; two companies of H.M. 93rd, 75th and 53rd, with the Irregular Cavalry, all under the command of Brigadier Hope. Their destination is Jellalabad. Went over the Alumbagh. It is disgustingly dirty, and overcrowded with men, elephants, bullocks, etc. Everything appears in confusion, and no order in pitching of tents or anything. It is a place quite safe against such an enemy as Pandy. About ten a.m. the force returned from Jellalabad. It was found evacuated. About fifteen hundred men were seen leaving it last night. It is to be blown up. The enemy brought out two guns, and kept firing at our advanced piquet on the left. Four of our guns turned out, but after waiting a short time they returned. Our piquet was strengthened, and Pandy kept firing a couple of shots now and then, doing little harm. This is the kind of fighting he likes, playing at long bowls; making a great deal of noise while he is in safety himself. When it comes to giving and taking hard knocks, he bolts immediately. One company of H.M. 93rd, the head-quarters, and three hundred men of H.M. 23rd, and two hundred of H.M. 82nd, came in to-day. One hundred and twenty of the Royal Engineers, and some Madras Engineers accompanied them—total, about seven hundred men. A demonstration towards our left front was made this evening, the Commander-in-Chief, with all his Staff, being present. It was to deceive the enemy, making him suppose our attack would be in that quarter. Pandy fired seven or eight shots at them, but all miraculously escaped unhurt. About twenty mortars came in to-day. They are to be manned by the R.A. All private tents were ordered into the Alumbagh to-day; one mess tent and one hospital tent being allowed for each regiment or troop.

November 14th. Our advanced guard started at 8.30 a.m. Our course is quite different from General Havelock's. He went the direct road from Alumbagh through the city. We leave it on the left, crossing country towards Dilkusha House, about three miles distant. The canal, the bridges across which have all been broken down, is the chief difficulty. The advanced guard proceeded until they reached the Dilkusha Park wall without meeting with any opposition. In one place a few Pandys were seen, but two shells sent them off. The 2nd Troop 3rd Brigade, with which I was, was a rear-guard. It was not until one p.m. that we even started. Pandy amused himself firing at us from a mile's distance. From his throwing away shot as he does, you would think his stock was never ending. While we were waiting, a battery of R.A., under Captain Middleton, two guns of a troop of Madras H.A., one company of H.M. 23rd, and two of the 82nd, with a troop of the Military Train came in. After leaving their tents they joined us as rear-guard. Passed Jellalabad on the right, about one mile. It is a mud fort with high walls, surrounded by a ditch. At the four corners are towers, and in the centre a stronghold. At the place where we crossed the road from it to Lucknow, a few Pandys were collected. They hid in the jungle and kept firing at us. A party of skirmishers were thrown out and drove them back without loss on either side. From this we turned to the right, across fields ankle deep in dust. It was scarcely possible to breathe the clouds were so dense. After innumerable stoppages we came to a nullah where several hackeries had broken down. Instead of assisting each other the drivers were sitting enjoying a pipe. After getting all the carts across we proceeded a little further and bivouacked in a nullah. Among the topes of trees and in the house of Dilkusha, the main column first met with opposition from the Pandys. We opened upon them with one light gun and two 18-pounders. After a very heavy cannonade our infantry advanced. Pandy evacuated the whole place, and retired *via* La Martiniere upon Lucknow. The whole force advanced, drove them from the jungle, and encamped in front of it. They were beneath a large grove of trees, with the Martiniere garden and a village in the rear. The right front and flank protected by the canal, at this place dry, Pandy having dammed it up. On the left was a large open space guarded by our guns. Towards four p.m. Pandy came out in force, and tried to retake the position. They got into a village on the banks of the canal and kept up a heavy musketry fire. From this, after a little, they were driven by salvos from the Naval Brigade, while H.M. 93rd and the Sikhs charged. One of our shrapnells is said to have killed nearly thirty men. They were all found in one heap. Here we lost Captain Wheatcroft, H.M. 6th D.G., doing duty with Lancers, and Lieutenant A. C. Mayne, Bengal Artillery. Only two guns, 6 or 9-pounders, were captured during the day. During the night all was very quiet. H.M. 75th are left to garrison Alumbagh, the detachments of H.M. 64th, 78th and 80th coming on with us.

November 15th (Sunday). At daybreak we on the rear-guard found we were only a mile from the Dilkusha Park, where all the heavy baggage and cattle remains. The house was one of the residences of the King of Oude. It has been turned into a field hospital. This establishment consists of Supt.-Surgeon Dickson, Surgeon Wilkie, Field Surgeon; Assistant-Surgeons F. Corbyn and O'Dowd, assistants. The house is situated on the most elevated piece of ground in the neighbourhood. On the right, about half a mile, runs the Goomtee, a very winding and currentless river. From the flat roof of the house the whole country is seen. The entrance is by a lofty staircase, leading to a portico with immense pillars. At each corner are lofty turrets. The rooms are large and high. The walls were hung with beautiful mirrors, but the Europeans and Sikhs from pure wantonness broke them. About half a mile to the right front, on the banks of the river, stands the immense pile of buildings, La Martiniere, its front is semicircular looking towards the river. A tall pillar in the middle of a tank is erected to General Martin, the founder. The centre consists of a mass of buildings surmounted on the top by an open crown of masonry like St. Giles' in Edinburgh. The tops of the walls and turrets are covered with statues, which look well at a little distance, but on a nearer approach are found to be made of mortar. It was a college for the education of half-caste children. They are all in the Residency. From the top a fine view of Lucknow with its mosques and palaces is obtained. Our headquarters are fixed here. The Residency can be distinctly seen. A semaphore has been erected, and telegraphic messages carried on. The side next the city was being fortified, the windows filled up and loopholes made. It had never entered Pandy's head our coming in another direction. Our force was bivouacked at the Lucknow side beneath trees, the road running through our centre. Our piquets were about half a mile in front. The enemy occupied the houses in front, and, taking advantage of the broken ground, annoyed us by skirmishes. Day and night the popping went on, little damage being done to either party. Now and then the Naval Brigade sent shells and rockets among them. About two p.m. two guns were brought out on our right flank. They came close up, hidden by the jungle, and threw shot among us. No sooner had our guns opened than they fled, the Sowars showing the example. From the top of La Martiniere numbers of Sowars and Pandys could be seen across the river, towards the bridge of the Fyzabad road. They kept moving about, but appear to have no guns. Our casualties small in spite of the constant musketry fire. At eight p.m. a salute of four guns was fired as a signal to the garrison that their relief was at hand.

November 16th. The troops started at nine a.m. We

crossed the bed of the canal, leaving La Martiniere on our right, and passed along the right bank of the Goomtee for some distance. The enemy were still moving about where we saw them yesterday. Across fields, jungly ground, and sandy roads in native villages we marched. Places scarcely broad enough for one gun, and overgrown with dense jungle, were passed through without a shot being fired. While winding through a narrow native bazaar our advanced guard of cavalry was attacked. This was Secunderabagh, a garden of the King's. As the column advanced the musketry increased. The confusion in the narrow streets was awful, bullets whistling about, officers hurrying to the rear to bring up the heavy guns and infantry, and native grooms blocking up the road with led horses. The 53rd, in front, kept up a musketry fire on the building, there being no entrance into it until it was breached. The building consisted of a large square with a garden in the centre, at each corner were turrets covered with earth. At each end was a gateway with towers. The walls, towers, etc., were loopholed. Before the west gateway a breastwork and ditch were made. At the east was a semicircular wall of brick. To the right of west entrance was a large hole with a 6-pounder gun pointing. It was defended by two thousand Pandys who had sworn to die. About twenty yards to the north was a large serai also occupied. Its walls were of mud, the roof of tiles. By dragging away a few of the latter, muskets could be pointed. The gateway was protected by an earthwork. When the 18-pounders with the R.A. were brought up, the fire was directed on the south-west turret. Captain Blunt's troop was ordered to fire at the west gate. After about half an hour's fire a large hole was made in the turrets. During all this time our troops were exposed to a most deadly fire, being only one hundred yards from the main building and twenty from the serai. Within a quarter of an hour two men were killed and fourteen wounded out of some fifty. The 53rd, 93rd and 4th Punjaubees were now drawn up, and when the breach was made, with a loud cheer in they rushed through a heavy fire. The enemy fought with desperation. They had a pair of colours, round which they flocked; these were captured by Colonel Ewart and Captain Burroughs, of the 93rd, although both were wounded in doing so. The place being surrounded by us, scarcely a man escaped the bullet or bayonet. In the east turret sixty men held out all day, and it was not until evening that they were all taken and killed. Among them were some Sikhs. Our Punjaubees spat in their faces, taunted them with being traitors, and then shot them. The Naval Brigade was brought to the front with the other heavy pieces, and a cannonade was kept up on the enemy's guns and the Shah Nusjhid, the next stronghold. Pandy is very badly off for pieces, and has no shells except some brass and zinc ones, which do not burst with effect. They brought out two guns on our left flank; one we captured, the other, though fired at for hours, could not be silenced. It kept sending shot into our hospital in the serai, but doing no harm. From one p.m. until five, the firing at the Shah Nusjhid was incessant. At the latter hour a general advance on our line was made. An 18-pounder was taken up close to the wall of the Shah Nusjhid. After half an hour's cannonade the musketry fire became so hot it was ordered to be withdrawn. The Highlanders, who had been lying down, were ordered to retire also. Brigadier Hope having heard of an entrance into the building, and not liking to retire, took fifty of the 93rd to examine it. He arrived, got on the walls with his men, extending them to the right and left. The remainder of the regiment being brought up, the place was soon in our hands. This occurred at sunset. As darkness fell, the musketry lessened and gradually died away. An accident, fatal in its results, occurred in the Secunderabagh, where the sixty Pandys had held out. A large quantity of powder was found. It was ordered to be removed by the 5th Fusiliers. Lieutenant Paul, 4th Punjaub Infantry, was superintending, when, from some unknown cause, it exploded, wounding and burning all the bystanders. Several, with the officer, have since died. After the explosion the building caught fire, and a rumour arose that powder existed at all the four corners. The field hospital, with the immense numbers of wounded, had been placed beneath the south wall. An immediate order was given for their removal, but before it could be half accomplished it was dark. The confusion was awful, no doctor knew where his men were; some were in one place, some in another. All were exposed without covering to the cold and dew. Many must have died from this who would otherwise have lived. One of the enemy's guns, an 18-pounder, across the Goomtee on our right, did a great deal of damage by the accurate fire it kept up. The first shot blew up a tumbrel of the Naval Brigade, wounding and killing several. Our loss was severe, but not more than might have been expected.

Royal Artillery.—Killed, Captain Hardie; wounded, Lieutenants Ford and Salmond, Assistant-Surgeon Veale, Captain Travers (slightly), Major Pennycuick (slightly).

All the officers of the Bengal Artillery escaped unhurt.

H.M. 53rd.—Wounded, Captain Hammond (severely).

H.M. 93rd.—Wounded, Captain Walton (severely), Lieutenant Monro (dangerously).

Killed, Lieutenant Dalzell, Lieutenant Lumsden, doing duty; wounded, Lieutenant-Colonel Ewart (slightly), Captain Burroughs (slightly), Lieutenant M'Namara (slightly), Lieutenant Cooper (severely), Lieutenant Wood (severely), Lieutenant Welch (severely), Lieutenant Goldsmith (severely).

H.M. 5th.—Killed, J. W. Benson, C.S. Volunteers.

H.M. 90th.—Wounded, Major Barnston (severely), Lieutenant Wynne (slightly), Lieutenant Powell (slightly).

Naval Brigade—Killed, Midshipman M. A. Daniell; wounded, Lieutenant Salmond (severely), Midshipman Lord Clinton (slightly).

2nd Punjaub Infantry.—Killed, Lieutenant Frankland; wounded, Lieutenant Watson (dangerously).

4th Punjaub Infantry.—Killed, Captain Paul, Lieutenant Oldfield; wounded, Lieutenant McQueen (severely).

1st Madras Fusiliers.—Wounded, Lieutenant Dobbs (slightly).

Sir Colin was struck by a spent ball. Wounded, Major Alison, military secretary (severely, arm amputated), Lieutenant Allison (slightly), A.D.C. Captain Hon. A. H. Anson, A.D.C. to General Grant (slightly).

Hodson's Horse—Wounded, Lieutenant Hackett (severely).

November 17th. Pandy's fire was much weaker this morning. Our heavy guns were advanced to the left and a heavy breaching fire kept up on the mess-house of H.M. 32nd. On the right our guns bore on the Moti Mahal, a large palace, the last building between us and the Residency. The 18-pounder on the other side of the river still kept annoying us. The Naval Brigade opened upon it, and at the third round dismounted it. The mess-house is a large stone building on an elevated spot, commanding all the neighbourhood. About twelve a.m. a magazine of the enemy's in it exploded. The mess is between the Nawab's Palace and the Shah Nusjhid, a little in front of both. On the city side, and to the left, is the Kaiser Bagh, the King's Palace. About three p.m. our infantry were assembled, and an advance made. With cheers the mess-house and Moti Mahal were taken. At the latter place the junction with the garrison, under Sir H. Havelock, was made. He and Sir James Outram, and five of his staff, rode out. In their short gallop three of the officers were wounded. The garrison are well, but badly off for tobacco, milk, etc. For two months they have been on half rations. Yesterday they made a sally, intending to join us, but, after losing twenty-five killed and wounded, they retired. We lost this evening Lieutenant-Colonel Biddulph, 45th N.I., the head of the Intelligence Department, and Lieutenant Thompson, H.M. 82nd. Went over the Secunderabagh this morning. The bodies are lying knee-deep in places. At one point, where the explosion occurred, hundreds are lying half burnt and burning. The smell is sickening. The Pandys chiefly belong to the 1st, 10th, 22nd, and 71st N.I. Several women are among the dead. The volleys had killed them also. At one gateway two hundred and seventy were counted; at the other, two hundred and fifty. It was intended to make this the field hospital, but the dead were so numerous it was impossible to remove them in time. It has, therefore, been placed for the present in the serai or native barrack alongside. After the Moti Mahal was taken, Pandy brought out three light guns with cavalry. They came so near that the Highlanders picked off the gunners and so many of the Sowars that they left the pieces and fled.

November 18th. The wounded, about two hundred and wenty in number, were sent with an escort to the Dilkusha House, which had been held by H.M. 8th. This movement was ordered from four or five shots having struck the building they were in; they came from the same gun on our right. Two of the Naval Brigade guns kept firing at it, but only stopped them firing it, but did not damage it. During last night Captain Peel's guns were put in battery, and opened about ten a.m. on the Kaiser Bagh, where Pandy holds his headquarters. Seven or eight mortars also threw shells into it. The firing was continuous all day, and a practicable breach made. Just at sunset Pandy came out, and tried to take Jack's guns. They were received with such a heavy cannonade that they retired. We took the European hospital in the evening. Pandy, on finding it slipping into our hands, set fire to it, expecting by this to drive us from it. The building, being thatched, burned very brightly, but did not drive us out; until morning it kept smouldering.

Brigadier Russell had a very narrow escape this evening. While standing behind a wall with Captain Bourchier, a round shot came and knocked them both down, hitting the Brigadier on the back of the neck. He totally lost the power of motion, but was quite sensible. The skin was only grazed. The sick and wounded in the garrison amount to five hundred; the efficient men to two thousand. A covered way is being made, by which the ladies and children can be removed without danger. The killed have been very numerous: fifteen officers of H.M. 32nd, nine of the 7th L.C., one of the 71st N.I. Almost all the Artillery officers are dead. Macfarlane still alive, having been twice wounded. Bryce died of cholera. The inmates have not been so badly off after all. They were on half rations, but it was regular. Some of the original garrison had taken in plenty of grain, filled all their cellars, etc. Mr. Gubbins, C.S., was one; and the kind treatment he bestowed on all those ill is the theme of admiration to all. He acted the "Good Samaritan," taking them into his house, and giving them food and wine, which was very scarce. Sixty of the wounded were removed this evening, and sent on in doolies to the Dilkusha. General Havelock's entrance was not such a glorious affair as we thought. They reached the Residency in utter confusion, having lost muskets, ammunition, and supplies. Instead of strengthening the garrison they weakened them, eating up all the supplies. In such a hurry did they rush in that thirty doolies with wounded men were left outside. No one could see them from the Residency, and the enemy did not dare to come so near, so the poor fellows died of starvation. The skeletons were found this morning. Selfishness seems to have been a great failing of the inmates. The sick died from want of stimulants, while some officers were revelling in champagne daily.

November 19th. Except the gun on our right, everything was quiet to-day. It cannot be silenced. It is said to be behind some houses, off the carriage, and tied by ropes to a tree; nothing but the flash can be seen. As they kept returning our shot, our fire was discontinued. The majority of the ladies and children came out to-day. After remaining in the Secunderabagh all day and getting food, they were sent off in doolies and carriages to the Dilkusha. The bodies in the Secunderabagh have been buried or covered with earth. Seventeen hundred were counted; not a bad bag; and will frighten Pandy from holding a position. Natives are seen leaving the city laden with burdens. In the Residency we have four state prisoners, one the brother of the King. All the crown jewels are there, besides twenty-five lacs of treasure. Besides these, immense quantities of loot are in our hands. Sir James Outram tried to prove we have no right to a share of the prize money; that the original garrison ought to get it all. If we had not come, what use would it have been to them? He says Havelock's was the relieving force, ours merely the reinforcements to it! Our men have got a good deal of loot from the dead Pandys, but more in the mess-house. It consists chiefly of gold mohurs, silver plate, etc. It has been decided that, after everything has been removed or destroyed in the garrison, we return with the ladies and wounded to Cawnpore. A force will probably be kept at Alumbagh.

November 20th. Still annoyed by the 24-pounders. It now fires at the Secunderabagh, not at the guns. Wherever Sir Colin goes they seem to know, as shots are always sent to that spot. Things are being quickly removed from the Residency. The ladies and women lived most of the time in tykanas. Sir H. Lawrence was killed by a shell which burst in his room and wounded him. Only two ladies were killed. One, a Miss Power, had her leg carried off by a round shot. Lieutenant Harrington, Bengal Artillery, was wounded to-day. The shot hit his neck and passed forward, stopping at the mastoid process. He had been recommended for the Victoria Cross, for bringing in a wounded man under a heavy fire. Pandy fired so well at the Secunderabagh that it drove Sir Colin to the Shah Nusjhid. Here, however, they found him out and laid their guns accordingly. As a proof how well Pandy aims—on the 17th a flag was erected on the top of the mess-house to let the garrison know our advance. With a 9-pounder they knocked it down twice. Two syces were wounded by the river gun and several horses killed. The H.A. has been removed to the rear of the building. The guns were being brought out to-day. Except this all is in *statu quo*. Pandy was seen bringing in four guns into the city from the other side of the river. Numbers of natives are seen going out and in. Maun Singh, the leader, is said to have several European men and women keeping as hostages. A Miss Jackson and Miss Christian are among the number.

November 21st. All the heavy guns which had carriages were removed to-day. The others will fall into Pandy's hands. The muskets, native guns, etc., will be destroyed. It is intended to blow up the Residency when we quit it. Several mines have been made. One beneath the Kaiser Bagh. A prisoner, caught to-day, states that the morning we began breaching it the European captives, including Miss Jackson, were shot. It is, perhaps, a great mercy, as the treatment they had undergone must have been awful. This Pandy says they muster strong in the palace, and that they have everything prepared if we assault it. He tells us that they are moving round to our left rear, and intend attacking the Dilkusha. A sudden order was given to Blunt's Troop and a battery of R.A. to escort heavy gun ammunition there and not return. We started about three p.m., but the sand was so deep and bullocks so scarce that sunset found us still on the way. We were all sent on piquet to the place where we came in on the 15th. The ladies and wounded are all comfortable; the former in tents, the latter in the house.

November 22nd (Sunday). The night attack did not take place, everything was quiet. Now and then a gun booming from Lucknow alone broke the stillness. About nine a.m. a dropping musketry fire commenced at our advanced posts. Our guns immediately turned out. When we got into the open, outside the wall of the park, a body of four or five hundred Pandys were seen crossing a field about one thousand yards distant. The first shot sent them running into the jungle. Some ahead, made for the village which comes quite close to the park wall. This was evidently the intended point of attack. Whenever they showed, two guns opened upon them. They tried to keep up a musketry fire at a thousand yards, but grape drove them off. They luckily had no guns, so made off as quickly as possible, we pursuing, but of course not coming up with them. Their Sowars cut up several grasscutters, and carried off some camels and elephants. A very large dâk came in yesterday with letters from up country. None for me, which is curious. Four thousand men are said to be at Cawnpore with General Wyndham, ready for the Gwalior force if they come. Armed steamers are also running on the river.

November 23rd. Last evening it was rumoured our force was to retire early this morning. The heavy guns were first withdrawn, and at two a.m. the whole army was on the march here. Pandy was quite unconscious of our movements and kept quite quiet. As much destruction as possible was done to the houses. One of the turrets of the Secunderabagh was completely levelled. The mines were all ready and matches applied. The garrison came out in twos and threes, formed line, and marched to the rear. The whole force reached Dilkusha in safety by daybreak. An accident occurred near La Martiniere. Some of our men were prowling about among some native huts. A store of powder got ignited and blew up, wounding a great many. Our headquarters are again in La Martiniere, and we hold a similar position to the 15th, except that all our heavy guns are at Dilkusha. A few shots have been passing between our piquets. Except this Pandy seems confounded, and is probably taking a squint at the places we hold. Major

Bank's house, which we held all to-day, was ordered to be evacuated during the night.

November 24th. The force was ordered to march at twelve a.m. The 1st troop 1st brigade was left with Sir J. Outram's Brigade, which had the honour of covering the retreat. I was with them. The whole of the troops and the large majority of the wounded were removed. No opposition was encountered, but the rear-guard did not reach Alumbagh until seven p.m. The force left behind consisted of H.M. 64th, 90th and 78th, in all two thousand men. We held La Martiniere and the ground to the left. A guard was also at Dilkusha. Two guns of the Naval Brigade kept down Pandy's fire. He tried several times to bring out a gun, but invariably failed. Sir Henry Havelock died to-day of dysentery. He had lived but a short time to enjoy his well-deserved honours. On the 17th he heard for the first time that the Queen had made him a K.C.B. He is universally regretted. Pandy fired a royal salute of twenty-one guns from the right of the Secunderabagh at sunset. Our retreat will be proclaimed over India as a defeat, and will consequently have a bad effect on our cause. It is intended to withdraw all the Europeans to the other side of the Ganges. To bed without dinner. Biscuits and rum being the only things to break fast with.

November 25th. We were to have started at daybreak, but it was not until ten a.m. the baggage was all packed. Pandy, in a very small body, kept popping at us, and no sooner had we entered the Dilkusha Park than he occupied La Martiniere. He followed us through the park, and sent after us a round shot as a farewell. Beyond this he did not follow. The heat and dust were awful, and, without food, the sun was felt with double power. Arrived at Alumbagh at 1.30 p.m. Found all the tents and camp in the same place as on the 14th. Nothing doing here. Pandy is quiet.

November 26th. Sir James Outram's Brigade stays behind here to occupy Alumbagh. It consists of H.M. 5th, 84th, 64th, 78th and 90th, the Regiment of Ferozepore, Olphert's Battery, Captain Maude's R.A. Battery, several heavy guns. The rest of the force, under Sir C. Campbell, proceeds to Cawnpore. The Gwalior fellows are said to be advancing with twelve heavy and twenty-four light guns. Supt.-Surgeon Dickson has been superseded, and C. Brown succeeds him. This is owing to some disobedience of orders about sending doolies to Dilkusha yesterday. Sir Colin had been visiting the hospitals. He gave Ferris, of the R.A., a dreadful jobation for some neglect. Saw John Carnegy to-day. He has escaped unhurt during all the siege. He looks very old and careworn. He is one of the prize agents to the force. Major North, H.M. 60th, is the other. They have charge of all the treasure, jewels, etc. The State prisoners are also in their hands.

November 27th. The advanced guard and baggage started from Alumbagh at eleven a.m., the rear-guard, with which I was, not until two p.m. From this place Cawnpore is distant forty-two miles. Heavy firing all day, very distant, supposed to be the Gwalior troops attacking Cawnpore. Our encamping ground was two miles beyond the Bunnee Bridge, or fourteen miles from Alumbagh. The bridge is held by a brigade of Madras troops. Reached our camp at nine p.m. All night the hackeries, etc., were coming in. We hear that Buckdar Khan is at Bareilly, that he has summoned all the Sepoys to join him there. He has fortified it, and intends not to let himself fall into the hands of the English. He says our "raj" is in the ascendant, but he will sell his life as dearly as possible.

November 28th. News came in late last night that Cawnpore had been attacked by the Gwalior force. Accordingly, we were ordered to start at six a.m. At first the H.A. and Cavalry were the only troops ordered off, but when further particulars were obtained, the whole force was held in readiness to make a forced march. The ladies are in great terror, hearing that Nana Sahib commands the rebels. We reached our old encamping ground of the 30th ult. at five pm. The firing commenced to-day at nine a.m., and was very heavy until the afternoon. Towards evening it became very weak. From what we can learn General Windham is hard pressed. He defeated the enemy the first day, capturing three guns. After this they retired, but being joined by the Nana with eight thousand men, they again advanced.

November 29th. Ordered to start at three a.m., but at that hour the Naval Brigade were advanced towards the river, while we remained until eight a.m. The heavy guns were in position on the left bank of the river to prevent the enemy from enfilading the bridge of boats. At first Brigadier Hope's Brigade was the only one that crossed over. It consists of 1st Brigade, seventeen Light Field Batteries,

H.M. 93rd, 53rd and 4th Sikhs. A squadron of the 9th Lancers and of Irregulars accompanied us. On crossing, we found all the city and most of the cantonments in the hands of the enemy. Numbers of houses were burning, the hotel among others. It seems that yesterday we suffered a great loss. The 64th Queen's, with others, charged the enemy's guns, took, it is said, sixteen, but when still in disorder the Sowars charged them, recapturing all the guns and killing a great many. Brigadier Wilson, H.M. 64th; the Quartermaster-General, Brigade-Major, and four officers of that regiment were killed. A panic then ensued, and our men all retired within our breastworks.. The enemy followed up and began throwing roundshot and shell into our entrenched position. The want of cavalry has been severely felt. We have always been successful, but lost our trophies by this alone. The troops here consist of—Rifle Brigade, four hundred men; H.M. 34th, four hundred; H.M. 88th, 64th and 82nd, part of each. Total—eighteen hundred infantry. General Windham is blamed by everyone. On the 26th he was encamped about four miles away watching the enemy's movements. During the previous night they had crossed the canal unnoticed, and had got all their guns into position. We charged them, took three, after which no attempt was made to follow up. The order was given to fall back upon the camp. When this was reached, the retreat was resumed, leaving tents, baggage, etc., in the enemy's hands. The Sowars charged the 34th on rear-guard, but they formed square and killed every man. Our troops fell back upon cantonments. The city was occupied the same evening by their Sowars. On our crossing the river heavy musketry fire was going on from the breastworks in front of the fort. The enemy were in the houses, some only eight hundred yards distant. Our brigade was moved across the canal, and halted on the plain near poor Wheeler's entrenchment. The enemy fired a few shot and shell at us, but did no harm. Saw the Rifle Brigade charging and capturing a bungalow, which was held by Pandy, and annoyed us greatly. Except a few shots from our entrenchment, and a few from Pandy at the bridge of boats, the day passed quietly enough. Musketry was going on between our advanced piquets. We bivouacked near the H.A. lines. The whole camp, ladies and wounded, were ordered across. All night baggage was arriving.

November 30th. The night passed quietly enough. Twice we were awakened by a heavy fire of musketry, but this soon died away. Our camp was pitched on the large plain near Wheeler's entrenchment, facing the city. My tent is within a few feet of the breastwork, in front of it. A spy who came in this morning tells us the enemy are encamped on the Maidan before the cavalry lines, where we were the end of last month; that they have forty guns. Last night we were told that they had retired, leaving only a rear-guard behind. Whichever report is true, we have remained all forenoon quiet. The fight here seems to have been most disgraceful. The first day the 82nd and 88th fled a perfect rabble into the fort, leaving the theatre with all their warm clothing. We only lost two men killed and eleven wounded, yet two thousand British infantry retired. The Colonel of the 82nd is chiefly blamed. As a contrast to this, shewing what Englishmen will do, if well disciplined: the following day four hundred of the Rifles and H.M. 34th defeated four thousand infantry and five hundred cavalry on this plain, capturing two 18-pounders and spiking two 24-pounders. They lost very few men. Their Colonel, Woodford, and one man being all the killed. H.M. 64th behaved also badly; they got into a liquor store, got drunk, left sixty wounded men to be cut up by the Sowars. The Naval Brigade have been firing all day at a breastwork the enemy were making, and which had a gun playing into our camp. A few rounds made Pandy withdraw his piece. Dâks from down country stopped. When we were at Lucknow no communication reached this place from the 16th to the 27th. This shows how vigilant their Sowars must be. General Windham sent fourteen letters to let us know he was attacked; only one reached. Everything remarkably quiet, now and then a gun alone breaking the silence. Pandy has left the natives intact in the city, having looted nothing.

December 1st. All the Sikh women in the city were murdered last night. Pandy has offered one thousand rupees for the contractor who is making harness for us. They have destroyed two complete battery sets. Besides the Nana, who is at present four or five miles away, the Gwalior force has a female relation of the Maharajah of Gwalior. They also have numbers of Mahratta women. The rebels are said to be entrenching themselves on the native parade behind the church. The number of infantry yesterday with General Windham amounted to two thousand one hundred and eighty-seven. Our force consists of seven hundred and seventy cavalry, four hundred artillery, with thirty guns, and about three thousand five hundred infantry. The enemy, taking courage from our inactivity, brought out some 9-pounders and began throwing shot and shrapnell into camp. This intention being known beforehand, our artillery was all ready. Bourchier's Battery and several of the Naval Brigade guns opened about eleven a.m., and soon silenced those of the enemy. The roundshot came into camp every now and then all day. Several natives were killed. Three of the 93rd (one officer, Captain Cornwall) were wounded by shrapnell. An elephant was struck in front of shoulder without piercing the skin. It ran a few yards and dropped down dead. The Naval Brigade guns have advanced to the canal and taken up a position there. Continual fire of musketry at our advanced posts. Colonel Woodford's body was found to-day and buried. The bodies of two European officers are said to be hanging from the gallows at the house where our poor women were murdered. They were probably found when dead. Such insults will not pass unpunished. A day of retribution is fast approaching, when it is to be hoped not a Pandy in Cawnpore will survive to tell the tale. General Windham is reported to have resigned his command and intends going home.

December 2nd. All quiet during the night except the peppering at our piquets. The ladies have all been removed to our rear, to the Foot Artillery barracks. Sir Colin Campbell is waiting for reinforcements from Futtypore. They are expected to-day or to-morrow. General Dupuis has arrived in camp. He commands all the R.A. in India. Lieutenant-Colonel Ewart lost his arm yesterday. He was sitting in a house and a roundshot came through. He belongs to H.M. 93rd. The ladies and most part of the wounded were to have started for Allahabad this evening, but at the last moment carriage was found to be defective, so they remained. H.M. 34th goes down on guard and probably some guns. Bowhill has been temporarily made Surgeon of the 3rd Brigade H.A. The troops on their way up country have been halted at Benares, some rising being expected there. Pandy remained very quiet all day. Our advanced piquet in the Mogul-ka-Serai is potting all day long. The Rifle Brigade and H.M. 88th have been formed into a brigade under Colonel Walpole.

December 3rd. Letter from hills, dated Meerut, October 26th, all quiet there. What a discontented creature man is, we are envying them in quarters, they are dying of *ennui* and wish to be with us. The inhabitants are leaving General-gunge, near the Sudder Bazaar, as our Sikhs got in and abused the native women. A battery of Royal Artillery, under Major Smith, with part of the Rifle Brigade with its bands, and a wing of H.M. 88th, came in this evening from Allahabad. More troops are on their way up, and will reach in a day or two. The ladies and wounded escorted by two Madras H.A. guns. A squadron of the 5th Punjaub Cavalry and H.M. 34th started for Futtypore at nine p.m. The two former go as far as the Choolee Bridge and return with H.M. 42nd. To-day it was even quieter than the last two. No round shot flying through camp to alarm everyone in his tent. The musketry is also very seldom heard.

December 4th. Still inactive, waiting for further reinforcements. Although now seven months since the outbreak, we can only muster about three thousand men to go into action with. This does not say much for the people at headquarters. Troops are detained at Benares and Calcutta, watching disarmed native corps, while we, where all the danger is, are allowed to wait patiently for the tardy march of three or four hundred men. The captors of Delhi are not to get prize money, but six months' *batta* instead. This will give a subaltern seven hundred rupees. The railway from Allahabad is now completed up to forty-seven miles from this. It is now at a standstill. The 13th N.I. are one of the most curious features of this mutiny. Only two hundred men left the lines the night of the outbreak; of the remainder, two hundred were taken into the Residency, the others sent to their homes. Of the two hundred who held the Bailie Guard during all the siege, seventy were killed and eighty wounded. The reason assigned by the officers is that they were at loggerheads with the 48th and 71st, also stationed at Lucknow. The 48th went first; the 13th, of course, took the opposite side. Such is the native character.

December 5th. All sorts of reports about Pandy's proceedings. One rumour is that he is retreating; the other that he is entrenching himself, and determined to hold out. To-day four hundred of H.M. 42nd came in, one hundred and fifty of the Rifle Brigade, and parts of H.M. 38th. They brought two 8-inch howitzers and two 9-pounders. All our sick from the field and regimental hospitals have been sent into the entrenchment, so it is generally supposed we will attack to-morrow. Pandy brought out nine guns about two p.m., and, under cover of the brick-kilns, began to cannonade our advanced piquet on the left. Blunt's Troop replied for some time, but the place becoming too hot, he was obliged to withdraw. One man was killed, another lost his leg. An 18-pounder fired into camp, and several shrapnell burst over it. No sooner had our artillery opened fire than they all withdrew.

December 6th. Night passed quietly. Our camp was struck at seven a.m. About ten a.m. the entrenchment opened with heavy guns, and they were ordered to keep up an incessent fire. At the same time, several heavy guns at the front of our camp also came into action. This was done to distract Pandy from the real point of attack, which was on his left flank. About 10.30, Brigadier Hope's Brigade came up and joined him beside the Native Cavalry hospital. It consisted of H.M. 42nd, 53rd, 82nd, 93rd, 23rd, and 4th Sikhs, the last leading. At the same time Captain Peel advanced with his heavy guns up the grand trunk road, and, when within seven hundred yards, opened upon the brick-kilns. Pandy was here in considerable numbers, but had no guns. The two troops of H.A. and all the cavalry moved off to the left, making a circuit of three miles to enable them to cross the canal by a bridge. Our object was to get possession of the Kalpee road, and prevent Pandy carrying off his guns. No one with us knew the way, so we wandered about over the country, and by good luck hit upon the bridge. On crossing it we saw the Kalpee road crowded with fugitives, camels, hackeries, etc., pursued by Bourchier's Battery. He had advanced up the grand trunk road, through a large camp of the enemy's, which was deserted, and passed on after the stream of fugitives. Our cavalry went on at the gallop, the Horse Artillery following as quickly as possible. For eight miles the pursuit was continued without drawing rein. Numbers of Sepoys, principally of the Gwalior contingent, were lying dead; hackeries, guns, ammunition, were left far behind. Looting was not thought of, nor was there time: to cut up the fugitives was the object. After giving the horses breathing time, on we went until the fourteenth milestone, where we halted, no more guns or waggons being in advance, everything having fallen into our hands. We halted a short time, and returned slowly to Cawnpore. We reached Pandy's camp at nine p.m. Here we bivouacked. The fighting in the city was better contested. The Rifles and H.M. 88th took every place up to the Subadar's Tank. Here they halted, but about sunset were attacked by the rebels in force. From behind houses Pandy brought out guns, and fired grape upon them. General Mansfield was slightly wounded, as also his A.D.C., Captain Mansfield. Darkness coming on, they were not driven out. In the morning the whole place was found deserted. About four p.m. the enemy's cavalry and infantry brought out two 9-pounders from near the brick-kilns, and began pounding the 23rd, who were in the camp. One 9-pounder, which was being dragged by a small party of the 53rd, was taken. The 23rd charged, and took the three with scarcely any loss. At this time Lieutenant Salmon, 7th L.C., was killed, while asleep under a tope of trees, by the Sowars. The rebels have two camps—one, the Nana's, at the Subadar's Tank; the other, that of the Gwalior force, where we bivouacked. The guns captured were one 18-pounder, nine 9-pounders, two 24-pound howitzers, three 8-inch mortars, and two 5½-inch—total, seventeen pieces. The result of this day's fighting is more glorious than even the most sanguine could have imagined. The cause of Pandy's flight seems to have been the complete surprise he got by our attacking his left flank. Seeing us making the circuit to his rear terrified him into flight. Our loss was very small; his about four hundred. By our keeping along the road, the rebels ran into the fields, where they were quite safe. However, it shows that he is a miserable foe to match against Englishmen properly led. The "Massacre Room" in the city has been cleaned out by the rebels, perhaps to prevent us making use of General Neill's plan, and compelling Brahmins to wash it out. The Nana's anger seems to have been expended upon the merchants' shops. They are all burnt, while what was unburnt of the Europeans' bungalows is untouched. Ensign Vincent, H.M. 8th, was killed to-day.

December 7th. The rebels from the city are said to have gone off to Bithoor, ten miles distant. This morning, as Lieutenant Probyn was placing his piquets of Irregulars, he was addressed by some Pandys in concealment. On going up he pretended to be one of their own Sowars. They told him they belonged to the 8th N.I., but were now in the

Nana's service. He told them to be off, or the Feringhee would be after them. He, in the meantime, got up some of his men, galloped after them, and killed eleven out of thirteen. Not a rebel remains in Cawnpore. Confidence is returning, and the shops are beginning to open. The quantity of ammunition, grain, etc., taken in this camp is immense. We were reduced to two days' supply; now we have abundance. About four thousand bullocks were captured and brought in. Our baggage came up during the day, and our tents were pitched about three p.m. A battery of Royal Artillery, under Major Le Mesurier, and five hundred infantry came in this evening from Futtypore.

December 8th. Brigadier Hope's Brigade, 1st troop 1st brigade H.A.; Captain Middleton's Battery, 6th company 13th battery; H.M. 9th Lancers, 5th Punjaub Cavalry, and Hodson's Horse, were ordered to march this morning. At twelve a.m. we started. Bithoor was generally supposed to be our destination, but our movements were to depend on what we heard on the way. On proceeding some six miles, we heard that Pandy was ahead with six guns. Thirteen miles out we halted from five p.m. to twelve p.m. At the latter hour we again started, and marched along the grand trunk road until eight a.m. Here we turned off along a country road, which led to a ghaut over the Ganges. We heard that a body of two thousand Pandys, without any guns, had gone this way. This long march was known to be the only way we could surprise Pandy. His information is always good, and obtained in time, while ours is miserably deficient. Our march was about twenty-seven miles.

December 9th. This hackerie track led through a dense jungle and narrow villages, which would have cost us a great deal of life if defended. Our good luck was, however, not absent; not a man opposed our progress. After proceeding about three miles we came upon the river, here about six hundred yards wide. From the high banks we saw the Pandys with their guns beside the ghaut—(Serai Ghaut). On seeing us they almost all bolted. The H.A. galloped forward and came into action. They were received with grape and shrapnell from all the pieces which were in position. One round was all. Whenever our shot began to enter their position they all bolted. One man alone fired a gun afterwards. The enemy's Sowars threatened the H.A., who at first were unsupported, but the Lancers coming up they retired as fast as their horses could carry them. Except the H.A. and two guns of Middleton's Battery, no other part of the force was engaged. Our cavalry pursued and cut up the Sepoys who went inland, but the majority crossed the river by the ghaut and escaped into Oude. The place where the guns were found was a high bank, with the river on one side and swampy ground in front. Only one road led to it. The Sikhs went over this, but found the camp totally deserted. The colours of the 7th, 8th, and 60th N.I. were captured. An 18-pounder was found deeply impacted in mud at the place where we first came upon the river. The camp contained lots of ammunition, hackeries, Government bullocks, but few valuables. The guns captured were one 18-pounder, eight 9-pounders, one 6-pounder (native), three 24-pound and two 12-pound howitzers. Total—fifteen pieces.

The mud was so soft along the water's edge that bullocks, carts, etc., sank in and could not be extricated. All the captured stores were removed on to firm ground, and there left with a piquet over them all night. Some fine shooting was going on at Pandys swimming across the river, but a man's head at six hundred yards is a small object to hit and so most escaped. We encamped at the river's side. All the baggage did not come up until the following morning. The villagers in this part are unfriendly. They denied the presence of Pandy. They have all been spared, which is a great pity.

December 10th. Halted to-day. Fatigue parties bringing up the guns. The 18-pounder was sunk up to the nave in thick tenacious mud. It required about fifty Highlanders with drag ropes to pull it out. Villagers have crossed the river to Pandy's camp in search of plunder. Little of value will be gathered after such perfect looters as the Sikhs. The Mehidpore contingent mutinied on the 7th November and killed two officers. The cavalry broke out in July. The artillery and infantry in November. Two hundred of the 73rd N.I. have been killed at Dacca. They refused to give up their arms. The 34th N.I. have mutinied at Chittagong. This occurred about the 20th ult. They went off towards Sylhet. Troops have been sent after in pursuit.

December 11th. Received orders from the Chief to march to Bithoor. The object is to destroy it and blow up the Nana's house. Started at twelve a.m. The intention was to go by a hackerie track. The advanced guard and camels went this way; the main column lost their way. Got on the grand trunk road and proceeded about five miles when they fell in with another track leading to Bithoor. We reached that place about five p.m. Two of Bourchier's guns and four hundred of H.M. 38th joined us. They have been sent out to take in the captured ordnance to Cawnpore. The guns did not get in until late at night, the hackeries not until morning.

December 12th. A letter from the Chief ordering the Lancers and Captain Middleton's Battery into Cawnpore immediately. This is owing to the news from Benares. A body of eighteen thousand men and eight guns are advancing on that station. By the time any troops can arrive from here things will be settled there one way or the other. Two troops of R.H.A. have been ordered here from Allahabad. A servant of the Nana's was caught to-day. He is willing, he says, to show us a covered-in well where ten lacs of treasures and jewels were buried by the Nana. Our Sappers are going to dig for it. The people here declare they never heard of the fifty thousand rupees offered for the capture of the arch-monster. He has thought better not to reveal this to his faithful followers. He is said to be a few miles across the river, with six guns and three regiments. His whereabouts no one here really knows. His movements are, of course, secret. Of his final capture there is little doubt, but it will not be by Europeans.

December 13th (Sunday). The Lancers left this yesterday. To-day, General Grant, the battery of R.A., the 38th Queen's, and all the captured guns started for Cawnpore. We shall probably remain here three or four days to finish the work of destruction. Went over the village of Bithoor. Many of the inhabitants have left, but still numbers of villainous-looking Mussulmen are prowling about. A piquet of the Highlanders are in the barracks formerly occupied by the Nana's soldiers. It consists of a square, the houses with verandahs looking inwards. The centre of the space is occupied by a small temple. This our Engineers are mining, it being the intention to blow it up. The Nana's abode was destroyed by Havelock. We are destroying other buildings of his. Bithoor is situated near the river. The village itself, like all Indian ones, is very dirty, without any redeeming point. The streets are narrow. The houses are built without any attempt at regularity. Some have their fronts, some their rear, and some their gable ends turned towards the thoroughfare. The trees are very fine about here and the crops luxuriant. Wherever nature is, ornament and beauty exists; where natives, everything that is ugly and dirty like their own dark minds.

December 14th. The labour of getting the treasure out of the well is found to be no easy matter. After removing the earth, forty feet of water was found to cover the prize. The Gwalior rebels tried to drain it by means of bullocks, but failed to make any impression on the quantity. Burning the houses of the Nana and his followers. Little loot procurable. The sound of distant firing heard all day, especially towards evening; the direction about Futtehgurh, or, more probably, from the rebels about Kanouge, who, we heard on our march down, were levying blackmail from all the neighbouring villages. They have six field guns. No news from any part, not even from Cawnpore. All going on favourably, it is supposed.

December 15th. The houses of the dependants of the Nana are being destroyed. His Moonshee's house contained a great many letters from various people. This person, by name Azimullah Khan, was sent home by the Nana to lay before the House of Commons his master's complaint, about two years ago. He was received in London as a great man, being *fêted* by the nobility and great people. The Peishwa, having no children, adopted Nana Sahib, a child of one of his Subadars. When the Peishwa died, Lord Dalhousie refused to continue the pension of eight lacs per annum, and told Nana Sahib, that having a large fortune, and being no child of the former recipient, the grant could not be continued to him. Azimullah Khan was sent home to represent the injustice of this. The letters are chiefly from young females, not of the lower classes, but apparently from some well-educated persons. This brute seems to have been trying to get a harem collected. Though all write in most affectionate terms of this fellow, yet most refuse, and say they could not renounce the Christian religion and become Hindoos. The extraordinary thing is their allowing such a person to hint at such a thing. One young lady (for from her letter you cannot call her anything else) writes to him at Constantinople, praying him to write, as he is constantly in her thoughts. One letter is to Oman Pasha, and has full particulars of our intentions regarding Persia. The last pages are lost, so the writer is unknown. What fools the English are, making more of this Moonshee than they would of any of their own countrymen; and see the result—cold-blooded massacre.

December 16th. Went over Bithoor. The shops are being reopened. Saw the wells where the treasure is. One has twenty feet of water, and is full of large pieces of wood, thrown in, it is supposed, by the Gwalior fellows when they found their efforts unavailing in extracting it. The Sepoys of the 13th, 48th, and 71st N.I., who remained faithful, are to be formed into a regiment of the line, to be called the "Regiment of Lucknow." All the garrison are to get six months' *batta*; the Sepoys, in addition, to get the order of merit, and to count three years of additional service. A man who was present came to-day and offered to show us the place. After a great deal of trouble, a few silver bangles, etc., wrapped up in a dirty rag, was all the treasure found. A cricket match was played to-day between the Lancers and the Artillery. The former came off victors.

December 17th. Jung Bahadoor, with nine thousand Ghoorkhas, is at Ghoruckpore, and intends marching on Fyzabad. A spy came in to-day from Agra. He says Brigadier Showers has defeated the Rohilcund mutineers near Etah, and captured eight guns. A force has left Cawnpore under Lieutenant-Colonel Walpole for Kalpee. Blunt's Troop accompanies it. The mosque we are going to blow up in Bithoor is said to be one of the oldest and most sacred in India. One at Kanouge is still older. It is situated in the barracks of the Nana's Sepoys. No news from any place. Weather beautifully cool at all hours; not the thick foggy mornings of Bengal.

December 18th. The force going to Kalpee proceed, it is said, *via* Etawah on Agra. We shall advance probably by Futtehgurh, on the same place. Sir Colin's despatch about Lucknow has arrived. The Bengal Artillery get great praise; the Royal very little. Nothing doing.

December 19th. Moved our camp about half a mile further forward, as our encampment has become very dirty. Showers' column defeated the Joudhpore legion near Nansud on the 16th November, capturing six guns. Lieutenant-Colonel Gerrard, 14th N.I., was the only officer killed. Assistant-Surgeon Clarke, 2nd Punjaub Infantry, has been tried for not attending to his men for three days, the 6th, 7th, and 8th ult. Sir Colin is furious, so he will probably be dismissed.

December 20th (Sunday). The 4th Punjaub Infantry left us to-day. They go to occupy Chowkepore, on the grand trunk road; it is sixteen miles out of Cawnpore. A grass-cutter of our troops was killed in a mysterious way a few days ago. It was at a place distant from our sentries. A man of the 93rd, of very bad character, is suspected. The native's tobacco pouch was found on him, and one cartridge was wanting from his pouch. Futtehgurh is generally supposed to be our first destination. Most contradictory rumours are given regarding it. One rumour is that several thousand armed men, with nearly forty pieces of cannon, are defending it. Another that there are only a few hundred, with four guns. Time will put us right.

December 21st. A Sepoy was caught in Bithoor yesterday. He had on his coat and belt, and was coolly washing his face at the river's side. He was immediately shot. Two others are said to be concealed. We have now at Cawnpore four hundred and fifty of the Naval Brigade. Our long inactivity arises, it is said, from our waiting until the 2nd D.G. arrive, and until a sufficient number of shoes are made at Cawnpore for the army. Courtmartials are frequent in the Chief's camp. The Colonel of H.M. 82nd has been tried for cowardice. The cause of General Windham's defeat is being thoroughly investigated.

December 22nd. Showers' column, with the 3rd troop 3rd brigade H.A., and two thousand men, was by last accounts at Allygurh. The well in Bithoor containing the supposed treasure cannot be drained. The water can be reduced to nine feet, but being so near the river, no sooner does the pumping cease than the water rapidly rises to fifteen feet. Outram's force has seen nothing of Pandy since we left. He occupies the Alumbagh, the Fort of Jellalabad, and some neighbouring villages. Everyone grows tired of this inactivity, there being nothing to break the monotony of the day. The remainder of the 42nd Highlanders arrived in camp this evening.

December 23rd. The mosque in Bithoor was blown up to-day at three p.m. The destruction was complete, the dome and all the walls falling in. Some treasure was got out of one well to-day. The value about seven hundred rupees. It consisted chiefly of silver squirts for throwing rose water. Laying the telegraph up the grand trunk road is being proceeded with. It is now complete for two miles beyond Chowkepore, or eighteen from Cawnpore. The 4th

Sikhs are to march to-day some miles further on to protect those engaged.

December 24th. The Chief's camp moved to Chowkepore this morning. This is probably to prevent the drinking to-morrow. He and his Staff have come to see the lions of Bithoor. Alumbagh, with its two hundred men, is much annoyed by the enemy. On an average one hundred shots are daily fired at them. General Windham is to command the Umballa division. Brigadier Inglis commands in Cawnpore. Brigadier Walpole's column has not as yet met any enemy. They have, however, captured and hanged some three commandants of what was the Gwalior force. Futtehgurh is garrisoned, it is said, by the late 41st N.I.

December 25th. Christmas Day. Fine cool days now, but wants the frost and snow, with roaring fires and the merry parties of the old country. In the Chief's camp, races, jumping, etc., were got up and prizes given; but in ours everything was sedate. It is the evening of this day which is generally kept most merrily. We had our dinner in great style, and it would not have been bad even on a table in England. A large quantity of golden vessels (sixty-seven) were got out of the well to-day. It will already well repay the trouble. Parties of H.M. 42nd and 93rd are down working, in all two hundred men. Thoughts of home, of course, strike in vividly on this day. What your relations are doing, and reminiscences of many a by-gone anniversary spent with friends now no more, makes one feel sad.

December 26th. We expected to march this morning, but the treasure has to be taken in to Cawnpore and the guard return before we are ready to move. The Chief's force was to leave Chowkepore this morning, so we shall be two day's behind all the way up, and lose all the glory to be obtained at Futtehgurh. The amount of treasure sent in to Cawnpore to-day amounts to 75½ lbs. gold and 256 lbs. of silver. Its value is, therefore, £4,493 5s. 1d. This evening nearly one cwt. of golden vessels was brought up. The 5th Punjaub Cavalry left this evening to join the Chief. The 53rd were joined by one hundred and fifty recruits from England to-day. They now muster nearly seven hundred men.

December 27th. The 88th Queen's came out to-day as a guard on the workers at the well. We start to-morrow morning. More silver and gold found to-day, so our labour will be well repaid.

December 28th. Started at seven a.m., and marched about sixteen miles to Poorah, which we reached at one p.m. The Chief is two marches ahead. Dâk carts running in the old style. Chowkeys every three or four miles. The country is evidently settling down. The villagers crowding out to see us pass. Pandy's days are numbered.

December 29th. Marched at seven a.m. Intended to stop at Uroual, thirteen miles off, but on our way received orders to join the Chief. Stopped four hours, but only proceeded a few miles further on and halted for the night. Colonel Seaton's column has defeated Buckdar Khan and captured thirteen guns at Gungeree. The 6th Carabiniers made a splendid charge and took some guns. Several (three) of their officers were killed and one wounded. He was marching on Mynpoorie, when, by the last accounts, he was attacked by the Rajah. Result not known. Dâk beginning to come in from up country.

December 30th. Started at ten a.m. to join the Chief only five miles distant. His camp is at Meeran-ka-Serai. A force left our brigade to destroy some boats on the Ganges. Two guns of the 1st troop 1st battalion H.A. and H.M. 53rd, with the 5th Punjaub Cavalry went. Another force, under Brigadier Greathead, has gone on a similar errand from this. Colonel Walpole's Brigade is at Etawah by the last accounts. He has met with no opposition. Heavy firing has been heard all the morning in the north-west direction, probably Seaton's column engaged. General Windham, with Brigadier Russell's Brigade, the 23rd and 82nd, is at Tutteea. The Rajah has a fort there and some guns. The place was found empty. The fort was blown up. The 53rd returned in the evening, having destroyed eight boats. A piquet of the enemy's Sowars were on the ghaut. Captain Hodson rode in from Brigadier Seaton's column at Mynpoorie. It was advancing on Baiwur. Mynpoorie was to be taken on the 27th. After firing one gun Pandy bolted, leaving six guns in our possession. One was an 8-inch howitzer, on a new carriage. The heavy firing heard Captain Hodson thinks at Futtehgurh, probably trying the range of several places.

December 31st. Marched at six a.m. Reached Gooshey-agunge, fourteen miles, about twelve a.m. Here the grand trunk road branches off to Futtehgurh. Hodson's piquet here was nearly surprised by Pandy last night, but their approach being heard of, they retired in time. The telegraph is complete from here to Calcutta. The iron bridge between this and Futtehgurh has been broken down by Pandy. As it crosses a deep watercourse, the Nuddie, it will detain us a day or two.

January 1st, 1858. The English mail telegraphed General Wilson has been made a baronet, with £1,000 per annum. Poor Havelock received the same. Sir J. Lawrence has been made a civil G.C.B.; Chamberlain, C.B. £500 has been given to General Mill's widow and to General Nicholson's mother. Windham joined us this morning from Tutteea. A force has been sent forward six miles towards Futtehgurh to occupy the bridge and enable the Engineers to repair it. Our force here, when Walpole and Seaton join, will be far the largest and finest army ever collected together in India. We have the 8th, 38th, 42nd, 23rd, 53rd, 64th, 93rd, and Rifle Brigade 2nd Battalion, in addition the 2nd and 4th Punjaub Infantry. Cavalry—Part of H.M. 6th and 9th Dragoons, Hodson's Horse, Mooltanee Horse. 1st troop 1st brigade H.A., 2nd troop 3rd brigade H.A., 3rd troop 3rd brigade H.A. Naval Brigade with six 24-pounder guns and five hundred sailors. Four Sikh heavy guns. 1st Company 3rd Battalion, and 17th L.F. Battery, two Royal Batteries. 1st European Bengal Fusiliers. What changes have occurred in India during 1857. At the commencement we were slumbering in apparent peace and quiet, unconscious of any danger, yet in a few months what a storm burst upon us! On the 10th May the first mutiny commenced, and for months afterwards nothing was heard of but regiments rising and killing their officers. One more horrible massacre, then another, struck every Englishman with horror, and "roused the vengeance blood alone could quell," until revenge was the cry which resounded from one end of the empire to the other. The army before Delhi was the only force left, and all eyes were turned towards it. Month after month passed, the siege drew its slow length along, and its termination appeared as far distant as ever. Reinforcements promised in July did not arrive; hope made the heart sick, and at last it became too apparent that Delhi must be taken by the army that had been so long before its walls. All forces disposable were hurried down by Sir J. Lawrence. A large siege train accompanied them. After six days' of open batteries, the proud city was stormed on the 14th and captured. On the 20th September it was completely evacuated. The arrival of Sir Colin Campbell, and the despatch of eighty thousand men, shows the deep interest taken in this rebellion. An ordeal more trying than anything undergone by any European nation. With a new year, and the numbers of men daily arriving at Cawnpore, the rebels will soon be chased out from one place to another until peace is restored. The only defeats we have sustained have arisen from incapacity in our commanders, not from ability on that of the enemy: Brigadier Polwhele, on the 5th July, at Agra; poor Wheeler's force at Cawnpore, on the 23rd June; and General Windham, the most disgraceful of all, at the same place, on the 27th and 28th November. Except these, our troops have been victorious in every encounter, even with ten times their number opposing. The country is now settling down. The inhabitants evidently find that our "raj" is returning. They are heartily tired of the Sepoys, who have plundered them on all hands. As a proof of the change of opinion, Outram's force is now obtaining quantities of provisions from the villagers. When we were there not an ounce could we get. Furruckabad is occupied still by five thousand men. They are in a great fright, and have changed their camp five times in three days. A great part of Rohilcund is ready to rise for us. Hindu Buksh and the Rampore Rajah are only waiting our advance on Futtehgurh. The Jeypur Rajah and the chief who commanded at the Hindan and Badli-ki-Serai, were hanged at Delhi on the 24th November.

January 2nd. The enemy came out and attacked the force at the bridge to-day. The road is now repaired; the beams were the only part burned. An entrenchment was made by Pandy to command the passage, but he evacuated it on the 31st. H.M. 53rd was on piquet at a bungalow about one hundred yards from the bridge on the Futtehgurh side. A village through which the road runs was about four hundred yards in advance. This the enemy occupied during the night, and early in the morning they opened with four guns upon the piquet and the party repairing the bridge. We had three guns of the Naval Brigade, a battery of R.A., Brigadier Hope's brigade, the 4th. The first shot made by Lieutenant Vaughan, N.B., broke the axle tree of a 9-pounder gun. The second blew up the ammunition waggon. Our troops were kept from crossing the bridge until reinforcements came up. Brigadier Greathed's brigade, the 3rd,

Lieutenant-Colonel Le Mesurier, R. Battery, and the remainder of the Naval Brigade left our camp at ten a.m. The enemy finding the village becoming too hot retired. After retreating some distance, they were joined by four guns. They again advanced. Our troops under fire of our pieces went on, drove the enemy out of the village without any loss on either side. Our cavalry made a detour to the left. This drove Pandy into a run, which we easily made him keep up. Some guns were well served and did considerable execution. The 8th Queen's while forming line were fired into, and had four men killed with one shot. H.M. 53rd lost seven killed and wounded with another. Our cavalry charged, the enemy as usual flying all over the country. The R.A. could do little, their harness continually breaking. The Infantry advanced up the road. Ultimately eight guns—the whole number—were taken. The heavy pieces were coloured a light blue, streaked at the muzzle with red. The carriages were quite new, never used; as was also an 18-pounder gun. The enemy's loss is supposed to be about one hundred and fifty. Ours was trifling. Captain Maxwell, Artillery, with Naval Brigade, was severely wounded. Lieutenant Younghusband, 5th P.C., was shot through the right lung. A palkee was taken in the pursuit. From its splendour the inmate must have been some leader. He was killed trying to escape from it. The Lancers got two colours belonging to N.I. Regiments. Lieutenant Roberts, Artillery, captured one belonging to the Nawab of Futtehgurh. The enemy's force is said to have been five hundred cavalry and two thousand infantry. The villagers about concealed their approach from us, Seaton's column was prepared, having heard of their leaving Futtehgurh. Colonel Seaton, Hodson, Light, etc., rode over to-day and found us. They return this evening. Their column advances from Bainour to-morrow. The whole of our camp started from Goosheyagunge at two p.m. We encamped at the twelfth milestone from Futtehgurh. The Kalee Nuddee is a very deep stream. It passes down by Bolundshur, and falls again into the Ganges below the bridge. The bridge is very narrow, of peculiar appearance, having small turrets on the top of each pier.

January 3rd. Explosions were heard in the Futtehgurh direction during the night. Marched at eleven a.m. It was generally rumoured that there would be no fighting as Pandy had fled. About three p.m. we entered the cantonments without meeting anyone. On the parade ground our camp was pitched. All the bungalows are of course burned down. A large Pandy encampment existed on the west of our camp among some trees. There were few tents left, but plenty of thatched huts. They had attempted to burn it all, but only a part had taken fire. A very fine new 24-pounder with carriage was found in position, with a sort of barricade formed of logs in front. They had evidently intended making a stand here, as a breastwork was in the course of construction in front. Yesterday's defeat took away all their courage. When the rabble came in they immediately prepared to bolt, all crossing over into Rohilcund. If it had not been for this fight, we might have had great difficulty in capturing it. The native town is very crowded, full of deep ravines, etc. For several miles along the road, gardens, jungle, etc., are on both sides. The bridge of boats is uninjured. The stacks of old seasoned wood belonging to the Agency untouched. This will save a great deal of money. The fort contains several guns, one a 32-pounder. A number of men and two guns are said still to be in the city, *i.e.*, Furruckabad. The 10th and 41st N.I. are the regiments that have for so many months been comfortably lodged here in the huts.

January 4th. The leader of the Pathans here, a great man under the Nawab, was delivered up by the villagers this morning. He commanded the two guns in the city yesterday. He was in prison when the mutiny commenced, and was then released. He had been condemned to fifteen years' imprisonment for some offence. He is to be hanged in chains this evening before the Kotwalee. Several European women have turned up in the city, but none of good character. One was married to the Nawab two days before he left, in the Mussulman form. She is said by some to be one of the Miss Goldies. This is not likely. One we know was so unfortunate as to fall alive into this brute's hands, and is probably an inmate of his harem. Colonel Walpole's Brigade came in to-day. Seaton's column is about twelve miles distant. H.M. 38th and two guns of Bourchier's Battery have been left to garrison Mynpoorie.

January 5th. Seaton's column arrived this morning. It consists of the Carabiniers (one hundred), Hodson's Horse (seven hundred and fifty), 3rd troop 3rd brigade Horse Artillery, two 18-pounders manned by Sikhs, 1st Fusiliers, and 7th Punjaub Infantry. The Englishwoman has turned out to be a Mrs. Burn, wife of an officer of the 10th N.I. killed here. She had previously lived with the Nawab, and after her husband's death returned to him.

January 6th. English letters and papers to the 24th September came in; all well. A column under Brigadier A. Hope started this morning. It consists of Major Le Mesurier, R.A. battery, two guns of 1st troop 1st Bengal Horse Artillery, three hundred of Hodson's Horse, one hundred of European Cavalry, H.M. 93rd, 42nd, and 4th Punjaub Infantry. They are going to Mhow and the villages in this district. These places have been most hostile to us and instrumental in killing the English. They are Pathans.

January 7th. The Nawab's palace has been partly destroyed by its owner before he fled. It is now being mined preparatory to being blown up. The view from it is very fine. It is built on an eminence near the river. A Zemindar who came in to give his allegiance to the Chief, from the other side of the river, had no sooner returned than he was seized by the villagers and both his arms chopped off. Sir Colin is to revenge him. The bazaar in the city is again open. We are far too lenient. The budmashes are selling beer, wine, cheroots, etc., which were doubtless looted from the unfortunate residents massacred here. The prices demanded are also extortionate; these cheroots are one hundred and fifty rupees per thousand.

January 8th. A force left this morning under Brigadier Hale, H.M. 82nd, consisting of two H.A. guns, one squadron Lancers, and one hundred Irregular Cavalry and H.M. 82nd.

They return this evening. Their destination is the other side of the river. Guns are reported to be concealed in the villages. The expedition that left this morning has returned, bringing in two guns, native ones, found in a village. A few miles from Allahabad there has been a fight. Since June a village has been occupied by malcontents. Several days ago they were attacked and three hundred killed. Our loss is said to be eight. A native has brought in news from Lucknow that Pandy is strongly fortifying the Kaiser Bagh, and is determined to stand or fall with it. A party of Pandys are said to be crossing into the Bolundshurin district. A force from Meerut is trying to intercept their return.

January 9th. Spies have come in from Bareilly and report its evacuation. The rebels are making for Lucknow. From this it is generally supposed we shall leave Rohilcund to some column from up country and retrace our steps to Oude. Hurdeo Buksh, of Dhurmapore, has come into camp. He preserved the lives of Mr. Edwards, C.S., and Mr. Probyn, collector of Futtehgurh, with his wife and children.

January 10th (Sunday). Rumours of Vakeels coming in from Maun Singh offering terms and restoring Oude to us. What his influence over the Sepoys can be, is unknown to us. This is probably a camp story. The Engineers are busy putting the fort in a proper state of defence. H.M. 82nd remains here to garrison.

January 11th. Weather very cold; more so than at any previous period. Mackinnon has got the Meerut circle. No news from any quarter. The last seven months have been so momentous that the want of excitement is felt now. Hope this quiet may continue for years to come.

January 12th. Clouds of dust flying about. Wind from the north-west piercingly cold. Hope's Brigade returned this morning. A European has arrived here from Lucknow. A woman is also rumoured as having come in. This appears very doubtful.

January 13th. Brigadier Walpole, with the 5th Brigade, left this morning on an expedition across the river. A battery of R.A. and some cavalry accompany him. They have taken provisions for seven days. Hope's Brigade did little more than hang a number of Pandys and Gazees who had fought against us at Puttiala. A convoy of provisions came in from Agra this morning. Several ladies, on their way down country with it, arrived here safely. Firing has been distinctly heard all day. It commenced about two p.m., and with long intermissions one gun kept firing until sunset. Generally supposed to be Pandy disputing with General Walpole the passage of the Ramgunga. This is a very large and deep branch of the Ganges. At this season it is probably fordable. It was crossed by a bridge of boats which Pandy has set fire to.

January 14th. Firing still heard off and on all day. Moved our camp this morning to near the American Presbyterian Church. We are to remain here until the end of the month. General Grant, Major Turner, Major Norman, and Captain Anson are off to Umballa for ten days. The heavy guns heard to-day arose from Pandy coming down to attack the piquet near the bridge over the Ramgunga. Our guns opening, Pandy soon bolted.

January 15th. Ordered to accompany the 2nd troop 3rd brigade Horse Artillery, which, with two guns of Naval Brigade, two hundred Hodson's Horse, and one Company H.M. 23rd, were proceeding to join Brigadier Walpole. The track (for there was no proper road) was very heavy. Several dry water courses had to be passed. The banks were steep and covered with deep sand. This delayed the progress of the heavy guns. Did not reach the camp, nine miles from Futtehgurh, until four p.m., although we started at nine a.m. The force now assembled here consists, in addition to ours, of an R.A. Battery, two Naval guns, H.M. 6th D.G., one squadron Hodson's Horse, one squadron Probyn's Cavalry, H.M. 23rd, 2nd and 3rd battalion Rifle Brigade. The Pandys are said to be numerous, but their numbers are probably exaggerated.

January 16th. Walked to the river's bank. It is a rapid stream, about forty yards across. The bank at this side is higher than on the other. It does not appear difficult to ferry across the infantry. The guns will be a greater difficulty. Pandy has seven guns. Only one good, a 9-pounder. They keep two in a village about a mile above the bridge, and the remainder among some houses on a hillock down the stream. Beside the latter a tall pillar rises. A few natives could be seen walking about the former place, none about the latter. Pandy only fired two shots this morning from behind the hillock. On our guns opening he retired. One of our piquets is three miles down the river, it guards the boats which have been collected here. Towards evening from this spot a large force of Pandys were seen marching to the east. Cavalry was not numerous. No guns could be detected. They are probably making for Oude.

January 17th (Sunday). Firing goes on at all hours. Pandy bolts out of some place and blazes away at about nine hundred yards, of course doing no harm. A part of Hodson's Horse has been away some time about Kanouge, watching for the Nana Sahib. By our coming over here it was thought he might attempt to cross the Ganges and get into the Mahratta country.

January 18th. Pandy fired two shots during the night, but touched no one. At sunrise began sending roundshot into Hodson's camp on our extreme right. One, unfortunately, smashed a Sowar's leg. The camp has consequently been removed to the rear. The rebels have erected a battery with two guns to command a ford down the river. It is supposed we will not cross the river at all, but return and join the Chief. Bukht Khan is commanding "over the water." Our spies inform us that not a Sepoy is at Bareilly. Several thousand Sowars are there, and twenty thousand Mussulmen matchlockmen. The 41st N.I., who bolted from Futtehgurh on our approach, are going there. A force has left Lucknow to retake Futtehgurh. They will probably change their mind before crossing the river. A reinforcement is expected to join the force opposed to us immediately. Saw J. Reade this morning. He is with the 2nd battalion Rifle Brigade. He was all through the Crimea with them. He expects to be promoted in a year's time, becoming a

Surgeon in five years. The Commissariat officer with this force turns out to be one of the Mylnes, of Mylnefield. Called on me this morning: he had seen my governor and all of them before leaving home.

January 19th. The Rifles are ordered to make pits about five hundred yards from the village where Pandy's guns are. They found a natural one which they occupied before day-break. Pandy tried to annoy them, and drive them out with grape and roundshot, but did not succeed. The enemy withdrew their guns and were silent all day. No casualty occurred on our side.

January 20th. Firing still going on from the rifle pits to Pandy's great annoyance, as he cannot fire a gun now. A brother of the Nawab of Furruckabad has been delivered up by the natives and summarily dealt with by us. A force is said to be assembling at Meerut under Brigadier Chamberlain. They are to march on Bareilly—we, it is supposed, go to Lucknow. Jung Bahadoor with his Ghoorkhas is clearing the district about Goruckpore. They are working upwards towards Fyzabad, so Pandy will soon be hemmed into Oude.

January 21st. High wind blowing with clouds of dust. Sir A. Wilson, Colonel Hogge, and Major Johnson are expected at Futtehgurh in a day or two. The first has got command of the Benares division. It is believed, however, he will join the Chief, and take charge of the large artillery force collecting against Lucknow.

January 22nd. Bukht Khan has been refused any command by the rebels. He has proved himself uniformly unsuccessful. A large siege train is on its way from Agra, so it is to be hoped we will soon advance into Oude. Got a home letter of October 24th; all well. Dr. Morris of the Sirmoor Battalion is dead. Dr. B. Smith has sent in an application for the appointment.

January 23rd. Very cold still. Heavy clouds hanging about, but no rain as yet. It is rumoured that we shall be encamped here for some weeks to come. A siege train has to come from Agra. Chamberlain with his column has to advance into Rohilcund.

January 24th (Sunday.) Very cloudy, cold and dusty. Rain began to fall about six p.m., and continued falling in heavy showers all day. Had a walk solus. What numbers of birds one meets with in a short stroll. Near one small pool, I recognised herons (two kinds), a kingfisher, snipe, plover (two kinds), sandpipers, tern, besides various others. It is extraordinary the opportunities one has for the study of natural history, and how few—none we may say in this country—take advantage of it. From what Hodson hears, Pandy is bolting from Bareilly and Rohilcund. They are determined, so the spies say, to stand or fall with Lucknow.

January 25th. Races are fixed to take place at Futteh-gurh to-day, patronised by the Chief. Early morning raining; sunrise fine, soon to be overcast with showers. The enemy has made a raid across the Ganges, burning Mhow and Shumshabad. These rascals were Pathans. A column is going out there. From Agra fifteen heavy guns are on their way down. Smith's R.A. battery remains at Futteh-gurh with two guns, detached to Mynpoorie. H.M. 38th leave the latter place and escort the siege train to Cawnpore. H.M. 8th take their post.

January 26th. Hodson's Horse received a sudden order of march last night. They are probably going towards Mhow. Probyn's Cavalry (2nd Punjaub) left for Futtehgurh this morning. Sir A. Wilson, bart., is to command all the artillery in the field, having two Brigadiers under him—Colonel Barker, R.A., and Major Turner, R.A. Sir J Outram writes:—"The enemy are leaving Lucknow and dispersing. The new levies are the only troops remaining in the city. The 1st Bengal Fusiliers have been ordered to Cawnpore."

January 27th. H.M. 6th D.G. go back to Meerut. A rumour is going the round of the camp at Futtehgurh that Jung Bahadoor, with his Ghoorkhas, has captured Fyzabad. If so, Pandy will be hemmed in on all sides except the north. Signs of a movement are beginning to be observed. Meetings of Brigadiers, etc. Outram's force has been twice attacked by the mutineers on the 12th and 16th ult. In both encounters Pandy was driven back with loss, while our loss was trivial. The leader of the enemy Beedeekedas Hoonooman—a Hindoo fanatic—was wounded and captured. The fifteen guns on their way from Agra are being escorted by two hundred of H.M. 38th, one hundred of the 3rd Europeans, two hundred and sixty Punjaub Pioneers, one hundred 1st Punjaub Irregulars—four guns, No. 21 L.F.B., with about fifteen hundred carts containing ammunition. The pieces consist of seven 24-pounders, one 10-inch howitzer, three 8-inch howitzers, and four 10-inch mortars. For each gun seven hundred and fifty rounds were provided, and five hundred for each howitzer and mortar.

January 28th. A column, as follows, left for Mhow, under Brigadier Hope, the night of the 26th :—H.M. 53rd and 42nd, H.M. 9th Lancers, two hundred Hodson's Horse, 1st troop 1st brigade Horse Artillery, 3rd troop 1st brigade Foot Artillery. News arrived here this morning of these having come up with the enemy, captured four guns and killed a great many. Captain Hodson and McDowell both severely wounded; Steel and Willis, 9th Lancers, slightly. Pandy only fired one round and bolted. Their Sowars were pursued, and being unable to cross the Ganges, were cut to pieces. Their loss is said to have been four hundred. An assistant-surgeon and six Sikhs were blown up.

January 29th. Poor McDowell is dead; he was struck by a roundshot. Materials for a bridge came here last night, so it appears we cross here after all. The place where the fight took place was a very sacred spot. The enemy who stood were all Gazees. The Assistant-Surgeon was Fairweather, of the 4th Sikhs. A Sikh, thinking a tumbrel contained treasure, fired his piece at the lock! Of course it blew up. Another explosion took place. The 53rd were throwing powder into a well when, from some cause, it went off. Eleven were burnt, six mortally.

January 30th. Tombs is on his way from Meerut to join us. His troop is probably with him. It is reported that we shall advance on Lucknow with one hundred guns. A great dinner was given last night at Futtehgurh to Sir

A. Wilson, K.C.B., and all the artillery in camp. The entertainers were the Engineers.

January 31st (Sunday). As the materials for the bridge have been taken back to Futtehgurh, so we are again in the dark regarding our movements. Pandy has been very busy all day placing a gun in position to annoy us. He has received reinforcements from Oude and Bareilly. Received orders from the Chief to march for Futtehgurh to-morrow morning before daylight, and leave the boats uninjured.

February 1st. Started at four a.m. Reached Futtehgurh about eight a.m. Pandy did not find out until everything was clear off. The Commander-in-Chief started very early this morning with the headquarters of Artillery and part of the Lancers, making forced marches towards Cawnpore. General Hope Grant, with his division, makes the same place by the usual stages. We halt here at least three days, destroy the bridge of boats, and follow the Chief down country.

February 2nd. Pandy did not find out our retreat until late. He sent one man across who reported our flight. The boats were then taken over to their bank. A few Sowars first crossed, who, with great caution, examined our encamping ground. Three guns were ferried over during the day. We shall probably allow them to get well over and then attack them. Villagers from this side the Ramgunga coming in. The bridge of boats across the Ganges here has been removed and fixed under the guns of the fort. Brigadier Franks has had a severe fight near Fyzabad. Particulars unknown.

February 3rd. Rumours of Outram having had another fight at Alumbagh with the usual result. The East India Company is abolished. The rulers are to be individuals who have been in India. They are to have seats in the Commons. The Governor-General is at Allahabad. The Chief goes to meet him there. They will probably return together and advance on Lucknow. Pandy it is said has recrossed the Ramgunga, being afraid of some trap.

February 4th. Marched at six a.m. Reached our old encamping ground, where our fight was on the 2nd January. It is twelve miles from Futtehgurh. Very warm to-day—the first of the hot weather. An expedition consisting of some Rifles, H.M. 79th, 7th Hussars, and 3rd D.G. have left Futtehgurh to attack the remains of the Gwalior force at Kalpee. At that place Pandy has seven guns.

February 5th. Marched at same hour as yesterday. Reached Jellalabad three miles on the Cawnpore side of Goosheyagunge, having come about eleven miles. Sir J. Outram is said to be hard pressed at Lucknow. The remainder of the 3rd battalion Rifle Brigade have been sent from Cawnpore to occupy Oonao, as the enemy are expected to attack the rear of our force.

February 6th. Marched at the same hour as yesterday. The march beat everything imaginable. It was impossible to see twenty yards ahead, and it was with great pain you could look up. Clouds of dust bedimmed every object, and covered you with a layer of mud. At our encamping ground everyone appeared with red eyes streaming with tears. We encamped a mile and a-half on the Cawnpore side of Meeran-ki-Serai.

The 7th Sikhs, under Captain Stafford, are here keeping open the communication. Hood, an old college friend, is Assistant-Surgeon. Went shooting—unsuccessful.

February 7th (Sunday). Usual hour marched. Went ten miles near to Unoul. Fine cool sunshiny morning.

February 8th. News from Lucknow is that the rebels are making a strong entrenchment in the open plain to the left of the Alumbagh. The queen-mother has persuaded them to do this, as she wishes the city spared. When we are beaten, they will be able to return and find houses. If they remain of this mind until our return, our victory will be much easier. All the Europeans on reaching Cawnpore are pushed across the river. We will probably do the same. The Commander-in-Chief is now at Allahabad. Two cavalry brigades have been formed, both under General Grant—first (Brigadier Little) consists of 9th Lancers, Hodson's Horse, 5th Punjaub Cavalry; second (Brigadier Campbell, 2nd D.G.) consists of H.M. 2nd D.G., 7th Hussars and 1st and 2nd Punjaub Cavalry. No news of the capture of Fyzabad, that has so often been rumoured. Marched at the usual hour. Reached Poorah about ten a.m., having come eleven miles. The Nana is said to be on the other side of the river attempting to cross, but is prevented by our troops watching all the ghauts. On our march we passed a body of men (Irregulars) raised at Agra by Captain Alexander. They are at Bithoor, looking after the rascals' motions.

February 9th. Struck tents at usual hour. Marched two miles beyond Chowbeepore—in all fifteen miles. Morning very close and warm; not a breath of air. No news.

February 10th. Received orders not to march into Cawnpore in one day. Some Commissariat difficulty was the reason. Started at six o'clock. Reached Kulianpore, seven miles distant, at eight a.m. No news from Cawnpore.

February 11th. Arrived at Cawnpore and encamped near the native cavalry lines, along the grand trunk road. The Chief has arrived from Allahabad and is still here. All the troops are encamped at Oonao, about six miles over the river. The siege train is still crossing. When joined by Colonel Franks and the Ghoorkhas, our army will number twenty-five thousand men. Great changes here since the 6th December. Barracks are being built, houses pulled down—everything preparing for the cantonment of an army. The Artillery is to be divided into two brigades—Brigadier Barker, R.A., commanding the heavy, and Brigadier Wood, R.A., the field divisions. The Horse Artillery present will be one troop of R.H.A., 1st troop 1st Bengal, 2nd troop 1st, 2nd troop 3rd brigade, 3rd troop 3rd brigade; two batteries R.A., under Major Le Mesurier and Captain Smith. The arrangement of the forces is as follows :—

ARTILLERY.

Major-General Sir A. Wilson, K.C.B., commanding; Major E. B. Johnson, A.A.G.; Lieutenant Biddulph, D.A.Q.M.G.

Horse Artillery—Brigadier Wood, C.B., commanding; Lieutenant Frith, Bengal Artillery, Brigade-Major. E troop Royal Horse Artillery, Major Anderson, C.B.; F troop Royal Horse Artillery, Lieutenant-Colonel D'Aguilar; 1st troop 1st brigade Bengal H.A., Captain Remmington; 2nd troop 1st brigade Bengal H.A., Major Tombs; 2nd troop 3rd brigade Bengal H.A., Captain Mackinnon; 3rd troop 3rd brigade Bengal H.A., Major Turner; 3rd company 14th battalion R.A. and No. 20 Light Foot Battery; 2nd company 3rd battalion R.A. and No. 12 Light Foot Battery.

Field and Siege Artillery—Lieutenant Hogge, director in Artillery and Ordnance Department; Brigadier Barker, R.A., commanding; Lieutenant A. Bunny, Brigade-Major. Royal Artillery—3rd company 8th battalion, 5th company 12th battalion, 6th company 11th battalion, 5th company 13th battalion. Bengal Artillery—4th company 1st battalion, 3rd company 5th battalion, 1st company 5th battalion, detachment recruits.

CAVALRY DIVISION.

Brigadier Hope Grant, C.B., commanding; Captain Hamilton, D.A.A.G.; Lieutenant Roberts, D.A.Q.M.G.

1st Brigade—Brigadier Little; Captain Sarel, Brigade-Major. H.M. 9th Lancers, 2nd battalion Military Train, 2nd Punjaub Cavalry, 5th Punjaub Cavalry, Wales' Horse.

2nd Brigade—Brigadier Campbell; Captain Forbes, Brigade-Major. H.M. 2nd D.G., 7th Hussars, 1st Punjaub Cavalry, Volunteer Horse, Hodson's Horse.

ENGINEER DIVISION.

Brigadier Napier, C.B., commanding; Lieutenant-Colonel Harness, commanding Royal Engineers; Captain Alexander

Taylor, commanding Bengal Engineers. 4th company Royal Engineers, 23rd company Royal Engineers, Punjaub Sappers and Miners, Corps of Pioneers.

I. INFANTRY DIVISION.

Major-General Sir J. Outram, G.C.B., commanding; Captain Dodson, D A.A.G.; Lieutenant Moorsom, D.A.Q.M.G.

1st Brigade—Brigadier Russell, commanding. H.M. 5th Fusiliers, H.M. 84th, 1st Madras Fusiliers.

2nd Brigade—Brigadier Franklin, commanding. H.M. 78th, H.M. 90th, Ferozepore Regiment.

II. INFANTRY DIVISION.

Major-General Lingard, C.B., commanding; Captain Shute, D.A.Q.M.G.

3rd Brigade—Brigadier Hamilton commanding; Captain Fendall, Brigade-Major. H.M. 34th, 38th, and 53rd.

4th Brigade—Brigadier Hon. A. Hope; Captain Cox, Brigade-Major. H.M. 42nd and 93rd, 4th Punjaub Infantry.

III. INFANTRY DIVISION.

Brigadier Walpole, commanding; Captain Barwell, 71st N.I., D.A.A.G.; Captain Carey, 17th N.I., D.A.Q.M.G.

5th Brigade—Brigadier Douglas. H.M. 23rd R.W.F., H.M. 99th, 1st Bengal Fusiliers.

6th Brigade—Brigadier Horsford. 2nd battalion Rifle Brigade; 3rd battalion Rifle Brigade; 2nd Punjaub Infantry.

A rumour that the Nana has eluded our piquets and crossed the Ganges and escaped, is incorrect. He sent a nephew to test the vigilance of our guards. He escaped. This will make our men more watchful for the future.

February 12th. The siege train has all crossed. The Naval Brigade left this morning. Blunt's Battery, the 3rd company 1st battalion, has gone to Ackberpore, twenty miles on the Kalpee road, to join H.M. 88th, and watch the remnant of the Gwalior mutineers on the Jumna. H.M. 75th are to come and garrison the fort here. No news. Our troops are all moving on Alumbagh. The road from this place thither is almost one continuous line of men, guns, horses, carts, etc.

February 13th. Received orders to start at 9.30 a.m. and march to Chowbeepore. The force is under General Walpole, and consists of the 2nd troop 3rd brigade H.A., two guns; 3rd troop 1st brigade Foot Artillery, one squadron 5th Punjaub Cavalry, the 2nd battalion Rifle Brigade, and the 2nd Punjaub Infantry. Our destination is unknown. We are, it is said, to join the force at Ackberpore, on the Kalpee road. Some of the mutineers are in some village, and intend assisting the Nana in escaping. Arrived at our old ground of the 9th ult. and encamped.

February 14th (Sunday). Started at three a.m. Very mysterious in all our movements. Reached the road that turns down to Serai Ghat at seven a.m. After resting an hour, our camp was marked out and we halted. H.M. 88th, with Blunt's Battery, are about eight miles off at Sheole. Some Pandys were in a village near there. It was the Nana's brother that escaped. He crossed by a ghaut guarded by native policemen. They have been arrested for conniving in the escape. The Nana is still on the other side, near this place. He has five elephants and thirteen hackeries laden with his property. A horse is always kept saddled for him. Two hundred Sowars are with him. We have detachments of troops at all the places up this road.

February 15th. Halted to-day. Out shooting, nothing but peacocks to be got. Killed my first quail.

February 16th. Marched at six a.m. Encamped at Poorah.

February 17th. News having arrived that the Nana had moved up the left bank of the river, we started at eight a.m. for Unoul. Arrived after a very hot march about one p.m. First day that has really been warm this year.

February 18th. General Grant with his cavalry tried to seize the Nana from the other side, but the rascal's information was too good. He escaped, and it is said has gone into Rohilcund, making for Bareilly. Telegraph from Calcutta informs us that all the Company's European troops are to be put under the Horse Guards. Colonel Inglis, the commander of the Lucknow garrison, has been made a Major-General.

February 19th. Halted again to-day. A few drops of rain fell this morning. This has lowered the temperature considerably. The two last days have been oppressively warm. Out shooting, no success. Flocks of geese, ducks, etc., on the Ganges, but they never give one the chance of a shot. The river at this place is alive with turtle. They push their noses out of the water for breath, and give a good object for the rifle. What silence reigns along the banks of the sacred stream! Nothing breaks in upon the solitude but the scream of some bird or the plash of some fish springing from the stream.

February 20th. Still waiting until Tombs' Troop arrived escorting the ladies. They reach Meeran-ka-Serai to-day. Maun Singh has delivered up all the European prisoners he had. Several ladies, including Miss Jackson, are among the numbers. He says he will take away all his soldiers from Lucknow, and is willing to treat for terms. This shows how desperate they think their cause, and being deserted by one of their leaders and his contingent, will terrify those still determined on dying with arms in their hands.

February 21st (Sunday). Marched at five a.m. Tombs' Troop with the ladies passed on during the night, making a forced march to Poorah, where we found them encamped. Captain Roper, H.M. 6th D.G., who was shot through the head (ball lodged) at the assault of Delhi, is still alive. He is on his way home. The Pandys near Kalpee attacked Colonel Maxwell's picket of H.M. 88th the other day. They brought out no guns. They were driven back with the loss of fifty men. Jung Bahadoor is at Belwah on the opposite bank of the Gograh from Fyzabad. His tardy movements arose from want of ammunition. They are awaiting its arrival from Benares. Eighty rounds per man is the whole they have at present. This will prevent their being in time for Lucknow.

February 22nd. Marched at five a.m. Reached our encamping ground of the 13th ult. about eleven a.m. The road in this part is very much cut up from the passing and repassing of the army. Clouds of dust cause every march to be worse than the last. With us are three hundred of the horse raised from the district around Mooltan. They are perfect wild men, great robbers, but probably good enough for cutting up Pandys. Some of the 8th Irregulars are here. This portion has throughout remained staunch, having escorted their officers to the hills.

February 23rd. Marched at 4.30 a.m. Reached Cawnpore about ten. The Commander-in-Chief and his Staff still here. Brigadier Franks has had an engagement with some rebels and captured eight guns. General H. Grant with the cavalry and some artillery are between Cawnpore and Futtehgurh, nearer the latter, following up the Nana.

February 24th. Heavy firing heard across the river. It is in the direction where General Grant was. No news has come in as yet. Late this evening news arrived that General Grant's Brigade has come on a party of Pandys in a mud fort. This they surrounded, and after some heavy firing, H.M. 53rd assaulted with success. Five hundred rebels were killed, and six guns, two 18-pounders, captured. Our loss was slight. Lieutenant Brockhurst, H.M. 53rd, and Midshipman Jones, Naval Brigade, wounded. Pandy was in a fort with only three gateways. An entrenchment with guns was before each. Our Horse Artillery and cavalry watched each. Two heavy guns breached the rear in half an hour, when it was assaulted.

February 25th. The ladies, escorted by a company of the Rifles and the Towana Horse, started for Allahabad early this morning. The 2nd troop 3rd brigade H. A. and the

8th Irregulars (200 men) started at 5.20 a.m. to join the siege train at Oonao. The distance was thought to be only a few miles. It turned out to be the warmest march this year, and about twelve miles. The siege train goes on in three divisions. The first left this this morning. Another goes to-morrow, while we follow with the last on the 27th. Firing heard at Alumbagh. No news of what is doing there. The civilians are all to be left behind at Cawnpore. Affairs will be carried on by martial law—the proper way in a country in the state this is.

February 26th. Two companies of H.M. 82nd and part of Hodson's Horse came from Cawnpore to-day. The former remain here with some Sikhs in a small entrenched place. The latter go on with us. H.M. 93rd with several companies of R.A. left this for Nawabgunge this morning. The 2nd division siege trains accompanied them. Rumours of General Grant having had another fight and chased the rebels into Lucknow.

February 27th. Started at eight a.m. The advanced guard at four a.m. Our progress was slow. A convoy returning to Cawnpore stopped the advance. Arrived at Nawabgunge at ten a.m. Here we found the 3rd battalion Rifle Brigade encamped. There has been a fight at Alumbagh. The artillery and cavalry had the chief hand in it. Pandy was caught in the open and six hundred slain, it is said. Two officers wounded, Lieutenant Gough, Hodson's Horse, and Colonel Berkeley, on Sir J. Outram's staff. Accounts from Lucknow all agree that Pandy is determined to fight in a day or two and then bolt. The Headquarter's

Staff, General Walpole's Brigade, and Tombs' Troop left Cawnpore this morning.

February 28th (Sunday). Marched at same hour as yesterday. Reached Buntra about 9.30. Here a large part of the army is encamped, and all the siege train. A distant and random gun is heard from Alumbagh. At the Bunnee Bridge the Madras Brigade is still encamped. They have entrenched the village, but have never been attacked. General Franks' division have had two fights lately; both successful. He has captured twenty-five guns and killed nearly two thousand rebels, with little loss on his side. He will join us at Lucknow about the 5th prox.

March 1st. Brigadier Horsford's Brigade, the 6th, with General Walpole, came in this morning. The whole army is here or at Alumbagh. The siege train is in the park here. The Naval Brigade has sixteen guns. We have forty-eight field pieces and about eighty heavy. An alarm in camp this forenoon. The enemy's Sowars were reported as coming down on our right rear. Everyone stood to their arms, but after waiting in breathless expectation for an hour we returned to our tents. Some of the honours for Delhi have come out by this mail. Major Tombs, Colonel Baird Smith, and Lieutenant Tritton, are C.B.

March 2nd. General Lugard's division, the 2nd, Little's Brigade of Cavalry, the 2nd troop 1st brigade, 3rd troop 3rd brigade, F. troop R.A., and four guns of the Naval Brigade, started at five a.m. Sir Colin accompanied them. Their destination is Dilkusha, as each man took a loaf of bread with him. General Grant's force joined late last night. Our troop will be kept on rear-guard with the Park at present. General Walpole's division is here also. The Dilkusha was taken this afternoon with no loss on our side. The enemy had only piquets there. One gun was captured. It is very extraordinary their not showing fight there. The place is very strong and commands the neighbouring country. Brigadier Little is the only officer mentioned as wounded, and he only slightly. The Naval Brigade have six 68-pounders throwing hollow shot, also eight rocket tubes.

March 3rd. H.M. 23rd and 79th, with the remainder of the Naval Brigade, marched late last night. Very heavy firing up to nine a.m. this morning. No news from the front. The general impression is that we are making a bridge across the Goomtee, so that we may enfilade all the batteries erected along the canal. Received an order late in the evening to march. Started at seven p.m. Our course was more to the south than on our last advance. Passed through the village of Jellalabad and past the fort. The former was Sir J. Outram's right flank. It has been strongly entrenched.

March 4th. Reached the neighbourhood of the Dilkusha at 1.30 a.m. Bivouacked alongside the 5th Brigade. The house of Dilkusha is under fire from the batteries around the Martiniere. Pandy has very strong entrenchments along the canal. The bridge across the Goomtee is not complete. Franks' column joined us to-day. Continual firing going on as if from the Dilkusha. We are only keeping down Pandy's fire until our preparations are complete. Tombs' Troop, with Campbell's Brigade of Cavalry, are ordered out on a secret expedition. They take all their camp equipage with them. The whole of our troop goes on piquet this evening. Our post was alongside the wall of the park in a large tope of trees parallel with the Martiniere. On our reaching it Pandy was tom-tomming in a most furious manner. In front of Banks' house and along the canal are several batteries. They are principally armed with 9-pounders. A constant fusillade goes on night and day. They have rifle pits in front of their entrenchments. The enemy made a rush upon some stray carts of the siege train and, it is said, captured six. Hodson's Horse immediately gave chase, but did not succeed in getting them again.

March 5th. Returned from piquet at sunrise. Our casualties have been very trivial since our advance. Tombs' Troop has gone to Alumbagh. The bridge across the Goomtee was completed to-day. Franks' column crosses to-day. It consists of H.M. 10th, 20th, and 97th, and six Ghoorkhas regiments. In all two thousand three hundred British, three thousand two hundred natives. We are, it is said, to await the arrival of Jung Bahadoor. He will arrive in a day or two at furthest. Heavy cannonade and musketry now and then towards the Martiniere. Orders came late at night to join the force under Sir J. Outram about to cross the river.

March 6th. Started at one a.m. The whole of General Walpole's division, Brigadier Hagart's Cavalry, three H.A. troops, and two R.A. batteries deployed over the bridge without a shot being fired by the enemy, although a heavy gun from the Martiniere, and six the rebels had brought into a village on the other side, commanded it. After marching along the left bank of the Goomtee for about a mile, we halted until daylight. Pandy was seen in small groups about the villages and topes of trees. About eight a.m. the advanced guard proceeded, followed by the rest of the column. After making a long circuit to the right, the cavalry and artillery were drawn up in a long line, the former in front. The country passed over was a large plain, dotted with topes of trees and fields, but generally very bare. It was intersected by numerous ravines. After advancing about a mile a party of rebels were seen trying to escape. We immediately gave chase, the cavalry leading. After a run of about two miles the guns halted and opened fire upon some of the enemy on the banks of the river. The 2nd D.G. and 2nd Punjaub Cavalry followed quite up to the city, and were with difficulty prevented from proceeding further. About sixty of the enemy were killed. The ravines gave shelter to Pandy, down which they ran, safe from any horsemen. Our loss was trifling. Pandy turned out in great numbers on seeing the dragoons so near. We had three men killed at this place. Major Smith, 2nd D.G., was one of them. His body was left on the ground. We waited for a short time and then turned to the right. This day's march was intended to clear this part of the enemy. We were to have gone on to cantonments about five miles distant, but the day being too far advanced we halted at a village called Ishmael Gunge, on the Fyzabad road. It was near that that Sir H. Lawrence went out to attack the rebels at Chinhut, and from whence he had to retire. The embankment over which his guns were turned by his mutinous gunners is near camp. Our tents not having arrived, we bivouacked about half a mile in front. It is through this part of the country that the enemy receive all their supplies. Our march here appears to have confounded Pandy. He had made no preparation for receiving us, his labour being all thrown away on the banks of the canal.

March 7th. Our troop was ordered to parade at nine a.m. to accompany the cavalry proceeding to reconnoitre. As we were leaving our lines without any previous intimation, roundshot came bounding through our camp. The troop galloped forward and got into action. The enemy in great numbers had advanced unseen up the ravines, and got into several villages in front. All our divisions were soon in front. The enemy kept sending shot and shell among our tents. Their infantry got into fields and hollows from which they kept up a fusillade. As soon as our guns opened they began retiring, and without any infantry coming up they bolted, although they had a fine opportunity of killing many of us by holding the broken ground. Their Sowars were drawn up flourishing their tulwars, but first of all they fled. The enemy left a gun and a limber in a village. This morning's work does not look as if they intended making a hard fight. They have very few horsed guns, but the broken ground prevented our cavalry taking advantage of their flight. We occupy their villages with piquets, and the ravines with riflemen. The cavalry and artillery now formed upon the road and proceeded towards cantonments. We started about twelve a.m., and were obliged to make numerous circuits to get over some nullahs or dykes. We did not reach our destination until three p.m. No one was seen. Stray individuals at long distances were observed watching us. The country here is beautifully cultivated, and fine crops are to be seen on every side. The tobacco fields are very carefully planted, like a nursery, with hedges surrounding them. We advanced into the lines of what was formerly the Oude Artillery, and found them all destroyed and deserted. A mud fort at one place was held by a few men, so was not attacked by us as it was too small a place to risk any lives. The only inhabitants of this now desert city was a large flock of sheep which were driven bodily into our camp. After reconnoitring, we returned by the same route, reaching our tents at 5.30 p.m. Franks' column had a fight the day before they joined us. The enemy were in a mud fort and fought desperately. We captured the outer part and several guns, but the interior was so strong we left it still occupied. We lost two officers of H.M. 97th, killed. The Delhi prize money is increased by twenty lacs taken from the Jhuggur Rajah. The sharers in it are all those who were at the assault, not those who arrived between the 14th and 20th. Fyzabad is said to be held by Maun Singh for us. Jung Bahadoor is daily expected, and has probably arrived at the Chief's camp. Sunday.

March 8th. A road between this and Dilkusha has been making this two days for the passage of the heavy guns. It is now completed. Last night twenty-eight siege pieces arrived. The Commander-in-Chief rode over this morning to superintend. The batteries will be made to-night. The Martiniere is to be carried this evening. Our Riflemen have advanced about a mile from this, and are gradually advancing. A battery of heavy guns is to be made in advance of our chief piquet, to drive the enemy out of a large, yellow bungalow on the plain. Everything quiet here to-day.

March 9th. At day-break our heavy guns opened on the Chukkur Kote bungalow, and continued firing about two hours. Pandy had no guns to reply with, except one small one across the river. The Rifles and 1st Fusiliers charged, and took the house with little difficulty. About two hundred Pandys were about it, but they bolted without firing a shot. About twenty of the rebels were surrounded in the building, and took shelter in an underground cellar from which they kept up a fire, killing several of our men. The house was at last set on fire, and they were ultimately all shot. The remainder of the infantry had been gradually advancing on the right through dense jungle and native houses. They met with no opposition. We all advanced, driving the Pandys across the river. Here our course was stayed. Our light guns came into action on the banks of the river opposite the Secunderabagh. Our Enfields told well here; the enemy being kept at a distance, their muskets could not reach. The whole left bank of the river was in our possession, and we commanded the iron suspension bridge. The view of the city of Lucknow from this part is very fine; one continuous range of domes and palaces overhang the river. Furthest down is the Secunderabagh, then the Kudda Mussoul, the Shah Najeef, the Moti Mahal, and the various palaces in the Residency. The top of the Kaiser Bagh is seen in the distance. Pandy has erected a large battery on the banks of the Goomtee close to the Moti Mahal. Four guns of the troop were ordered back to join the cavalry in protecting the camp. A few of the enemy's Sowars appeared away to the right. They succeeded in cutting up one or two camel men, but bolted on our cavalry appearing. The Chief found the Martiniere evacuated in the evening. Several guns were found there. On this side the river Pandy came out in great numbers, and attempted to drive us back. This, of course, they did not succeed in doing. Their cavalry, principally the 7th L.C, showed as if they intended charging our guns, but did not summon up sufficient courage. The enemy were in a village, and annoyed our advanced piquet greatly. A small party of the 79th Highlanders were sent forward, who cleared the place, killing about fifty men; not being strong enough to hold it, they retired. It had such a good effect that the Pandys did not return during the night. The only officer killed to-day was Lieutenant Anderson, with the Sikhs. Lieutenant George, of the 1st Europeans, was dangerously wounded. He was shot by one of the Pandys in the yellow bungalow.

March 10th. The Chief took the whole line of the enemy's batteries this morning without the loss of a man. It is said Sir W. Peel was wounded this forenoon. It being reported that people were leaving the city by the Seetapore road, all the cavalry and two of the H.A. guns were sent to stop them. After being out all day, they only cut up about thirty budmashes. We suffered a great loss in Major Sandford, 3rd L.C. He went prowling about a village with an orderly, and was shot dead by some Pandys in a mud enclosure. He had heard of his promotion for bravery at Delhi only the day before. We shifted our camp to the sandy plain, close to the yellow bungalow this morning. This building appears to have been a race stand. We have got several batteries along the banks of the river. Pandy's fire very little in reply. The Chief's headquarters are in Banks' bungalow. This afternoon the heavy guns with him were pounding to the left of the Secunderabagh. A havildar, taken yesterday, told the Chief we would find this far more difficult to take than Delhi. Maun Singh has delivered himself up to Colonel Macgregor with Jung Bahadoor. He came in this morning. The Ghoorkhas are encamped three miles from the Chief. Nothing doing on this side but firing from the heavy guns. Very few Pandys appear to be either in the Kudda Mussoul or Shah Nujeef.

March 11th. The Chief's force holds the Secunderabagh, and are working up towards the Kaiser Bagh. We have got five mortars at the Padshahi Bagh, opposite the Moti Mahal, playing into the various buildings. Close to this we erected a new battery last night with five heavy guns. Pandy has been at a great deal of trouble making entrenchments since our last visit here. He has enclosed the Moti Mahal, the mess house, and Kaiser Bagh, in one long line of batteries. There are no guns in position at this side; we enfilade the whole from this side, so he must evacuate it all. On this side the river we advanced up to the bridges, driving the Pandys over the river. The enemy were in native houses in narrow streets. From these our rifles and infantry turned them out with no great loss on our side. Two officers of the 2nd battalion were killed, Captain Thin and Lieutenant Cooper, the latter mortally wounded. Lieutenant Moorsom, H.M. 52nd, on Sir J. Outram's staff, was also killed. A Pandy rushed out of a house, applied his musket to Moorsom's head and blew his brains out. We now hold all this bank, and command the Residency and all the large buildings. The Chief's force made good progress to-day. The Kudda Mussoul and Shah Nujeef were taken. Very heavy musketry fire about four p.m. The Mess-house, Pandy still holds. No news of what is doing there reaches us, or of what casualties. It is generally rumoured our loss is small. One roundshot this evening killed three and wounded four men in our mortar battery. The most extraordinary thing is the few guns Pandy has. Three or four are all that fire during the day. We took two on our advance to the bridges. He may have a great many in the Kaiser Bagh, but as yet they are silent. It is said Major Hodson is mortally wounded. If so, he is a great loss, being one of the first cavalry officers in India. Our cavalry made a demonstration towards cantonments to-day.

March 12th. Heavy cannonade this morning. Said to be the sailors 68's pounding the line of entrenchments. It was capturing the Begum Kotee that the heavy musketry fire was heard last night. In it five hundred and eighteen Pandys were killed. This was the number carried out and buried. Our loss was thirteen killed and twenty-eight wounded. Two officers of H.M. 93rd were killed—Captain McDonald and Lieutenant Sergison. Lieutenant Powlett, of Green's Sikhs, was wounded. Captain Hodson was mortally wounded at the same time. He is a great loss. Everything is very quiet to-day. We have made no advance. Heavy batteries are being erected to breach the Kaiser Bagh. A melancholy accident occurred to-day. An officer of the Naval Brigade foolishly rode in front of one of our mortar batteries when firing. A mortar was exploded, and blew off his head. We, the Horse Artillery, are having a very easy time of it. Nothing to do but remain quietly in camp. A great deal of loot has been got in the captured buildings, principally shawls, etc. We are pounding away from this side, and our mortars are throwing shells into the Kaiser Bagh. It is said numbers are flying from the city. Few Pandys, it is hoped, will escape. Our camp is pitched in a most unpleasant place. Clouds of sand are continually flying about. You have either to bear being well powdered, or by shutting up the tent becoming melted and resolved into a dew.

March 13th. We are approaching the Kaiser Bagh by saps. The Ghoorkhas are working round towards the Char-bagh, so as to open communication with the Alumbagh. The Begum Kotee is to the left of Banks' bungalow. A village further on near the canal was taken by the Ghoorkhas. The Imaum Bara near it was being breached all day. As soon as a practicable entrance was made, it was found that an inner wall still prevented our assaulting it. Green's regiment of Sikhs has lost already thirty-eight wounded and killed. Our mortars keep up a continuous fire day and night. Letters from home down to the 23rd January; all well.

March 14th (Sunday). The Kaiser Bagh was captured to-day without any loss. It was taken by a rush, and without any orders. Pandy did not attempt a stand. Forty heavy guns are said to have been found. Two young ladies, Miss Jackson and Miss Orr, were also there. What must their feelings have been, after being in such demon's hands for eight months, to see a European face again! The whole of the cavalry and our troops made a reconnoitring party; we went through cantonments and up to the Moosa Bagh, where a large body of Pandys were, with two guns. They kept firing at us, but from too long a distance. Did not reach camp until 7.30 p.m. As we approached our camp frequent explosions were seen, probably loose powder lying about. Our division was to have forced the river by the iron bridge to-day, but the enemy were so numerous and the place so strong, that the attempt was delayed until the houses had been shelled.

March 15th. At daybreak our heavy guns opened, but in a short time it was found that the large mass of the enemy had bolted during the night, leaving only a few determined rascals primed with "bang" to fight to the last. They are said to have taken up an entrenched position, and as being determined to sell their lives dearly. The extraordinary thing is the ease with which we have taken Lucknow. Since November the rebels have been doing nothing but preparing for us, yet they allow themselves to be driven out with scarcely any resistance. The ladies have not been found yet, but they are in some part of the city quite safe. As soon as the glorious news reached us, we were ordered to be formed into a pursuing column under Sir J. H. Grant. It consists of H.M. 2nd D.G., 2nd and 5th Punjaub Cavalry, 1st troop 1st brigade Horse Artillery, 2nd troop 3rd brigade Horse Artillery. The 5th brigade of Infantry join us. We started about one p.m. Our destination is first Sitapore, about fifty miles from Lucknow, then to Bareilly, where we join the column under General Renny, on its way from Meerut. Four heavy guns also accompany us. Passed through cantonments and encamped about eight miles out. The rebels are supposed to have gone towards Rohilcund. They can show little fight now, having few guns. It will be a pursuit and attack on villages, etc. The majority will probably disperse to their homes where the police will hunt them out.

March 16th. We were to have marched at five a.m., but orders came from the Chief late last night for us to halt, as he could not spare the infantry as yet. Pandy still showing opposition in the city. The enemy's Sowars have been cutting up our followers going into Lucknow. A Sowar from the Chief was killed, and his despatch taken. This contained the news that a large body of the enemy were making off between cantonments and our camp. About twenty thousand men and two guns are said to have gone towards Baraitch. Both bridges—the stone and iron—are in our possession, with all the buildings between. A good deal of firing during the day. Warm weather now commences in earnest.

March 17th. Marched at seven a.m. Returned and encamped upon the parade ground next the artillery lines.

Very heavy firing all night; gradually dying away towards daybreak. Several very loud explosions during the day, especially one about two p.m. It is rumoured a mine was sprung, and about two hundred of our men, principally Sikhs, carried up. The city is now totally deserted, only a few men are left, it is said, to fire the mines. It is truly lamentable losing men in this way—men before whom the enemy do not dare to stand, and who are slain by an unseen foe. The cantonments here are totally destroyed. The Suddur Bazaar is untouched, and said to be full of loot. The quantity of treasure found in Lucknow is said to be immense. Jewels, shawls, etc., can be bought for a trifle. Silver is selling at twenty-three rupees per seer. Its value is about eighty. Fine Cashmere shawls going for one and two rupees. Diamonds, pearls, and rubies are got in quantities, and sold for a few rupees.

March 18th. Our loss in Lucknow has been fifteen officers killed, and about six hundred killed and wounded. The number of Pandys is computed to be two thousand five hundred. A few of the rebels still hold what is called the "choke," a part of the native city consisting of large pucka houses in a mass. Lieutenant S. Chalmers, 33rd N.I., was shot yesterday by a European sentry. On being challenged he said, "Commissariat-Sahib." The soldier fired and wounded him. The explosion yesterday, when forty men (not two hundred) were blown up, took place when powder was being thrown into a well. Lieutenant Brownlow, Bengal Engineers, and Lieutenant Clark, R.E., were killed. The casualties were chiefly among the Sappers. As soon as the city is completely in our possession the army is to be broken up. Already officers are returning to their staff appointments. Sir A. Wilson left to-day for England. Lieutenant-Colonel Turner for Futtehgurh. Our troop is to go into cantonments with the 9th Lancers, probably to Umballa. We march *via* Bareilly and Moradabad.

March 19th. An advance from all sides was made to-day, which resulted in the final capture of the whole city. A great mass of Pandys were collected around the "bagh." Sir J. Outram came up the right bank of the river. The Chief moved through the city. Our cavalry force kept this side, while Brigadier Campbell's ought to have made a detour in the rear from Alumbagh. The last did not arrive, so the Pandys bolted without fighting. The only officer mentioned as wounded is Captain Hutchinson, 9th Lancers. He was wounded, it is feared dangerously, in the eye by a spear. Thus terminates the capture of Lucknow after thirteen days' fighting. After all the preparations made, and the hosts of the enemy, they have proved themselves despicable foes, cruel and unrelenting against unarmed men and women; while they have showed themselves arrant cowards when opposed to Europeans. Their religion has failed them, the proud proclamations of their leaders, and the anathemas of their priests have not inspired them with courage. The mark of Cain, the murderer, is upon them. The only resource left them is to seek for shelter from the pursuing sword. The two ladies were found to-day. Whether they were well or badly treated is unknown. Latterly they were concealed by an Armenian. We have captured some sixty guns and quantities of ammunition. The fiends have desecrated the graves of our race. The very bones have been cast out. What mercy can be shown to such monsters who can torture the body when alive, and approach the tomb with the same devilish rage. Surely a day of vengeance is approaching, when the righteous deserts of such deeds will fall upon their heads.

March 20th. Rode into Lucknow. Went over the iron suspension bridge into the city. Passed through the Bailie Guard and part of the Residency. It is one mass of ruins. A few pillars and walls still standing erect, make the destruction look complete. What a rain of bullets, shot and shell, must have been poured upon this place to produce such effects. Every wall, almost every stone, bears the mark of some missile. This quarter is completely destroyed beyond repair. One palace after another stretches from this up to the Kaiser Bagh. They are all built in squares, each with a large space in the centre, with fountains. The verandahs are large, spacious, and cool. The domes and spires have been originally grand, now they are battered and tottering. All these, however, sink into insignificance when compared with the Kaiser Bagh and the Rainbow Palace. To equal them you must go to the palaces of France, which are similarly constructed, but less gorgeously. Through archways you enter into one immense square, with flower-beds on all sides. Facing you is the large arch, the rainbow, many coloured, over the principal entrance to the palace. You ascend by narrow stairs to the royal apartments. What a sight you behold there. The floors are strewn with large mirrors, candelabra, sofas, tables, all smashed. The remains of oil paintings, with the chief part cut out, still hang on the walls. The roofs of all the rooms are decorated with the royal arms. Two mermaids, with beautiful Grecian profiles, are supporting the crown, round which a halo of light springs. The inner rooms at rear of this belong to the zenana. Here dresses, silks, and other portions of female attire are lying strewn about, mixed up with pieces of shell, shot, etc. The rooms are generally small but lofty, furnished with English goods. The interior of the square with the gardens is very fine. On all sides are small mosques, approached beneath arches of the vine. Beautiful marble statues and fountains are scattered among the trees—Cupids, Venus, Hercules, etc., are very common and finely sculptured. In the centre of this is a large open summer-house, formerly a favourite haunt of the King's, we can imagine; now it is turned into officers' quarters. The domes of the palaces are all gilt, the buildings of a bright yellow. In every direction you turn, it reminds you more and more of Versailles, or some other Imperial residence. This beautiful structure has been seriously injured by our fire. The most remote corner has not escaped, pieces of shell are to be picked up in most improbable places. Every gateway, almost every dome and window, is barricaded and loopholed. The buildings included in the Kaiser Bagh are nearly a mile square. Squares upon squares, temples, mosques, barracks, are all included under this name. The exterior of this stronghold has been rendered very strong. Immense earthworks, with brick bastions at all commanding points, while a ditch about ten feet deep surrounds it on all sides. The walls are all ventilated and loopholed. If properly defended it ought to have detained us an indefinite time. Their guns swept all the approaches, and a fire before which nothing could live might have been poured upon the assailants from the house-tops. What was the case: a rush, without orders, of a few men captured this Malakoff. Passing on from this, about half a mile on, you come to Banks' bungalow. Here, also, every ingenuity has been made use of to prevent it being captured. Walls have been loopholed on a level with the ground, that the cowardly Pandys' might lie flat and shoot down their opponents. In front of this is the canal full of water. One continuous line of batteries extends from here past the Martiniere to the Goomtee. The canal is impassible on foot; the banks are steep, strong bastions have been built at the bridges, and the arches cut away. The earthworks are very thick and lofty. At the rear of them a deep ditch runs which was to receive all the mortar shells from us without injury to the defenders. This was captured without the loss of a man. After visiting all these spots our success seems miraculous. How men, in the desperate state these Sepoys are, did not fight behind such works is incredible. The flank movement upset all their plans. Confusion reigned where everything ought to have been in order; terror instead of courage; want of confidence instead of implicit obedience. This is what the ladies state: the Sepoys were continually moving guns about, talking and shouting to one another, obeying no one but following their own inclinations. Our fire disturbed and frightened them and prevented them settling any plans. The Secunderabagh has been left untouched. The heaps of

Pandys in the east room, over whom we heaped earth, lie a festering mass. All the trees outside the garden have been cut down, probably to furnish barricades.

March 21st (Sunday). The reason Brigadier Campbell did not arrive on the 19th ult., in time, was owing to his losing the way. A village strongly defended by the enemy also detained them. Tombs' Troop, while in action near it, were suddenly charged by a body of fanatics, each armed with two swords. Grape was poured into them, but the dense jungle prevented its telling to advantage. The 7th Hussars charged them with success, but lost four officers and eight men wounded. One officer lost an arm and leg. He was thrown from his horse and cut up. Among the guns taken from Pandy were several cast by General Martin, who founded the Martiniere, dated 1789. They are of very thick metal, but small bore. Armed rebels still in the city. Lieutenant Cape, 30th N.I., and a soldier were cut up in the city, when wandering about. An attack was made to-day to rout them out. Captain Wilde, 4th Punjaub Infantry, was severely wounded in face. The Moulvie leads the rebels. About fifty were killed to-day. The army is being gradually broken up. H.M. 5th and 78th have returned to Cawnpore. Lugard's division (the II.) remains here. The 1st troop 1st brigade Horse Artillery, E troop Royal Artillery, Maude's Battalion, Olphert's Battalion, and 2nd Artillery Companies garrison Lucknow. Jung Bahadoor made a farewell visit to the Chief yesterday morning. A salute of nineteen guns was fired in his honour. He and his Ghoorkhas have started on their way to Nepaul.

March 22nd. Captain Wale, 48th N.I., commanding a regiment of Horse, raised by himself, was killed yesterday at the head of his men leading on a charge. One hundred and fifty Pandys were killed. Lieutenant Thackwell, 15th N.I., was killed, along with Lieutenant Cape, in the city. The English mail telegraphed. Lord Palmerston brought in his new India Bill on the 12th February. By this the Home Government of India is to consist of a Secretary of State with eight Councillors. The latter are to be persons who have been in India. All European troops are to be under the Horse Guards. All appointments, at present in the gift of the Court of Directors, fall to the Ministry. The civil service is to be competitive. Cadetships are in the gift of the Councillors. Our tents were all struck and sent into General Walpole's camp at nine p.m. Were obliged to wait until the infantry and heavy guns arrived.

March 23rd. Marched at one a.m. We proceeded in a north-westerly direction. The infantry with us were those of the 5th Brigade, under Brigadier Horsford. H.M. 53rd escorted the four heavy guns accompanying us. After marching about two miles over a very broken and narrow track, we had to halt, because the siege pieces had lost their way. It was not until seven a.m. they made their appearance. We again started and proceeded four miles over an immense plain with beautiful topes of trees. At nine a.m. we halted beneath a large mangoe grove, and did not move until three p.m., the infantry being weary and the day very warm. Our destination was a village about twelve miles from Lucknow where several thousand budmashes with guns were assembling. This long halt in the morning gave them timely warning, of which they made use. At three p.m. we once more moved off and reached the village about five p.m. It is situated on an elevated piece of ground on the right of the road. Its name is Koorsee. No sooner had our advanced guards come near it than large bodies of the enemy were seen making off across the fields. The Cavalry and Horse Artillery went in pursuit, while we in the main column followed as fast as possible. We left the village on our right and galloped towards the south-west. A few matchlockmen still held the place and fired at us passing, without doing any injury. The enemy made no attempt at a stand, but made off towards a nuddee, about two miles distant. The two guns of the 2nd troop 3rd brigade Horse Artillery, alone came into action. One of the limbers, belonging to the 1st troop 1st brigade Horse Artillery, blew up in an unaccountable way from concussion, killing the two lascars sitting on it. The 1st and 2nd Punjaub Cavalry cut up about a hundred and fifty real Sepoys, and pursued them to the nullah. The Sepoys were desperate, and waited until the cavalry were within a few yards and then fired. In consequence of this our loss was more than usual. Lieutenant Macdonnell, 14th N.I., Adjutant of the 2nd Punjaub Cavalry, was shot dead while in the act of cutting down a man. Lieutenant Cosserat, Madras Infantry, was severely wounded. Poor Macdonnell is lamented by all. He has been with us since Delhi, and done good service. We captured fifteen guns in all, and quantities of ammunition, etc. Among the pieces were two of our 9-pounders, and two 5½-inch mortars. The remainder were native, of all sizes and shapes, from small 3-pounders to long heavy 12-pounders. If we had arrived a few hours earlier, we would have got a greater number of Sepoys. They had just commenced retreating, the guns, etc., being all on the road. Our infantry did not arrive until all was over. Like all the actions Sir J. Grant commands in, the cavalry and horse artillery did all the work. Five or six Sowars of the 2nd Punjaub Cavalry were killed and wounded. The infantry halted on the road with the heavy guns, while we bivouacked on the Maidan, the road to camp being unknown. A hard fight was expected from the force sent, yet the result shows how cowed Pandy is now. He did not fire once, although he had so many guns. A great many women were with the Sepoys. Our men spared them all.

March 24th. After getting bullocks to drag the captured guns, we started on our return about eight a.m. Yesterday about fifty camels, three elephants, and an innumerable number of bullocks were taken. On reaching the tope where we halted yesterday, we had breakfast, and again proceeded at three p.m. Reached cantonments about six p.m. As our troop was resting, about half-a-mile from it, under some trees, a nest of hornets was disturbed. Thousands of them immediately attacked man and horse. The latter ran off with guns and wagons. Two waggons were turned topsy-turvy. One gun that ran off came to a sudden stop, the trail of the gun having snapt like a reed and capsized. It was an awful and, at the same time, ludicrous sight. Horses maddened, charging through men and horses. Luckily all escaped unhurt, except the stings. One of our grasscutters brought in mortally wounded by a private of the 53rd. The native refused to give up his pony at the command of the European. The city is now quite empty. We have taken, including yesterday, one hundred and twenty-eight guns at Lucknow. Spies told us that they had a hundred and thirty-two horse guns we know they took with them from the Muchee Bagh. Nothing doing. When the police are organised and order commences, the army will break up. Sir J. Grant has been made a Major-General, and has got a good service pension of £100 per annum. Our tents arrived about nine p.m. Our camp is on the front parade ground, before what was formerly the house of the Resident of Lucknow.

March 25th. Weather still keeping moderate. Only 94° in a hill tent, afternoon. No movement spoken of yet. When it does come it will be sudden. It is, however, provoking, wasting away what remains of the cold season here, when so much is yet to be done.

March 26th. The Zemindars about here are sending in their turbans in token of submission. This is a good sign. They will probably be employed in delivering up the Pandys. It seems generally to be believed that some compromise will be made with the rebels. Commissioners have, however, been appointed for the sole purpose of hunting them down, as done with the Thugs. The city is gradually being re-occupied. Police have been enrolled, so order will soon be restored, after seven months mutiny.

March 27th. Grasscutter shot on the 24th, died last night. No prospect of detecting the murderer. Letters from home to the 3rd February. All well. Major Brind has arrived to take command of the 3rd brigade Horse Artillery. He has received no brevet for Delhi, although he did no ordinary man's work. This has been an act of omission and will be soon rectified, it is hoped.

March 28th. Until the Moulvie is caught, all natives agree that it will be impossible to restore order. An attack, it has been said, has been made by Pandy on our small force at Oonao; at least the telegraph has been cut, and communication stopped. Sir H. Rose's advance is delayed from scarcity of provisions. The rebels have again appeared in force in the Azimgurh direction, and besieged the Naval Brigade in Ghoruckpore. Lugard, Major-General, with H.M. 10th, 34th, and 84th, with the Military Train, eight heavy guns, and a battery of Madras Artillery, start to-morrow morning to quiet that district. It is becoming the universal belief that Rohilcund will be left untouched until the cold weather, that all our endeavours will be turned toward pacifying Oude. Sir T. Grant has been ordered in to take command of Lucknow, vacant by General Lugard's departure. Rode into the city to-day. Went over the stone bridge. On the opposite side, at the bridge head, is the Muchee Bhawun, the place held by Pandy after the capture of the Kaiser Bagh. It is an exceedingly small place, but very strong. It commands the broad street leading down to the city. Sir H. Lawrence held it until the day of the defeat at Chinhut. When he reached the Residency he issued orders for its evacuation and destruction. This was done, and both forces joined. Both forces would have been destroyed had it been held. From this place a broad road leads through a high archway past the Imaum Bara, which is situated on the left. This building has been praised by travellers as the finest edifice in India. This ill-deserved commendation is accounted for, from its being inaccessible to Europeans. No heretics were allowed within the sacred precincts. It is the tomb of a former King of Oude, Asophad Dowlah. The entrance is through a lofty arched gateway. This leads to a square, from which steps and another larger and wider arch takes you into an inner and more capacious space. Directly opposite you is the Mausoleum with a marble throne. The architecture is admirable, but the mud and lime, of which it principally consists, detracts from the beauty. The left side of the square is formed by a large dome, with two immense minarets, at least one hundred and fifty feet high. From the top of this the view on a clear day is beautiful. The whole city of Lucknow lies below you. The eye can recognize the Alumbagh, Dilkusha, the cantonments, and all the palaces and domes of Lucknow. This building is at present occupied by H.M. 79th. It is a curious and startling sound to hear the bagpipes re-echoing through the arches of this sacred spot. Sunday.

March 29th. Went to see Tombs' Troop yesterday. They are encamped at the Moosa Bagh with the 7th Hussars, H.M. 5th and 78th foot. Brigadier Campbell is blamed by everyone for his conduct on the 19th. The Moulvie would have fallen into our hands if the pursuit had been continued. He has been remanded to command his own regiment, the 2nd D.G. They consequently go in and exchange places with the 7th Brigade. Hagart comes out in command of the force here.

March 30th. General Walpole's division—at least that part of it consisting of Rifles and Sikhs—joined us to-day. The whole of the field force is to be encamped here previous to starting. The 2nd troop 1st Brigade and 2nd troop 3rd Brigade are under orders to march. A camel corps from Agra, under Captain Patten, 3rd Europeans, came in to-day, and encamped with the Rifles. As yet they are only armed with swords, so will be of little use except for the conveyance of Europeans. No one knows as yet the point towards which our march will be directed. All the troops, except what remains as the garrison of Lucknow, join us here. Saw a shield and sword of the King of Oude, taken from the Kaiser Bagh by Lieutenant Fisher, 2nd Sikhs. The former is inlaid with clusters of rubies and topazes. The latter has the handle formed of porcelain, with flowers beautifully sculptured. The whole army has been reconstructed. The divisions are broken up. The field force in Oude is to consist of two infantry brigades under General Walpole. H.M. 42nd, 93rd, 79th, and 4th Sikhs form the Highland Brigade, under the Hon. A. Hope. The 2nd and 3rd Rifle Battalions, and the 1st Europeans, constitute the second under Brigadier Horsford. The cavalry is commanded by Brigadier Hagart. The regiments are the 7th Hussars, 9th Lancers, 2nd Punjaub Cavalry, etc.; all the Naval Brigade; the 2nd troop 1st brigade, 2nd troop 3rd brigade, 3rd troop 3rd brigade Horse Artillery, and some royal batteries from the artillery force. Lucknow is formed into a divisional command, and Sir J. H. Grant has got it. The garrison consists of H.M. 20th, 23rd, 38th, 53rd, 90th, and 1st Madras Fusiliers. The cavalry—H.M. 2nd D.G., 1st and 5th Punjaub Cavalry, Hodson's Horse. The 1st troop 1st Brigade, and F troop Royal Artillery, are the Horse Artillery force.

March 31st. Our force at Azimgurh is said to be in a bad way, being short of provisions, and surrounded by myriads of rebels. The 37th Queen's went out to prevent them coming into the city, but were driven back by overwhelming numbers. Troops from Allahabad and Benares have been sent to relieve them. The 4th L.C. have been disbanded, it having been discovered, during the trial of the King of Delhi, that they were among the chief instigators of the mutiny. They have been disarmed at Umballa since June. Rumours of the defeat of Lord Palmerston on the Alien Bill and elevation of the Earl of Derby are rife in camp. If this proves correct the East India Company will probably have a new lease of office, modified of course.

April 1st. The headquarters, 3rd brigade, and 3rd troop 3rd brigade Horse Artillery, joined us to-day. Major Brind commands the whole. Bareilly is again spoken of as our destination, while the other brigade advances on Fyzabad. The death of Louis Napoleon by a fall from his horse is rumoured in all the newspapers. If true, this disaster would cause an immediate blaze in Europe. Republicanism would again become rampant, and its pernicious doctrines spread like lightning through Europe. Weather now very warm. The thermometer reached 100° in a hill tent. A presage of still greater temperature. Sales of prize property are being daily held in the city. Nothing of great value has been got as yet.

April 2nd. Good Friday. Rode into Lucknow. The Field Hospital has been removed from Dilkusha to the Chatta Munzil; the chief camp to the "Tara Kote," the observatory. Hundreds of coolies are busy in demolishing the earthen works erected by Pandy. Rumours of our brigade starting on Monday. De Renzy has been appointed to Simla. D. B. Smith is applying for the Residency at Indore. A party of Pandys planned an attack upon the wounded proceeding to Cawnpore the day before last, but the convoy probably frightened them.

April 3rd. The Muchee Bhawun is to be turned into the fort of Lucknow; it commands both bridges. Broad and straight streets are to be made through the city. People are not returning to the city in such numbers as was expected. The Dilkusha and Moosa Bagh are spoken of as outposts to be held. No rumours of moving.

April 4th (Easter Sunday). The affair at Azimgurh appears to have been disastrous; similar to the Cawnpore retreat. Our troops were attacked by overwhelming numbers, and retired, leaving their baggage and tents in the enemy's hands. Such are the defeats we must expect. No sooner do we concentrate troops on one point than Pandy attacks our detachments in another. A salute was fired to-day in honour of Sir J. Outram's departure, he having gone to take his seat in Council. Mr. Mont-

17

gomery is Chief Commissioner in Oude; Mr. Denison of Lucknow.

April 5th. Had a long letter from J. Henderson. He is near Nagpore, at a place called Raipore. The natives seem much more hostile to our Government in that quarter than here. In districts where no Sepoys are found, the same enmity exists as in Bengal. Hot winds have commenced, with clouds of dust. Temperature consequently low. Dr. Tice, of H.M. service, accompanies this force as Supt.-Surgeon. Kotah has again been captured by our arms. No particulars given. Jhansi is closely besieged. The batteries are open and we are shelling the fort. Part of the town is in our hands. The Rajah being friendly, joined our forces.

April 6th. The small party of our men in Azimgurh have made a sally, but were again driven back by overwhelming numbers. Lugard's division ought to be approaching to relieve it. A large force of the enemy—supposed to be the Kalpee force—tried to raise the siege of Jhansi. Sir H. Rose, however, turned round, defeated them, capturing fourteen guns, two of which were heavy siege artillery. A mad elephant paid our camp a visit last night, causing great alarm. It kept charging the Mahouts and natives. It was at last driven away by spears, and walked deliberately into the jungle, having previously smashed a cart to pieces and thrown or driven a bullock into a well.

April 7th. A force consisting of the following corps starts to-morrow morning for the Moosa Bagh, to remain there until further orders:—The 2nd troop 1st brigade, 3rd troop 3rd brigade, and a heavy gun battery of Bengal Artillery,

H.M. 9th L.C., 2nd Punjaub Cavalry, the Highland Brigade with the 4th Punjaub Infantry. They take two months provisions for Europeans, and seven days for natives. Their destination supposed to be Bareilly *via* Shajehanpore. No news of our moving. Some say we march direct to Umballa, others that we go *via* Sitapore and join the other column this side Bareilly. All the Engineers have left us, however, and the Goomtee requires to be crossed by a bridge, none being in existence above this.

April 8th. Brigadier Seaton, with a column from Futtehgurh, has had a very successful engagement with the rebels near Bowgong (?) The enemy were defeated, with the loss of three guns. Their flight was so precipitous that they burned the bridge they had erected over the Ramgunga. The news from all quarters are good. Jhansi has fallen. Azimgurh is relieved. Prize sales still going on in the city. The officers and men, however, retain the most valuable. One officer of the 42nd Highlanders has loot to the value of £70,000. Another's prize is said to be £40,000. Why does Sir Colin not compel them to restore it to the proper quarter?

April 9th. The force proceeding to Bareilly marched this morning from the Moosa Bagh. Our force was expected to march to-morrow towards Fyzabad, but it has been delayed. H.M. 38th has joined us in place of the 3rd battalion Rifle Brigade, who remain in Lucknow from sickness. They have buried fifteen men since coming out here. The 2nd Battalion have lost none. This can only be accounted for from the latter being old seasoned Crimean warriors.

April 10th. Six months' *batta* has been given to the army of Lucknow in addition to that for Delhi. This has disappointed us all, for if we were entitled to it this time, how much more ought we to have got it for our victorious march from Delhi and relief of Lucknow? A great quantity of prize money has been collected here. Ten lacs are said to have been dug up here this morning. We expect to march to-morrow. Destination supposed to be Fyzabad, where the Moulvie is seeking shelter. The force proceeding there consists of 2nd troop 3rd brigade Horse Artillery, Captain Middleton's Battery R.A., Captain Talbot's Royal Artillery Heavy Battery, one squadron H.M. 2nd D.G., H.M. 7th Hussars, Wale's Horse, one hundred men Hodson's Horse, Infantry Brigade under Brigadier Horsford, H.M. 2nd Rifle Battalion, H.M. 38th, 1st European Fusiliers, 5th Punjaub Infantry. The whole under the command of Major-General Grant, K.C.B. Several companies of Sappers accompany us with a pontoon train.

April 11th (Sunday). Marched at four a.m. Proceeded as far as the Bukshi Talow, where we halted on the 15th March. We encamped about a quarter of a mile beyond it. We are expected to surprise the Begum and Moulvie in some villages, as if they had no communication regarding our movements. Our being astir will have a good moral effect in quieting the country. The Sikhs are becoming very independent. It appears that they consider the defeat of Pandy arises solely from their assistance. They believe we surpass them in fighting, but conclude that if it took us a year to conquer a foe they have often met, and on all occasions defeated, they the Sikhs would be able to hold out an indefinite period with every chance of ultimate success. Time will show.

April 12th. Marched at five a.m. The road being very bad for heavy guns, as it passed through villages, we did not reach our encamping ground until 12 a.m. The march was dreadfully warm. A hot wind blowing like a furnace. On our way, a Rajah of some neighbouring place delivered himself up to us. He says the country is quiet, and no Sepoys near. The Moulvie is at a place eight miles from this, with several thousand men, principally Ghazees, and a few guns. It is very doubtful whether he will await our arrival as we have given him plenty of time to escape. Passed several villages on our way, which were perfect models of the Oude forts. They are all square, with a tower at one corner, and surrounded by a dense impassable bamboo jungle. The large square is divided into several smaller ones. Being formed of mud, shells alone make any impression on the walls.

April 13th. Started at four a.m. After proceeding two miles our guns on advanced guard came across a large body of Sowars. They were in line, and immediately charged down upon the guns, but their leader being slain, and the grape coming unpleasantly near, they bolted, pursued by Wale's Horse. A large body of their cavalry made a wide circuit, and at a gallop advanced on our column. The Horse Artillery kept sending round shot, shell, etc., among them, and had the effect of sending one half to the rear. The remainder pressed on, but, unfortunately, alighted on the place where two companies of the Bengal Fusiliers were in line. By them they were received by two volleys, which had the effect of stopping their career, and turning it into flight. The 7th Hussars at this moment charged, riding through and through them, and causing considerable loss. They, however, had Lieutenant Topham wounded, and eight men, of whom three have died. While this was going on in the rear, the 2nd Battalion Rifles advanced on the village in front, where the enemy's infantry were. This was only an outpost. The main body were behind a nullah impassable for guns. The Rifles, proceeded by skirmishers, advanced without firing a shot until within a short distance. Then they opened fire, and, with a rush, drove the enemy out. No attempt at a stand was made, but the whole body scattered as only Pandy can. As soon as the Sowars had disappeared we advanced. On the horizon a few horsemen were seen watching us, but the majority had disappeared. After carefully reconnoitring a dense jungle in front, we found the headquarters of the Moulvie deserted. The village of Baree, where he has been for some time, retains traces of the encampment of a large force. It is a very beautiful village with several large tanks and beautiful groves of mangoes. A magazine containing some powder and numbers of sandbags was discovered. The inhabitants had all gone off. Our camp was pitched about half a mile beyond it.

April 14th. Marched at four a.m. Up to this place we had proceeded straight north from Lucknow, along the Sitapore road; now we turned sharp to the east, and advanced across country yesterday. We hear that the charge of cavalry was headed by the Moulvie himself, that he was wounded, and fled with only forty followers. The force that came against us consisted of one thousand cavalry and five thousand infantry. Spies tell us they were so disorganised that the former made for Sitapore without drawing rein, expecting the cavalry after them. The infantry scattered all over the country. Encamped after a ten-mile march at a village called Burwah (?). The country here is covered with jungle, consisting of small shrubs, and here and there a large topé. Agriculture is bad. Villages numerous but small. A half-caste named Phillips came in to-day; he belonged to the magistrate's office at Sitapore, escaped, and has remained concealed ever since.

April 15th. Marched at four a.m. A slight shower fell this evening, which increased instead of lowering the temperature. On the way heard that a body of Pandys intended showing fight, but it soon turned out a false alarm. During the night they thought better of it, and bolted at daybreak. They were commanded by the Nawab of Mahomedabad, and had two small guns with them. They made off towards the place where the Begum is, and towards which we are marching. The country hereabouts is very fine; the topes of mangoes magnificent. The village of Mahomedabad, where we encamped, after marching eight miles, was the residence of the Rajah. When compared with the surrounding miserable mud hovels it looks a palace. It has turrets, and three stories, so it towers over everything near. The interior of the house contained several clocks; one a Parisian one with a statuette of Napoleon on it. What a curious thing this figure of a man so famous in European history, being found in a house in Oude, where the fame of his name had probably never reached. This part of Oude has never been surveyed. In the maps a blank alone marks this quarter. The Nawab's abode was mined and blown up this evening. The villagers in this district appear quite neutral. They swarm around their huts and look apathetically at the passing column. Conciliation is being followed by us. No looting, although with difficulty prevented, is allowed. The natives in this district are principally Poorbeeas, and, as a consequence, inoffensive.

April 16th. At usual hour marched. Country still bears the same aspect—jungleless, but the plain is flat and extensive. Passed through a very large village, called Pyntapore, with a mud fort. The streets are very narrow, short, and winding. Our strong force prevents any opposition in these places. The maidan beyond this is more broken. Numerous dry nullahs had to be crossed, a sign of a neighbouring river. Encamped after an eight mile march at Bilher, also a large place. It also has a mud fort with four circular bastions, and a ditch. The houses, of course, come quite up to the wall, and present fine cover for the assailants. Brigadier Seaton has had another fight about Futtehgurh. The rebels from Lucknow and Bareilly are attempting to cross the Ganges at Shumshabad and make for Central India. Our troops in Azimgurh have been relieved from Ghazipore. The chief assemblage of rebels in Oude is opposite Fyzabad, on the left bank of the Gogra.

Our troops are advancing to meet them. The budmashes there number, it is said, fifteen thousand men and twenty guns. Affairs are looking bright on all sides. Wherever Pandy has a force, we have one pursuing or watching it. We are now close upon the stronghold of the Begum. It is in the Doab, between the Chouka and Gogra, almost at the point of their confluence. The former we have to cross. It is only about waist deep, so can be forded. The force of rebels here are strong in cavalry, and have about ten guns. If we can get them into this point of land, the bag will be very great. This Begum is Huzzrut Mehal, a wife of Wajid Ali, late King of Oude, now in Fort William. Her son, Binjees Kudur, *alias* Ramzan Ali Khan, was elevated to the throne by the unanimous voice of the rebel soldiery. He is quite a boy, and is governed by his mother and her paramour, Mummoo Khan. The Moulvie is an enemy of this clique.

April 17th. The force halted to-day, but all the cavalry and the 2nd troop 3rd brigade Horse Artillery, made a reconnaisance towards the river Chouka. Its object was to examine the Rampoor Ghat, over which we intend crossing. It was found to be about four feet deep. No enemy was seen, they having withdrawn their outposts from this side, probably expecting us to advance to-day. The news from the villagers was that the Sepoys were leaving the Begum for Baraitch, but that the Nujeeb's matchlockmen were remaining. We hear the Moulvie is at Fyzabad. A European is in custody for having killed two men and a woman in Bilher, yesterday. He demanded money, which they refused from poverty. It will be difficult to convict him from want of witnesses.

April 18th (Sunday). At the usual hour marched. As we have to await orders from Sir Colin, before attacking the Begum's stronghold, we marched south-east to a large village called Tilwah, where some two thousand budmashes had been collected. They made off on our approach. We encamped on a beautiful grassy maidan, after a short march of seven miles. The country in this neighbourhood is very fine, the plain covered with grass, over which the eye can range uninterruptedly for five or six miles all round, unless where some large topes obstruct some more distant objects. Numerous small villages surrounded by dense bamboo jungle dot this plain. A Sikh was to-day sentenced to death for shooting and wounding two villagers. The sentence has been commuted to transportation for life. A force of two guns with cavalry were sent out in the evening to reconnoitre a village three miles off. It was found deserted, although spies brought in word that it was full of budmashes.

April 19th. Usual hour marched. Proceeded seven miles to Ramnuggur, a large place, the residence of a Rajah unfriendly to us. The rebels left it some days previously. On our approaching it a Sowar on a camel was seen making off, as also some armed footmen. The cavalry overtook and killed several, others made for a large serai, from which they opened fire on our troops. The Sowar and all the villagers say the rebels have evacuated Bitowlie, the Begum's abode, and are making towards Fyzabad. All the cavalry with Middleton's battery of Royal Artillery, started this afternoon to bring away four guns which the rebels left behind. After great difficulty they crossed the largest stream of the Chouka, but an island in the centre covered with sand, several feet deep, baffled all their endeavours to proceed. They consequently returned, after being within a mile and a-half of the fort.

April 20th. Halted to-day. Lord Derby's new Indian Bill is telegraphed as having passed, probably only the first reading. It is very similar to Lord Palmerston's, but differs slightly in details. The house belonging to the Rajah of Ramnuggur, was blown up this evening. Not an article of value was found in it.

April 21st. Marched as usual. Reached our encamping ground at Mussowlie about nine a.m. We are on our return to Lucknow, but expect to halt either at Nawabgunge or Chinhut until further orders. Our camp is on the edge of a nuddee, about three feet deep, swarming with teal. Rumours of a fight with Brigadier-General Walpole's column. It attacked a fort and took it, but only after a very severe loss, more than its capture was worth. No particulars given.

April 22nd. Started at five a.m. in the expectation of having a fight at a place called Jungheerabad. The Ghoorkhas had been afraid to attack it, and great preparations for defence had been made. The Rajah sent in yesterday asking our terms. These were—delivery of himself and guns into our hands. As we were starting, a palkie arrived with the man, an old rascal about eighty years of age. He informed us that all his guns had been sent off to Nawabgunge, where they were awaiting our arrival. He was allowed to go away. As we passed within a short distance, General Grant thought it advisable to reconnoitre. After passing through a dense impassable bamboo jungle, with only a footpath to guide them, a bastion was found in front of a house. On exploring the jungle, much against the will of the guides, a masked battery and three guns was found. Having broken faith with us, his house and jungle were set on fire. The fort itself, still deeper in this labyrinth, was reached by us. We arrived at Nawabgunge, after coming nine miles, and found no guns awaiting us. The Ghoorkhas, who have been here about a month, left this morning in the Fyzabad direction. They are about eight thousand strong, have two thousand sick, principally from small-pox. With them are four thousand five hundred carts, besides elephants and camels; as they tell off one man for each of them, about a thousand only are ready for fighting. Very sad news from Walpole's column. He went off to a mud fort called Rookwah, where a Rajah, Narput Singh, with several hundred men and six small native guns were. Without any reconnoitring the heavy guns began pounding at the walls. After an engagement of eight hours duration, it was still held, and our men retired. The infantry, consisting of H.M. 42nd, and the 4th Sikhs, assaulted it, but a deep ditch drove them back with great loss. It was impassable on this side, while on the other an entrance, through which a troop of Horse Artillery might have ridden in line, was found next day. The loss was immense; forty Sikhs out of one hundred and twenty were killed and wounded; almost a similar number of the 42nd fell. The Highlanders got up to the ditch, but further advance was impossible. Their dead were left where they fell. To crown all this mismanagement, cavalry were ordered to protect the rear through dense jungle. No attempt was made to prevent escape. During the night the Rajah with his harem, treasure, guns, and Sepoys, made off unharmed. Our loss is—Killed, Brigadier the Hon. A. Hope, H.M. 93rd; Lieutenants Douglas and Bramley, H.M. 42nd; Lieutenant Willoughby, 4th Sikhs; wounded, Lieutenant Harrington, Artillery, dangerously. The fall of Brigadier Hope is irreparable. The best and most beloved Brigadier has fallen. In what a melancholy way cut off—from the incapacity of his Chief. Everyone looked up to him as a future leader. His quiet unassuming manner, his kind word for everyone, even of the lowest rank, endeared him to all. Surely Brigadier-General Walpole's command has terminated! Admiral Byng was shot for a much more trivial offence. The brother of the Home Secretary will be hauled through, although a less influential man would be lost. The death of Hope is a murder of omission, if not of commission. The descendant of a race of warriors, the son of the famous Sir J. Hope, who succeeded Sir J. Moore at Corunna, to fall from the stupidity of a senior, will call down on the head of the culprit (or ought to do so) unending infamy.

April 23rd. A force left camp this morning to destroy the fort partly burnt yesterday. It was found deserted, was mined and blown up. Nothing talked of but Walpole's defeat. An unanimous vote of censure is passed on him, and if he was in our hands no pity would be shown.

April 24th. The 1st Bengal Fusiliers, the squadron of H.M. 2nd D.G., the Punjaub Sappers, and the R.E., left this morning with all the sick for Lucknow. The Fusiliers leave us because the regiment is so unhealthy. Eighty men were in hospital. They relieve a Queen's corps, which comes to join us.

April 25th (Sunday). Nothing doing. Weather oppressively warm, not a breath of air during the day. Firing or explosions heard several times to-day. Camp very dirty. Men still healthy in spite of this, and the remains of dead Ghoorkhas round our encampment.

April 26th. Marched at four a.m. Dust storm last night. Instead of the thunder showers of Meerut, we have in this part these clouds of dust. Proceeded about thirteen miles to Chinhut, the scene of Sir H. Lawrence's unfortunate battle in July. News of a fight near Futtehgurh. Pandy made no attempt at a stand. The 9th Lancers, in pursuit, are said to have killed four hundred and fifty. We expected to remain at this place some weeks, but a sudden order came this morning to march to-morrow to Dilkusha. This arises from the moveable column of the garrison of Lucknow having proceeded to Bunnee, it being threatened. The telegraph wire has been cut, and bodies of maurauders are wandering about. Lugard's column has had two fights; one on entering the Azimgurh, the other on the 19th ult. Lieutenant Havelock, nephew of Sir Henry, was killed in one.

April 27th. Started at usual hour. Crossed the Goomtee by a bridge of boats below the Dilkusha house. The park is now dreadfully dirty from the quantity of troops that have at various times encamped on it. Clouds of dust also flying about. Received the unwelcome news that we were to march in two days for Roy Bareilly, a place eighty miles from this. No European is said to have been there. It is almost due south of Lucknow. Bodies of the rebels are collecting in that quarter. Communication with Cawnpore is said to be stopped by rebels. We are to take provisions for two months, and are not to return here. Fyzabad will probably be garrisoned by us. Dreadful dust storm during the night, followed by thunder, lightning, and rain. No further news, except that it is the present intention for us to take what houses we can in Roy Bareilly, and make ourselves as comfortable as possible until the cold weather.

April 28th. At five a.m. marched. Morning very cool and pleasant. Instead of going direct to Alumbagh over country, we went all through the city and down the Cawnpore road. The bridge at Charbagh across the canal, which at this place is very deep, delayed us some time. The rebels broke it down after Havelock passed. It has only lately been repaired by a fragile-looking wooden erection. This proved sufficient to bear the heavy guns. Encamped about two miles beyond Alumbagh. This place is in a perfect state yet, the fortifications, ditches, etc. Pandy's zig-zags that he made are also still perfect. General Sir J. Grant comes in command of our column.

April 29th. At five a.m. marched. Proceeded to Bunnee, where we encamped just beyond the bridge. On the Lucknow side, the 20th, 23rd, and 53rd, with Artillery and Cavalry were in camp. They return to Lucknow to-morrow morning. The 27th Madras Native Infantry are still in the entrenchment in the village of Bunnee. For five months they have been there without seeing a shot fired. It is not known whether we proceed to Roy Bareilly direct, or attack a body of Pandys to the north of this.

April 30th. Sad news to-day. Sir William Peel, K.C.B., died at Cawnpore, on the 26th, of smallpox. One of the most unassuming of men, as brave as a lion, cool and daring to excess. After passing through a short but brilliant career has been cut off, and his name added to the long list of great men dead. The news from Behar is very bad. Koer Singh has entered Arrah again, and the whole district is in his hands. He appeared at some place above Dinapore. A force was immediately sent after him. A part of it fell into an ambush, and two hundred of H.M. 38th with ten officers were killed. Two guns were lost by us. It was against this rascal that H.M. 10th lost so severely in a similar manner. Marched at 4.30 a.m. Proceeded about two miles along the Cawnpore road, then turned to the left, going in a southerly direction, made a long circuit, and encamped after a march of about seven miles. The camel corps left Bunnee this morning, on its way to Busserut Gunge. They are to keep the communication open with Cawnpore. Koer Singh is said to have been wounded, and lost an arm at the ambuscade.

May 1st. Halted to-day, part of our baggage having gone on to Cawnpore yesterday. This place is called Kantha. The capture of Jhansi, by Sir H. Rose, seems to have been a well conducted affair. The Nana's brother, Tantia Topee, brought a large force to relieve the garrison. His men seem to have fought well; they withstood two charges of our cavalry, at the third they bolted. H.M. 86th lost several officers killed, and all but one wounded. The enemy blew up the magazine when our men got into it, and killed a great many. The treasure taken has been immense. This fighting lasted three days. The 2nd April was the hardest engagement.

May 2nd (Sunday). Marched to Poorwah, nine miles distant. The Pandys have been at this place for some time, in a large "pucka" fort, but bolted a day or two ago. No stand is expected in our course, except from Ram Singh, a large Zemindar, near the Ganges, who seized the boats with the unfortunate inmates and returned them to the Nana at Cawnpore. He has sworn, it is said, to die in his fort.

May 3rd. Koer Singh is dead from the effects of his wound. The man who commands the rebels in this district has issued a proclamation calling upon the inhabitants not to believe our orders, as whenever the country is settled we intend compelling them to become Christians. A very sudden death in hospital to-day. A man named Lyster, a recruit, was under treatment for fever; about four p.m. was seized with sunstroke, and died in three hours. Halted to-day. The Sappers were employed in destroying the fort. Pandy's Sowars are hovering about and attempting to capture our elephants.

May 4th. Marched at usual hour. Proceeded only a short way and encamped at Morawan. Passed a village where a body of Pandys were yesterday. They left last night. We burnt it in passing. Day intensely warm. A brevet is issued for the relief of Lucknow. Generals Mansfield and Cotton are made K.C.B. The late Brigadier Hope, Colonel Hale, H.M. 82nd, C.B., etc. A medal for this campaign, with a clasp for Delhi, and another for Havelock's force, has been authorised. None as yet for our relief. Major J. Baird has been made a Lieutenant-Colonel and C.B. Dr. J. C. Browne, also a C.B.

May 5th. Force halted to-day. We, with some cavalry and infantry, proceeded to a fort two miles from this. The Rajah came in yesterday, and his men bolted. Our expedition was to destroy the place and bring away any guns concealed. We found one 4-pounder gun on carriage, and two camel guns. The village was set on fire. Apparatus for casting round shot and making gun carriages was destroyed. Returned to camp about ten a.m. This Rajah has been fined five thousand rupees for burning houses in a village yesterday, and five thousand rupees for deceiving us regarding the guns, he having affirmed that he had none. A great many matchlocks and tulwars were carried off by us.

May 6th. An extra six months *batta* has been given us for Delhi; in all, fourteen hundred rupees. Marched to Derpaulgunge, about seven miles. Country very jungly, badly cultivated, with plenty of water. A body of Pandys are in the village, a few miles from this. We pay them a visit to-morrow morning. The chief rebel in this quarter is called Banee Madho. He is the individual who we hear daily is a few miles in front, but regularly makes off on our approach. The other rascal in the district is Ram Buksh, whose place is on the banks of the Ganges. He it was who murdered some of the fugitives from Cawnpore, and sent back to the Nana a boat containing others. He is anxious to come in, but his men, who are greatly in arrears of pay, are unwilling to part with him. Mr. Tucker, the Commissioner with us, has also intimated that he will receive no mercy from us. The sentence of the King of Delhi has been published. He is to be transported for life to the new penal settlement at the Andaman Islands.

May 7th. Shajehanpore was entered by the Chief's force without opposition on the 29th ult. The station, of course, is all destroyed. The rebels with the Nana are, it is said, determined to fight at Bareilly, and intend trying their luck this time on the open plain. There has been a fight somewhere near Moradabad. General N. Penny commanded, and he is mentioned as killed. No particulars. The Carabiniers charged and lost four officers wounded, and several men killed. Marched at usual hour. The Pandys were known to be only a few *coss* * ahead; however, none were seen. We burnt several villages on our way. On the banks of a deep nullah we found large preparations for an immense fortification, which we have destroyed. Passed large salt manufactories on our way. The mode of preparing it is as follows:—The soil is heaped up into mounds, water is poured through this and collected in a trough. This in its passage dissolves the salt, which is afterwards collected by means of evaporation. The salt thus made is very

* A *coss* is two miles.

coarse and pungent, containing some acid. Halted after six miles march, at a place called Sugdeopore.

May 8th. Halted to-day, in order that the fort near here might be destroyed. It has been planned by some man well acquainted with engineering. It is masked on three sides by jungle. The villagers in this district are very friendly. The budmashes have been looting them. Another death in hospital to-day from sunstroke—C. Callaghan, stable orderly, nineteen years residence in India. No remedies of any use. Nineteen men have been buried this week from *ictus solis* alone. Warm east wind blowing night and day.

May 9th (Sunday). Marched to Nuggur, six miles distant. Our course is now south-west towards the Ganges. Dust storm last night with great deal of lightning. Day consequently cool. Pandy Sowars still loitering about us; keeping well out, but cutting up stray grasscutters.

May 10th. Marched at three a.m., having a longer march. Our destination was the stronghold of Ram Buksh, near the Ganges. Found that he had fled. On the way the villagers told us that a force of several hundred Sowars, eight hundred infantry, and three small guns passed along the road three days ago. They also said that the budmashes were leaving him and returning to their villages. Captain Reid joined us yesterday from Lucknow. No rebels were seen or heard of on his way. This says a great deal for the effect produced by our march, and of the friendly intentions of the natives. First anniversary of the mutiny of Meerut. What a tempest has blown over the land! What numbers of officers and ladies have fallen. What a labour is still before us. Things are, however, settling down, and peace is returning to large districts. This place is called Dungeogeera.

May 11th. Halted. Destroying Ram Buksh's village and several about here. They were first given up to loot. About two miles from our camp is the Hindoo Temple, in which fourteen of our countrymen sought shelter after their boat ran aground. Guns were brought against it; but not until their ammunition failed did Pandy prevail, and it was only by smoking them out that our brave fellows were forced out. They made a rush, but out of the number, five only reached the river, about a mile distant. Rumours of Banee Madho being near this with ten thousand men (?) Whatever truth there may be in this, we march at eleven p.m. The fort here, which we destroyed, is a strong place, being surrounded by a deep ditch and jungle.

May 12th. We started at midnight, and returned by the same road as on the 10th, to Nuggur. Our march was intended to be about twenty miles, but the night was so dark, the country so wooded, and there being no road, the army went straggling all over the country. Various attempts to collect it were made, but all failed. We halted until day break, and then moved on to our encamping ground. Struck our tents again at two p.m. Banee Madho is only three *coss* from us. The baggage with two guns, some cavalry and infantry, were collected around the village in rear. The day was intensely hot, not a breath of wind blowing. The effect of this was most disastrous, men were dropping down, some dead, some insensible. Above twenty soldiers were sent back. We continued our march in battle array, the cavalry on the flanks, then the artillery and the infantry in the centre. After proceeding about four miles, large bodies of Pandys were seen hovering about the topes of trees. The country here is very broken, mounds of earth, villages, nullahs, and large mangoe topes intercepting the view. Two small pieces opened upon our advanced guard, but did no harm. Our right flank was immediately moved rapidly forward, the guns galloped to the front, opened fire, and silenced the guns. Pandy made no attempt at a stand. Their cavalry showed front on our right flank, but on our guns being turned towards them they retired. One gun, with waggon complete, was abandoned by them. Our artillery kept advancing and firing at the retreating rebels, who were in immense numbers. Our cavalry could do nothing, the country being so broken. A nullah stopped our progress, but from its banks a heavy fire was kept up. This nullah contained water, of no depth, however, but the opposite bank was covered with dense jungle, from which they could only be driven by skirmishers. While this part was being reconnoitred, a large body appeared on our right, around a village called Simore, which was in truth their centre. The nullah ran round it. Our guns cannonaded it for some time, but were unable to silence the musketry fire. One company of H.M. 38th advanced as skirmishers, and kept it under. It was the intention to assault this place, but an attack on the left prevented any infantry coming up. The Pandys from their overwhelming numbers, extending above two miles, kept moving round our flank. On the left they advanced within a short distance of the 7th Sikhs, who were behind a mound. They, with a cheer, rushed at them, first giving a volley, then using their tulwars. About fifty budmashes were killed at this one place. The Rifle Brigade then advanced through the jungle, driving the enemy out and capturing two guns ; one a 12-pounder, the other a mortar. The latter was abandoned from want of bullocks to bring it in. Darkness coming on, they and all the infantry were withdrawn behind the nullah. On the right, Pandy seeing we did not advance, got courage and advanced up the nullahs to our flank. Having no infantry to drive them back, the artillery and cavalry retired, followed by their skirmishers. At this time darkness coming on, the musketry ceased. We joined the infantry and bivouacked for the night, strong picquets being thrown out all round. This affair, although so unsatisfactory, had a beneficial effect. Four guns were captured, and Pandy, except on the right, driven back at all points. Another hour's daylight would have completed the defeat. Our want was infantry, and the sudden attack on the left, alone prevented their coming. Our loss was trifling from the enemy, but the sun made deadly attacks on the infantry. About forty men of the Rifles alone fell out, incapable of going on. Three men of the 38th dropped down dead. The force was completely done up by the long marching. The enemy's Sowars cut up a sergeant of the Rifles in a doolie. They also cut up several grasscutters, etc. One of these was found in the morning with his hand cut off and wounds in all parts of his body.

May 13th. A loose horse during the night caused great alarm. The piquets fired; the natives rushed in through the sleeping infantry, who started up, seized their rifles and knocked down their neighbours. Captain Gibbons, R.A., because he wore a white pugerie was knocked down. In the scuffle his revolver went off, wounding him severely in the thigh. The rest of the night passed quietly. As soon as it was light started for camp, as fears were entertained regarding the baggage. Pandy still occupied the same village, but did not molest us. Reached camp about eight a.m. No enemy appeared there. This was the hottest day we have had yet. Not a breath of air. The deaths from sunstroke are very numerous. Above twenty men were buried this evening. Bareilly is in our hands. It was evacuated, all but a small fort on the parade ground. The rebels are making for Oude. Shajehanpore, where we left civilians and a small party of men, was attacked by a large force of Pandys with twelve guns. They were, however, driven off, and the place relieved. The Begum has occupied Nawabgunge, where we were on the 22nd ult. She has, it is said, twenty-five thousand men. She intends driving us out of Lucknow, and again occupying the Kaiser Bagh. The news brought in to-day of yesterday's fight is, that the Pandys are greatly disheartened, having retired a *coss;* that they lost three hundred men, among whom was Sewruthun Singh, the fellow who was building the fort which was destroyed by us on the 8th ult. Halted to-day.

May 14th. The news from Lucknow has obliged us to return there without delay: we start to-morrow and go direct. On our troops approaching Bareilly, a large party of Ghazees rushed through the 42nd Highlanders. They came with such overwhelming force that nothing could withstand the onset. Above six hundred were killed—the whole body. No news of how many Highlanders fell. Four European women have been rescued there, probably half-castes. It was the Moulvie who commanded in the attack on Shajehanpore. Banee Madho and his men are plucking up courage, and intend attacking us. Koer Singh's men are fortifying themselves in a dense game preserve at Jugdespore. Sir E. Lugard is on his way to attack them.

May 15th. Started at 4.30 a.m. Marched to Sugdeopore, our old encamping ground. In addition to the rebels at Nawabgunge, about twelve thousand are said to be at Baree. The mortality in Lucknow is very great, about eighteen per cent. are on the sick list. Smallpox is raging. Captain Forster, one of the prize agents, lately died of it.

May 16th (Sunday). Same hour as yesterday marched. Banee Madho is only six miles off. If we had not such strict orders about pressing on to Lucknow, we would attack him. Encamped near Poorwah. The people of Calcutta are still panic-stricken. A rumour is going the round of the bazaars there, that in a short time "something white will disappear." This, of course, is referred to the Europeans. From whatever cause, uneasiness is being felt. The natives are all bolting from Lucknow. No coolie can be got to work at the fortifications. The rebels have given out that they will murder every native in our employ.

May 17th. Halted, as Pandy considered we were bolting

from him. Sir H. Rose has had another fight on his way to Kalpee. Brigadier Walpole was wounded in two places, by the Ghazees, at Bareilly. Major Norman was wounded by a round shot on ankle.

May 18th. Marched to Kantha at usual hour. News from Lucknow more favourable. Sir E. Lugard has driven the enemy out of Jugdespore. They have bolted to the south. The Commander-in-Chief is at Meerut. Tombs' Troop returns there. Weather has become very cool and cloudy, with a strong east wind blowing.

May 19th. Marched to Bunnee. This force is to encamp at Manao, the old cantonments, in tents. They are to be thatched, and every precaution taken against the rains. The papers acquaint us with the murder of Major J. Waterfield, 38th N.I., A.A.G., at Meerut, while travelling in a dâk gharrie, along the grand trunk road. Some mutineers were crossing the Doab and fell in with him. Captain Fanshawe, accompanying him, escaped. The 4th N.I. have been caught plotting against the lives of their officers, at Hosheyarpore. Several have been hanged. They were disarmed nearly a year ago.

May 20th. Marched to near Jellalabad. This road is now covered with carts, etc., travelling to and from Lucknow. A different sight from the first time we marched up.

May 21st. Marched over country to Dilkusha, and crossed the river, encamping on a plain in front of the Martiniere. Our stay here is not to be long. We go to Nawabgunge to prevent the rebels crossing the Gogra. It was all false about a large force being assembled there. The mortality in Lucknow is very great. The week before last it was fifty-nine—all European. Last week forty-nine. This, with our deaths for three weeks, which were seventy-five, amounts to one hundred and eighty-three. If this goes on England will have a greater drain than she can withstand.

May 22nd. Lost another man from *ictus solis* last night. Went to the first sale of the state jewels this morning in Lucknow. Prices very high. Natives were the chief purchasers. The city is still very deserted. The streets are now in good repair. The pulling down of houses, etc., is going on rapidly. Good news this evening. We are to go into the quarters occupied by the 1st troop 1st brigade, while they go out on this expedition.

May 23rd (Sunday). Went over the Kaiser Bagh, where we are to live. The quarters are good, but rather confined. The nights are said to be fearfully warm, the days cool. The weather on this side of the river is intensely warm, with a strong hot wind blowing.

May 24th. A salute was fired this morning, in honour of Her Majesty's birthday. Two columns left Lucknow to-day. The one we belonged to returns towards Cawnpore. Sir J. H. Grant goes again in command. Banee Madho is said to be at Poorwah, and threatening to stop all our communications. The other force is encamped at Manao for the present. We took up our quarters this evening. Found it until sunset cooler, after that warmer, than in tents. Got the offer of the Staff here from Dr. Brown; at once accepted it.

May 25th. Kalpee was taken by Sir H. Rose with little loss on our side. The rebels have fled in the direction of

Jalaon. His campaign has been most wonderful; across the whole continent of India he has marched, and fought innumerable fights, defeating the rebels on all occasions. Dust storm to-day with a few drops of rain. Temperature fallen from 103° to 96°.

May 26th. Called on Major Carnegie to-day. He lives at the Katwallee, in the centre of the Choka. He is now the Deputy-Commissioner of Lucknow. This native city is an extraordinary place. The streets short, very narrow and winding. The noise of natives squabbling is continuous.

May 27th. The Chief has had a fight near Shajehanpore. No particulars known. The Moulvie is still in that part with swarms of cavalry. The Rajah of Kuppurtollah is on his way down from the Punjaub with about two thousand men. He is to assist us in settling Oude. There are several thousand of our Sikh levies with him.

May 28th. Sir J. Grant is at Nawabgunge, on the Cawnpore road. Talbot's company, with heavy guns, goes out to join him. We hear Banee Madho's men have dug up the bodies of our poor men, who died of sunstroke, and have paraded their skulls, singing pæans, etc., and bragging of their great deeds. Grant's force is losing a great many men. The 1st troop 1st brigade alone, have had five deaths. Even H.M. 53rd, old seasoned men, are dying fast. Already ninety men are said to have dropped down.

May 29th. Lieutenant-Colonel Parnell's force, encamped near cantonments, is going on some expedition in a day or two. Grant's still at Nawabgunge. Poorwah is to be occupied during the rains by one thousand Sikhs, with three light guns. Fortifications are to be made, armed with heavy pieces. Weather has become much cooler.

May 30th (Sunday). First anniversary of the first battle on the Hindan. This was the first meeting of England's soldiers with the cowardly mutineers. How often have they been opposed since and with what uniform success! The last twelvemonths has seen the reoccupation of every place in the hands of the mutineers. No strongholds remain to them, no unity binds them together; and although it may be long before the last body of rebels is dispersed, yet its dispersion is certain. Bareilly is to be garrisoned by the 3rd troop 3rd brigade A.F.A. company with heavy guns; 2nd Punjaub Cavalry; H.M. 42nd and 93rd Highlanders. Brigadier Jones with H.M. 60th and 79th have gone to Shajehanpore to relieve it, and attack the hosts of rebels surrounding it. The Chief has joined them there, and some fighting, result unknown, has ensued.

May 31st. The Chief has returned to Futtehgurh. He is to spend the rains at Allahabad, so rumour goes. Shahjehanpore was relieved on the 11th ult. Mahomdie is the rebels' headquarters in Rohilcund. The Moulvie has left it and gone to Sandu to assist the rascals there. He is the most troublesome and clever enemy we have had since Koer Singh's death. Bringing priestcraft to bear, he carries all the evil-disposed with him, promising honour here, and eternal happiness hereafter.

June 1st. A native rumour has been prevalent here for some time, that a rise would be made to-day, and all Europeans murdered; of course there was no attempt. A rascal with one thousand men and three H.A. guns has appeared on the grand trunk road, between Cawnpore and Futtypore. The rebels have taken a new method with us. Instead of cutting the telegraph wires and stopping the dâks, by which we soon become cognisant of their movements, they now do nothing and allow traffic to go on. By this means they can march while we are in perfect ignorance. Panics are the order of the day. There is one in Calcutta, Dacca, Allahabad, and, as usual, in Agra. The hot weather causes this brooding over calamities supposed to be impending.

June 2nd. The rains that were threatening have cleared off. Days are again hot, with a strong west wind blowing. Grant's column has gone to Poorwah. H.M. 53rd are to be hutted at Nawabgunge, on the Cawnpore road. Nothing doing here. The Engineers are busy blowing up houses, etc., all day long. Broad streets are being carried straight through the city.

June 3rd. Went over the Muchee Bhawun and the fortifications erecting there. Beginning from the east, a strong earthen fort commands the iron bridge. It is so far completed that guns are in position. The Muchee Bhawun is greatly strengthened. The high walls, along the foot of which the street runs, are left intact. The side next the city has been totally changed. Piles of buildings have been levelled, and earthworks made in their place. A lofty battery, armed already with 68 and 24-pounders, is erected in the centre of the fort on a high inclined plane, commanding all the city. This part is connected with the great Imaum Bara. At the stone bridge, on the rising ground on the right bank, another strong redoubt has been made. Such an undertaking must have a beneficial effect in allaying any turbulent feelings in the city, by showing that we are in earnest, and intend holding what we have got. No news.

June 4th. Mahomdie has been found evacuated. The enemy, headed by the Moulvie, made an attack on our force at Shahjehanpore, but were repulsed. They have gone, it is said, towards Lucknow. A pursuing column, under Colonel Robertson, is following the rebels from Kalpee. Their principal body has gone towards Gwalior. This causes some uneasiness. The Maharajah's troops are not trustworthy, and they have been tampered with by spies of the Nana. This brute being the adopted son of the Peishwa has great influence there. Numbers of his followers are attempting to cross the Doab, but as yet they have been prevented. A Brigade of Sir H. Rose's army go to Gwalior and canton there. This will restore confidence. The last accounts from Sir J. Grant's column are that he was then only five miles from the rebels.

June 5th. News came in to-day of the capture of Gwalior by the rebels. The Maharajah's troops joined the mutineers. The whole of the city was by the last accounts in their hands, but the fort was still held by some faithful Thakoors. The Maharajah has fled to Agra. His body-guard fought for some time until two hundred were cut up. If the fort falls, one of the strongest fortresses in India will be in their possession, and will entail great trouble on us. Sir H. Rose's force was only fifteen miles distant at Mahomdie, when this occurred. If he can relieve those inside, affairs will soon look bright again. A party of two thousand Sepoys, with three H.A. guns, have crossed the Doab and Ganges from Kalpee and joined Banee Madho. It is this awful heat that alone prevents our chastising these predatory bands.

June 6th (Sunday). The rebels on the east at Nawabgunge number two thousand men, with twelve small guns. This is the news brought by some Syces detained by them. Letters from home, dated April 16th and 22nd—all well.

June 7th. The fort of Gwalior is in the hands of the rebels. They number ten thousand men. They have placed seven guns in position; have summoned the neighbouring Rajahs to join them. It is doubtful whether they will await the arrival of Sir H. Rose, there being no escape if they shut themselves up. They have piquets of cavalry watching the Agra road. Several of the Sirdars are joining the Maharajah. He went out against the enemy, and drew up his army in three divisions. The left at once joined the enemy, the right soon followed, but the centre fought well for some time until overpowered by numbers. It consisted principally of his body-guard, and was led by him in person.

June 8th. First anniversary of Badli-ka-Serai and advance on Delhi. Never did Pandy fight as he did on that morning, but the action was never doubtful. The superiority of the West over the East was proved, and it has been confirmed on every subsequent occasion. How splendid our disasters have been! The earthwork at Cawnpore will remain a memorial of the endurance and bravery of the British soldiers. How frequently have the two nations met—never on equal terms—yet every place in the rebel's hands has been wrested from him, and he is now a wanderer and an outcast. No news of any kind. Tombs' Troop goes back to Meerut.

June 9th. Grant's column arrived to-day. A salute was fired this morning announcing the arrival of the Kuppurtollah Rajah. His force is encamped at Bunnee. The enemy in the direction we are going are very numerous, much more than was at first imagined. Stragglers are constantly joining them. They number, it is said, ten thousand men. Our force at Chinhut is not considered strong enough to attack.

June 11th. Brigadier-General Napier, B.E., commands the army proceeding against Gwalior. The rebels under Tantia Topee have raised the green flag. Bhurtpore is still quiet. Several of the Maharajah's Sowars have crossed the Chumbul and are waiting to join us. The mutineers are putting the fort in a state of defence. Meade's Horse, Captain Light, with four guns, and the 3rd Europeans (four hundred men) have gone towards the Chumbul. Tombs' Troop is ordered to Agra, as is also Le Mesurier's R.A. battery.

June 12th. Marched at three a.m., and proceeded about three miles beyond Chinhut. The change is far from agreeable. The heat was great and the dust in clouds. Our force is very strong. One troop H.A., Major Carleton's battery, Gibbons' R.A. battery; about fifteen hundred cavalry, consisting of 2nd D.G., 7th Hussars, Hodson's Horse (five hundred), and Wale's Horse; the 2nd and 3rd Rifle Battalions, parts of two Sikh corps, and H.M. 90th. The enemy in front number, it is said, sixteen thousand men. Some bolted

19

yesterday, the remainder will probably stand. We start at eleven p.m. The Moulvie of Fyzabad is said to command, and the Begum is, or was there.

June 13th. Our progress was slow and tiresome. About three a.m. we turned off the pucka road, and went north so as to get between the fort of Jungheerabad, destroyed by us on April 23rd, and Nawabgunge. We advanced about two miles when our advance guard was stopped by a challenge of "who goes dere." We accordingly halted until daybreak. As soon as it became light we again advanced, but the enemy immediately opened on us with musketry. There was a strong piquet of them here, consisting of cavalry, infantry, and several guns. The two former were in a deep nullah, with broken watercourses running into it. Our guns opened, but of course did no harm. The popping still kept on, and it was only by ordering a company of Rifles forward that they were driven out, and that without attempting to stand. They bolted and joined their main body on the right, some to the left, where there was a strong battery of guns and swarms of Sowars. Our force was rapidly moved forward, and a gun was found deserted. On making this forward movement the enemy tried to turn our right flank, and at one time we were completely surrounded except in rear. The enemy had a number of guns—some heavy ones—but being always fired high, did little damage. As soon as our infantry came up we formed towards the right, where large bodies of the enemy were in villages. Gibbons' R.A. battery, some cavalry, and two companies of Rifles kept the enemy from attacking our left flank and silenced their guns. For some time the cannonade was very heavy, the enemy's guns being in the village. The infantry, 2nd Rifle Brigade, went in at a charge, and the number killed there was only surpassed by the Secunderabagh. The enemy fought as they have rarely done, and in some places even came out to meet our men. One body of about two hundred—probably Ghazees—came charging, but the 7th Hussars rode through and through them twice, cutting up the majority. At another village they advanced bravely, and were only driven back by grape and the fall of their leader. The enemy now made off eastward to the Gogra. Our cavalry pursued some distance. Nawabgunge was evacuated by them without any fighting. Pursuit was kept up for about a mile beyond, and several guns captured, but the day was hot and the men knocked up with the night's march, so that no pursuit was made. Hodson's Horse and Wale's refused to charge, although the enemy in front were only in small numbers. It is to be hoped this arises from cowardice and from nothing else. The number of guns captured was seven. The effect of this very successful affair must have a beneficial result. This large body, which has defied us so long, and even boasted of recapturing Lucknow, so easily dispersed, will allay the feeling of insecurity of our powers, now prevalent among the natives. Our tents had been ordered to start at daybreak, but this was countermanded. We, therefore, were bivouacked under trees. The heat of this day surpassed even that usual at this season. The wind, when it did blow, was like the blast of a furnace. The consequence was men were being struck down on all sides, some from sunstroke, others from the heat alone. The camp with the sick left Chinhut at twelve a.m. Among my men two were dead on reaching us, and another dying. In the troop itself one Sergeant Bickerstaff was in *articulo mortis*, and in a few hours was dead. Thus four men died, and seventeen men admitted to hospital out of eighty men. The night was equally close, and unfortunately the troop was in a tope. One man was seized during the night. This sickness and mortality does not arise from the heat alone. The Rifles were all day alongside us, yet they only lost two. This troop is done up. The men's nervous system has been over-excited during the last year. Now there is the consequent depression predisposing to such attacks.

June 14th. Another case of sunstroke last night; was waiting on him from one a.m., and as a consequence was quite done up. Heat very great. Eighteen men in hospital, out of eighty-nine. Marched at four a.m., on our return to Lucknow. We got to the cantonments, and are to be hutted there. Encamped as on 12th. H.M. 90th, the 2nd D.G., and some Irregulars are here. They go in with us to-morrow. Dust storm in the evening which lowered the temperature.

June 15th. Marched at three a.m. Proceeded to Aleygunge, half way on the road to cantonments. Encamped in a large tope of trees. News from Gwalior good on the whole. The rebels are quarrelling for pay, and not fortifying the fort. Sir H. Rose is rapidly advancing from Kalpee, and a brigade from Agra. The rebels have proclaimed the Nana as Peishwa, who is to be obeyed as King; the Ranee of Jhansi is Commander-in-Chief, Tantia Topee, Regent. Several cases of sunstroke to-day; all recovered. Letters and papers from home, up to the 9th May.

June 16th. On the 13th we killed the Rajah of Ahnowlee by a round shot. His body was found. Grant is to follow them and prevent them crossing the Gogra. Parts of the 1st Madras Fusiliers and of the Regiment of Ferozepore, go to join him to-morrow. Several severe thunderstorms during last night; the presage of the rains.

June 17th. Pandy has made a raid and carried off all the stud horses and brood mares from Ghazeepore. Days very hot. No wind blowing. The Oude proclamation of Lord Canning, confiscating all the land, except that of six thalookdars, is causing great excitement at home. A dispatch has been sent out to order the Government not to carry it out to its full extent. Some hope from this that his lordship will resign.

June 18th. Twenty-four years of age to-day. How unprofitably they have been spent! What a change from this time last year! What scenes have I gone through! How much has been done, and how much still remains undone! Rumours of Grant's column having had another fight to-day have come in to us, but no particulars. Very warm; little or no wind; in a damp atmosphere.

June 19th. Rode into Lucknow. All the men of the troop doing well. No news in there. By this day's date we hear from Shajehanpore, that the Moulvie, the Fyzabad one, the plotter and originator of all the late disturbances, has been killed by the Sowar of some Rajah, and his head sent in. This is generally believed here. If true, it is of the greatest benefit to us, in the future pacification of Oude. That affairs have taken a favorable turn at present is certain, in spite of Gwalior. Tej Singh, the rebel Rajah of Mynpoorie, has given himself up to us. The news from Gwalior good. The Maharajah has gone to join Sir H. Rose. His old army, it is said, are regretting the step they took. Tantia Topee, the rebel leader, has left, probably to excite rebellion somewhere else. A rebel force has been sent out to stop Rose's force. They do not appear to have made up their minds for a stand, as they are doing little with the fort. Bhurtpore still quiet. Rose's column expected to reach Gwalior about the 17th inst. The Agra column has crossed the Chumbul, but it is not thought they will advance further, the Kalpee force being sufficient.

June 20th (Sunday). Grant's force have never left Nawabgunge, and consequently have had no fighting. The guns we used to hear, chiefly at night, were fired by the rascal of the fort of Jungheerabad. By this means he imagined to frighten us. He has, however, without being attacked, made off. None of the rebels now remain on this side of the Gogra. Rains still keeping off. Heavy masses of cloud floating about. The heat this year appears to have been uncommon. In Calcutta all business is stopped, and the deaths are very great. At Dacca, old residents are panting, even with punkahs, etc.

June 21st. The news from Gwalior still favourable. Scindiah's army is partly returning to him, and partly disbanding to their homes. The advanced guard of Sir H.

Rose's force have already had a brush with the enemy and defeated it. The Agra force is to advance on Gwalior. The Moulvie's death is confirmed. He went against a Rajah and demanded two *Tessildars*. This the Rajah refused, advanced with his men, and after three hours fighting defeated the rebels, and killed their leader. All eyes are turned to Gwalior. No one doubts that it will be taken soon, but every one is anxious to know where the rebels, if they escape, will make for.

June 22nd. The force left at Nawabgunge consists of F Troop R.A.; Gibbons' R.A. Battery; H.M. 7th Hussars; parts of Hodson's and Wale's Horse; 2nd Rifle Battalion; 5th Sikh Infantry; 1st Madras Fusiliers. The remainder joined us this morning. Gwalior is taken. Sir H. Rose captured it, after five hours fighting. The Cavalry and H.A. gone in pursuit. This is all the news received as yet. The Ranee of Jhansi was killed; how, or by whom, telegraph does not say.

June 23rd. No further news from Gwalior. English mail is in. Lord Ellenborough has resigned. This arises from his having published a secret dispatch sent to Lord Canning, censuring him for his Oude proclamation. When the mail left there was every prospect of a dissolution. In the Lords, the Earl of Shaftesbury's motion, censuring the publication, was defeated by a majority of nine. In the Commons, however, it is generally believed Mr. Cardwell's motion will be carried against Ministers. In that case a dissolution will probably ensue.

June 24th. Rode into Lucknow. Men doing well. The convalescents are to start in a few days for the hills.

June 25th. Weather keeping very cool. An east wind has been blowing uninterruptedly for three nights and days. Gwalior was taken on the 17th inst. On the 16th the enemy were driven from the suburbs. On the following day from the city, with the loss of four guns. They evacuated the fort. The Ranee was killed charging at the head of the cavalry. Brigadier Napier went in pursuit at the head of our cavalry, with infantry on camels. They came up with the enemy, captured twenty-five guns and killed a great many.

June 26th. Heavy thunderstorms to-day, but very partial. Only one officer was killed at Gwalior, Lieutenant Rose, 25th Bombay N.I. He led the storming party against the fort, which was held by some fanatics. The rebels have crossed the Chumbul about thirty miles from Dholepore. Some of them had arrived at a place called Sur Muttra, only forty miles from Bhurtpore. They may attempt to raise a disturbance there, but the people appear friendly. The news of the fall of Gwalior has had a first-rate effect on the native mind. They had made up their minds that it would not fall for some time, but the speedy capture and flight of the rebels have at last opened the eyes of the most bigoted and proved that there is something more than "*ikbal*" attending the Company's raj.

June 27th. This day last year the rains commenced at Delhi. This morning there was every appearance of its being true this year also. It rained about two hours in the morning, then cleared up. In the afternoon a dust storm. The sick are not going to the hills. Vans are not procurable for them. Sunday. Our huts are to be ready by the 9th prox., it is said.

June 28th. Heavy thunderstorms with rain, but none of any duration. No news from any quarter. Got several books, the works of Sydney Smith, Borrow's Bible in Spain, etc., etc. The want of literature to while away the time is the greatest drawback to this monotonous life.

June 29th. Rained very heavily this morning. No further news from Gwalior. The Portuguese women who were left behind, and whose husbands fled with the Maharajah, have been kindly treated by the rebels, at least they did them no harm. The force at cantonments will consist of 2nd troop 3rd brigade Horse Artillery, 2nd company 3rd battery Foot Artillery, H.M. 2nd Dragoon Guards, Hodson's Horse, H.M. 38th, part 90th L.I., and the 3rd battalion Rifle Brigade. The whole is commanded by Colonel Parnell, C.B., 90th L.I.

June 30th. We have now got into the season of the year when such a thing as news cannot be procured, and one day is as like the day before it as one pea to another. The only particle of difference is one day it rains in showers, another continuously. Our life is unvaried and monotonous in the extreme. Things get into working order, and they go on smoothly and glibly without interruption.

July 1st. We moved our quarters to-day. The men into huts, while we remain in our tents. We are pitched in a compound on the walks, with the prospect of a ruinous bungalow in front, fast crumbling into decay from the effects of wind and rain. Each residence is worse than another here, almost all being built of mud. The huts for the men consist of long huts raised from the ground, open on all sides, and covered over with thatch.

July 2nd. The rebels have attacked the jail at Gyah and liberated all the prisoners. This occurred on the 21st ult. The rebels from Gwalior are making for Manupore, in a miserable plight. They intended halting at Hindoun, but the advance of our force from Dholepore set them off again. Nothing doing here.

July 3rd. Mr. Cardwell withdrew his vote of censure, on the 21st of May, without a division. This is equivalent to laying guilt on Lord Canning's shoulders. The Government, however, spoke highly of him and his policy. The most curious thing about this debate is the total break up of the Liberals. Sir J. Graham was found siding with ministers and abusing his former colleagues.

July 4th (Sunday). Another English mail in. Turner has been made a Colonel; Blunt, a Lieutenant-Colonel, and Light, a Major. Awfully hot. No appearance of rain. A case of sunstroke last night; patient recovered.

July 5th. Still the same paucity of news. The Begum is said to be assembling a force to attack the Rajah who killed the Moulvie, to avenge his death. This Rajah, although he did not assist officers in their flight, yet never did any overt act. He has been forgiven, and the fifty thousand rupees have been given him, although it was only offered to anyone bringing in the Moulvie alive.

July 6th. Lord Stanley has been made President of the Board of Control, and Sir E. L. Bulwer Secretary for the

Colonies. The Government have pledged themselves to support Lord Canning, but not his policy; which he has been induced to follow, they say, by the advice of his Council. It is still doubtful whether he will resign or not. If he does not, he has a chance of making amends for past errors. The General Assembly of the Scotch Church have petitioned Parliament not to interfere with religion in India. If that means that Government is not to assist missionaries, nor to prevent as many coming as choose, it will cause us a world of trouble to keep fanaticism within proper limits.

July 7th. No news. Weather still oppressively warm. No appearance of rain.

July 9th. Rode into Lucknow. Called on Dr. McClelland, who has just come up from Benares where he was staying. The rain commenced to-day in real earnest. About two p.m. dense masses of clouds came rolling up from the west, preceded by pillars of dust. The sight was grand and not easily forgotten. About 2.30 the storm burst over us with great fury, hiding everything at first in dust, but soon followed by deluges of rain. From that hour until five p.m. it continued without cessation, vivid flashes with thunder accompanying it. The whole country around was soon one sheet of water, excepting where there were roads, or where a piece of rising ground reared its head like an island. During the whole night it continued drizzling. No sooner had darkness fallen than the air resounded with the croaking of myriads of frogs. In one spot the deep and sonorous bass of the male was replied to by the shriller soprano of the female. This pæan lasted uninterruptedly, now however dying away, and again awakening with redoubled fury. With all this turmoil going on in the water, on the dry land the beetles and crickets hummed their unvarying song. The air was full of flying ants, bugs and *hoc genus omnium*. Everything is wet; the interior of your tent damp. You yourself damp and out of spirits.

July 10th. The morning succeeding such a day as yesterday is very beautiful. The dawn breaks among heavy black clouds, still unwilling to yield the field to the approaching sun. No sooner have his rays begun to pierce them and to tinge them with varied hues than, affected by his benign influence, they fade and vanish. Then nature shows its beauteous face surrounded by the glories of an awakened creation—herbs, grasses, etc., spring into being at the touch of the magician's hand. What was a desert a short time previously is a garden covered with luxuriant growth; what was a dry and sandy desert of yesterday is a garden of Eden to-day.

July 11th (Sunday). Very warm. No news.

July 12th. The Gwalior fugitives are making for Tonk. General Roberts, with a large Bombay force, is in pursuit. The Nana is said to have crossed the Gogra, and is in a bad way. He has sold, so natives say, jewels valued at £1,000,000 for ten thousand rupees—a ruby the finest in existence.

July 13th. The rebels in Oude are said to number sixty-six thousand men, with about fifty guns. The largest body are across the Gogra, with the Begum and her paramour, and number forty thousand men. A large proportion of this force does not consist of Sepoys, but armed budmashes. The General, Sir J. H. Grant, inspected the barracks, hospitals, etc., this morning.

July 14th. An order has been issued for every corps here to be in readiness to start by the 5th October next. A telegram from England tell us that thirty thousand more men were under orders for India. They were all to leave before the end of this month. The Rajah of Powayne is said to be surrounded on all sides by the enemy. A force from Shajehanpore will probably relieve him.

July 15th. On a committee all day, examining hospital apprentices in Lucknow. The English mail of the 17th June telegraphed Naples had yielded, and given compensation to the two English Engineers for £3,000. The Indian resolutions are rapidly passing; Lord John Russell and Lord Palmerston in vain attempted opposition to Ministers; a majority of eighty-four was on the Ministerial side. Colonel Berkeley, 32nd L.I., has captured a fort near Allahabad, on the frontier of Oude, and killed a number of rebels.

July 16th. A force is to proceed to Fyzabad immediately. That at Nawabgunge will probably go, while we go out there. The cause of this sudden move is that Maun Singh is surrounded and in difficulties. He defeated the Pandys with the loss to them of seven hundred (?), so rumour says. This, of course, is very annoying. Everyone has been building houses, and no sooner are they ready for living in than their owners are ordered out.

July 17th. No further news of moving. The weather during the last week has been very uncommon, even to that inhabitant of all lands and climates, "the oldest resident."

One continuous gale from the east has been blowing, with little intermission for above a week. Days, of course, are cool, but no rain having fallen makes people look forward to a famine, which must be the result. However, there is time enough for a deluge in the next two months.

July 18th (Sunday). We march on Tuesday morning for Nawabgunge. Whether we go on from there is as yet a mystery. The Rajah of Kuppurtollah goes on still further and keeps up the communication between Lucknow and Fyzabad. Letters from home, dated June 2nd—all well

July 19th. Raining nearly all day, a foretaste of what we may expect on our march. The 1st Europeans left Lucknow, escorting heavy guns to Nawabgunge. The order for us to march at three a.m. to-morrow morning was annulled on account of the rain.

July 20th. Rained heavily during the night. Hodson's Horse left this morning for Nawabgunge. They go on to Fyzabad. The Kuppurtollah Rajah, goes to Duriabad, twenty miles beyond Nawabgunge.

July 21st. Marched at three a.m. Morning at first doubtful, turned out fine. Halted first beyond the village Chinhut. The Nana, it appears, has crossed the Gogra, and joined the Begum. He has requested to be put in command of all her forces but has been refused. The Begum wrote to Maun Singh, telling him to come over and join her. Although still playing a double game, he applied for assistance from us first. Our marching will probably decide him in still remaining loyal to us.

July 22nd. Marched at three a.m. Reached Nawabgunge

about eight a.m. Morning very warm, without wind. Found the rear-guard of Grant's column only moving off the ground. The huts they were building are not entirely finished, and compared with what we have left are miserable places. There are no bricks here so they had to make them of mud alone. We have pitched our tents and will probably remain in them altogether. Heavy firing heard all morning. Some petty chief, in a small fort, attempting to frighten us from advancing further. Grant's Column are at Dadia.

July 23rd. A part of the 2nd D.G. and the whole of the Rajah of Kuppurtollah's force marched this morning to join Grant's column at Duriabad. They remain there on the General's advance. Awfully hot now, day and night. No news.

July 24th. The Calcutta dâk has not arrived for two days. The rains, which are very heavy down country, have delayed it. Walked over our battle-field of the 13th June. The appearance of everything is changed. The crops are high now, where there was nothing but grass before. Skeletons of men and horses whiten the ground here and there.

July 25th (Sunday). Rained heavily last evening, as well as during the night. The ground where we are is very flat, but there are several nullahs and jheels into which the water is drained. General Grant has reached Duriabad quite safe, Pandy bolting at his approach. Maun Singh sends word that he is surrounded by great numbers of the enemy, and that he himself is badly off for ammunition and provisions.

July 26th. Captain Rattray has captured Sungram Singh, who has been keeping the country about Depree in a constant state of alarm. He sent out eight picked Sikhs, who brought him in alive and killed all his family. Banee Madho and Rugonath Singh with thirteen thousand five hundred men and seventeen guns have marched, it is supposed, towards Pertabgurh.

July 27th. Orders came this morning for the Ferozepore Regiment and two guns of Horse Artillery to proceed and join the General. They start to-morrow morning. McLeod goes in command. Strong gale blowing to-day. No one here has ever seen such cool rains and with so few storms.

July 28th. Tombs' Troop has returned to Meerut, while ours is still out and no prospect of getting into any station. Had a letter from J. Henderson. He is still at Kamptee, with the 33rd Madras N.I. No news.

July 29th. No news from anywhere. Still cold, with showers of rain and a gale of wind.

July 30th. H.M. 53rd, with two guns of the 2nd troop 3rd brigade Foot Artillery, arrived here this morning *en route* to Duriabad, where they remain.

July 31st. Damp, rainy day. The 53rd left this morning. Grant's force has arrived at Fyzabad without fighting. Pandy made off across the Gogra.

August 1st (Sunday). Another dull, rainy day. The Moulvie Mahomed is said to have advanced to a place called Futtypore, about twenty miles from this. He, like many other chiefs, is being treated with, and shows an inclination to come to terms.

August 2nd. Grant's force on reaching Fyzabad was in time to give the rebels a few rounds as they were crossing the Gogra. He has since gone to Shahgunge, Maun Singh's fort, and exchanged pugeries with him. The rebels are still causing us great annoyance about Arrah. They are in the Jugdespore jungle, from which they make raids in all directions. On the 21st ult. a party appeared on the grand trunk road, near Jehanabad, and robbed the mail. A detachment of H.M. 73rd, proceeding to Benares, fell in with them and killed several. Since this happened, the Camel corps and some Sikh cavalry have been sent down to keep the road clear.

August 3rd. The Shazada Feroze Shah attacked a thannah, near Bunnee, a few days ago, and carried off the Thannadar. Since then he has surrounded a part of one of our police corps near Sundeela. H.M. 88th, with a battery of Royal Artillery, have gone out to relieve them. Had an attack of remittent fever to-day.

August 4th. Raining nearly all day. Rumours are rife of Grant having proceeded to Sultanpore to visit a Rajah who is friendly to us. The revenue is being collected in this district. Pandy, during his reign, levied blackmail from some villages. We at present are regardless of this, and demand full arrears. It is the intention, however, to remit it back again when peace is restored.

August 5th. Damp rainy day. News of a party of rebels, with eleven small guns, attempting to cross between this and Duriabad, came in to-day. The spies brought word that the rain prevented them moving. A strong patrol of cavalry was immediately sent out. It appears that on our reaching Fyzabad, Pandy made off in three bodies—two to different places on the Gogra, and the third to Sultanpore. It is the last who are now returning and attempting to join their friends.

August 6th. English mail of July 2nd in. Hogge, Bourchier, Remmington are made C.B.'s; Olpherts has got the V.C.; Probyn and Watson, late of the 2nd and 1st Punjaub Cavalry, have both got V.C. Rained all morning.

August 7th. The Pandys, who were supposed to be near this, attempting to cross the road near Fyzabad, are on their way to join the Begum. Firing heard all yesterday; very heavy for some time. Spies inform us it was a quarrel among some rebels about twenty miles north-east of this. They are Rajpoots. Cause unknown. Good news from Rohilcund. Hurdeo Buksh captured Sandu, near Futteh-gurh, for us, and he reports that the people of the district have offered to come in and lay down their arms. Though apparently of no great moment, it shows us how the wind lies.

August 8th (Sunday). John Carnegie was here yesterday. He was on his way to Duriabad, where he is appointed Deputy Commissioner. He went on this morning.

August 9th. Very ill all last night and to-day with intermittent fever. No news. Firing heard this morning to the east.

August 10th. The rains have stopped the force proceeding to Sultanpore. General Grant returns to Lucknow. The Pandys made a descent near the other Nawabgunge on a police thannah and killed forty men. Elated with their success, they attacked another. Here, however, they were resisted and driven off. They again approached with guns. This time Brigadier Evelegh was prepared; attacked them, killing several, and capturing one gun.

August 11th. An attempted mutiny at Dhera-Ishmael-Khan has been discovered. The 39th N.I. (disarmed) were sent there. They plotted with some Poorbeeas in a Sikh corps, and were almost ready when an accomplice confessed. They intended murdering all the Europeans, then marching on Mooltan. This shows how ignorant these men are still of the turn affairs have taken, and how deeply-rooted this mutinous spirit is. Captain Ross, the Assistant-Commissioner, has succeeded in capturing, in a village north of this, the wives and family of the Moulvie of Kyrabad, one of the leaders against us. They were sent into Lucknow to-day.

August 12th. The force that was on the Duriabad road have gone back to Sultanpore, leaving a piquet of fifteen hundred men to keep open their course for flight. It is about sixteen miles from this. H.M. 2nd D.G., with us, have gone to reconnoitre. The force destined for Sultanpore has left Fyzabad. It consists of 1st Madras Fusiliers, Vaughan's Punjaub Infantry (7th), R.H.A one troop, parts of H.M. 7th Hussars, Hodson's Horse, etc.

August 13th. Rained very heavily all last night. The country is more flooded than it has ever been yet. Rumours of Jung Bahadoor playing us false are spreading. If he does rebel there is not much fear of the result. An army that cannot march above ten miles a day cannot be formidable.

August 14th. The 1st Bengal Fusiliers left this morning in the midst of the rain for Duriabad, to take the place of H.M. 53rd, ordered on to Fyzabad. We have only the 90th with us now. A party of rebels, numbering nearly three thousand men and four guns, have appeared about thirteen miles to the east of this, and intend, it is said, to attack one of our thannahs. The country is so flooded that it is impassable for guns.

August 15th (Sunday). Colonel Berkeley's Saraon field force are still out near Allahabad. They have captured three forts, killing six hundred rebels in one of them. First fair day for long.

August 16th. A wing of H.M. 88th joined us this morning. Sundeela has been captured by a police corps without any assistance. This speaks well for their efficiency. Sultanpore is in our hands. A few shots were fired, but no casualty on our side.

August 17th. Another attack of fever; in bed all day. Rumours of the death of the Puttiala Rajah by poison, and an extensive rebellion of the Malwah Sikhs are current. Nothing official is as yet received. If true, it arises from one of the old hereditary family quarrels. The party whom we recognise as the descendants of the kings are not acknowledged as such by a large party. It is this sect that have mutinied. The conspiracy at Dhera-Ghazee-Khan was among them also.

August 18th. The Malwah Sikhs are the inhabitants of what was formerly the "protected Sikh states." They live on the east of the Sutlej, and are called Poorbeeas by those on the west. The affair at Sultanpore was as follows :—The rebels fled across the Goomtee on our approach after exchanging a few shots. When we tried to follow them, they opened from batteries upon our advancing troops. We desisted from crossing. The old game that we played at the Ramgunga is going on; long bowls without injuring either party. Our people are collecting boats, and reinforcements have been sent on from Fyzabad, consisting of the 2nd Battalion Rifles and two guns of Johnston's R.A. battery. A party of rebels are threatening a thannah of ours near Suftergunge, on the Duriabad road, eleven miles from this. Carnegie has gone out with a force to disperse them.

August 19th. The rebels, who are about thirteen miles east of this, attacked our thannah at Dewah last night. Like natives, they neglected to shut the entrance, or it was left open by treachery. About ten p.m. the Pandys rushed in, the police fled; seven or eight were killed, eight dreadfully wounded, while the remainder sought shelter in an inner building, which Pandy did not dare attack. After committing these feats he retired, afraid of our coming up. The mysterious thing is, the Thannadar and Subadar have both disappeared. They were not taken prisoners, the police say, so it is probable they proved traitors. Busy all day, dressing and amputating the wounded.

August 20th. The Pandys who attacked the thannah yesterday have gone to Futtypore, near the Gogra, where there is an assemblage of rebels. The Begum is now crossing over to this side of the river. Where she is going and what she intends doing is still unknown. The people who were at Dewah are in such a fright that the Thannadar has been obliged to shut up the thannah and come into camp. Some of the regular police, who are armed with matchlocks, will probably occupy it.

August 21st. The cause of the rumour of the rising among the Malwah Sikhs arose from some family squabble. This has been settled, so everything is quiet. Brigadier Berkeley's Saraon force is to join Brigadier Horsford's at or near Sultanpore. Communication with Fyzabad is being opened by steamers from below. Already a dâk runs between it and Jaunpore.

August 22nd (Sunday). General Grant, with the whole of the force at Fyzabad, and the heavy guns, have gone on to Sultanpore. A wing of H.M. 53rd remain behind with Maun Singh in the fort at Shahgunge. Some rebels, whose headquarters are fourteen miles south of this, made a raid in our direction yesterday, attacked a village, and meeting with no opposition, carried off forty of the inhabitants as prisoners. The two guns of this troop have remained behind at Fyzabad. The country is very much flooded. The heavy guns have caused great delay to General Grant.

August 23rd. The Begum has quarrelled with her paramour, Mummoo Khan, who has since left her. She has taken a man named Davy Bux to act as *Cavaliere servente*. Mummoo Khan is, through a vakeel, trying to make terms with us, but we decline having any terms with him. Brigadier Berkeley's force are under orders to march to Purtabgurh, on the road to Sultanpore. General Roberts with his column has at last come up with the remains of the

Gwalior rebels. He defeated them, capturing all their guns and ammunition, etc., and killing about seven hundred.

August 24th. Heavy firing all morning towards the north. It turned out to be a Zemindar called Fukeer Bux, who was besieged in his fort by some budmashes. He had before being shut up got assistance from Futtypore—a great nest of the rebels. The reinforcements are commanded by the Moulvie. The assailants numbered three thousand, and three guns. The Moulvie Mahommed commands at Futtypore. He has about eight thousand Sepoys, Nujeebs, and rabble. He is opposed to the Begum.

August 25th. This fight still going on to the north of this. Rumours of a large body of budmashes having advanced to within twelve miles of this are rife, but not believed. No news from any other quarter.

August 26th. Our force has crossed the Goomtee at Sultanpore. No sooner had the heavy guns opened than Pandy bolted.

August 27th. A force consisting of two Horse Artillery guns, fifty of H.M. 2nd D.G., one hundred Hodson's Horse, and one hundred and fifty of H.M. 90th, on elephants, started at two a.m., to chastise a Thalookdar to the north of this. After going fifteen miles they came suddenly upon a large and very strong mud fort, defended by about two hundred men. A parley was opened with them, but they refused admission, their "malek" being absent. Colonel Smith, who was in command, instead of retiring, ordered the guns to open fire, without any object in view. After a few rounds he retired without loss. The enemy's cavalry were hovering about the horizon. The fault was in firing at all. It gives these rascals an opportunity of claiming a victory.

August 29th (Sunday). First really bad day since coming here. Letter from Nicholson yesterday. He is in the Commissariat Department now, and a Dep. Assistant Com. General at Sasseram.

August 30th. English news down to the 2nd instant came with a rapidity that is truly wonderful. The Indian Bill has passed both houses: the Queen's consent will, of course, be given, and to-morrow the momentous change comes into operation. The wording of the proclamation in this country is left to the Governor-General. The force which had crossed the Goomtee is surrounded by rebels, who, however, keep at a respectful distance. The thannah of Dewah was again attacked by the rebels, but this time they were beaten off. This evening, in expectation of another attack, the courage of the police ebbed; they evacuated the thannah and came into camp.

August 31st. This day closes the career of the East India Company. From being a small commercial community confined to the banks of the Hugli, it became the governor of the greatest and brightest possession in England's crown. It carried the name and might of England to the foot of the Himalayas, dictated to and overcame the most powerful confederacies of Asia, and was at last destroyed by internal mutiny. Old and effete as this enormous government became, its interests were always sustained by the vigour and courage of its servants. A service that has produced a Clive, a Hastings, a Metcalf, and in the last year a Lawrence, a Neill, and a Nicholson, cannot have been despicable, and its rule cannot have been hurtful. Its crimes and errors have been great. Its power has often been used unjustly. The native has, in many instances, been trampled under foot; justice has been one-sided; interest and the benefit of the white has overwhelmed the considerations of right; might has become right. No one can look at the past history of the Company without being proud of belonging to a people who could form such an empire without the aid of kings and courts, and govern nations differing from one another in every respect but one—hatred to us. This hatred was not derived from any misdeeds of ours, but from the feeling inherent when white and black, Christian and Mussulman, meet. In spite of all the abuse heaped on the head of this government, its executive is retained. The native army is again being restored; the revenue is still collected as of old; nothing but the name is altered. Now we are servants of Her Majesty's Indian Government, instead of being in the Honourable East India Company's service. The change will be little felt by us, it is hoped. Our pay, pension, etc., are not touched; our duties and terms of service are the same. Those coming after us will probably benefit, rather than lose, by the new Bill. The thannah of Dewah has been abandoned by us. The police have been marching down from Sundeela, but their progress has been stopped by a fort, in attacking which Mr. Cavanagh was wounded. The Begum is still at Boondee. The Thalookdars, still friendly to her, plunder the villagers and support her followers. A commissary of ordnance has been shot by a Sepoy.

September 1st. The last few days have been showery. Last night it began to rain about twelve p.m., and continued incessantly until seven a.m. The country is more flooded to-day than it has been this year. Another fight has been going on to the south of this. Moosub Ali, whose dwelling is across the Goomtee, makes raids on this side, as on the 22nd, plundering the villagers. Yesterday he did so, and came to a village belonging to a petty Rajah called Ram Bux, who refused to allow him to loot, or even to give him money. It ended in a fierce cannonade, which went on long after dark, without much loss probably on either side.

September 2nd. Nothing but rain all last night. The brevet for Lucknow has come out. General Franks is made a K.C.B.; Tombs a full Colonel; Mackinnon, commanding our troop, a Major, etc., etc.

September 3rd. Moosub Ali still fighting to the south of this. A column is in process of formation to start about the 15th prox. in a northerly direction from Lucknow. We are certain to be of the number. Its object will be to clear this district of the rebels. The contingent from Duriabad went out a few days ago, surrounded a village, and killed some one hundred and eighty budmashes. This is behaviour we did not expect, as they have only been drilled since they joined us.

September 4th. Rained almost all last night, and this morning it was pouring a heavy thunder shower, with very vivid lightning.

September 5th (Sunday). First fine day for nearly a week. Thermometer at its highest is now only 93°, and has gone down to 78° when the rain is falling. News of a fight at Phillibhit, north of Bareilly. The rebels had three guns, and numbered several thousand. A force, consisting of five officers and five hundred men, were sent against them. They defeated them, killing about three hundred, capturing all the guns, camp, etc. Three officers were wounded, among whom is Major Sam Browne commanding 2nd Punjaub Cavalry; he has lost an arm. News of a party of rebels, six thousand strong and three guns, trying to make their way from Sultanpore to join the Begum, has been brought in. Now they are eighteen miles from Sultanpore across the Goomtee. We have received orders to march and intercept them on their crossing the river.

September 6th. General Grant expects to be at Lucknow by the 19th prox., probably to organise a column. The Begum is said to have left Boondee and gone north. Her treasury is empty, and her Sepoys get no pay. She is beginning to raise money upon the present crops at the rate of two annas per rupee. The rebels are making an entrenchment at Poorwah, but with what object it is difficult to say. The Saraon force seems to be the one intended to do some important service soon. It consists of H.M. 13th, 32nd, 54th, 73rd, 79th, etc., etc., three regiments of Sikhs, and several batteries, cavalry corps, etc. It is commanded by Brigadier Pinckney, H.M. 73rd, but will probably be directed by Sir Colin in person.

September 7th. It is rumoured that the Begum has sent Waleedad Khan, of Malagurh, to Nepaul, offering Jung Bahadoor all the country to Goruckpore. The remains of the

Gwalior rebels have crossed the Chumbul, and attacked a chief, whose troops deserted him. He has been obliged to come to terms with them. Excitement in camp to-day. Spies came in with the information that we were to be attacked in the afternoon by ten thousand men. This, of course, proved false. The origin of it was, the Moulvie, who was at Futtypore, north of this, has got on the move somewhere.

September 8th. The Atlantic Cable is at last safely lodged at the bottom of the ocean and England is in direct communication with America, at least so a telegram says. News of a serious affair at Mooltan has arrived. The 62nd and 69th N.I., both disarmed, have broken out, having had arms concealed. They were assisted by some native artillery, and they attempted to seize the guns. Luckily the other troops, a Belooch Battalion, the 6th Irregulars, behaved well. The Bombay Fusiliers and the above killed about four hundred and chased the remainder out of the station. They were making for the Sutlej, and are pursued by Horse Artillery and Cavalry. Rewards are offered for any prisoners brought in, so few will escape. The cause of this is unknown to us, having only received a telegram with the news.

September 9th. Purtabgurh has been occupied by the Saraon Brigade without opposition. Banee Madho, by his retreat, has left all that country open to us. This chief, who refuses terms and sends back the message that he will fight to the death, has been severely wounded in the thigh at Sultanpore. He is now near the Goomtee, encamped on the Kandhoo Nuddee, a very strong position, over which there is no crossing except by a bridge. The Moulvie Mahommed, commanding at Futtypore, to our east, is still there, and does not seem inclined to attack us. The depôts of two Police Corps are on their way to raise recruits at Fyzabad, and those from the lowest caste are to be preferred. About Fyzabad the Brahmins are opposing this innovation on the rights of the privileged classes.

September 10th. We shall probably remain here until the Saraon Brigade compel the enemy to make for the Gogra. We, of course, will intercept them if possible. When that is accomplished we shall probably clear the country to the north, taking and demolishing forts, placing thannahs, etc. A body of the rebels numbering five thousand men and five guns have crossed the Goomtee and advanced to within eight miles of this, to the south. Their leader is Moosub Ali. They are evidently trying to cross over to Bahramghat and join the Begum. The fugitives from Sultanpore have retired to Amathee, the Rajah of which was their leader when attacked by our people. Colonel Robertson has again come up with the fugitives in Central India and completely routed them. They are now completely disheartened, having lost everything, and are now an unarmed mob. Tantia Topee has again made himself comfortable and dangerous to us. Thalia Patha (?), which they occupied through the treachery of the Rajah's men, contained three lacs of rupees, about thirty guns, and complete equipment for their men. The Nana has again been proclaimed King. The Rajah himself has escaped to Neemuch.

September 11th. The news of the outbreak at Mooltan was as follows: the 62nd N.I. was to have been re-armed; the 69th N.I. disbanded. Some evil-designed person spread the report that the latter would all be killed *en route* to Lahore, as only a few were to be discharged at a time. On the forenoon of the 31st ult. the 69th made a sudden rush on the guns of a battery of R.A. at twelve a.m., the midday gun being the signal. They were joined by the men of what was formerly a native troop, the 4th troop, 3rd brigade Horse Artillery, but since the Mutiny it has become European. The Artillery immediately rushed from their barracks and having their carbines and swords soon drove back the Sepoys, who were only armed with legs of charpoys, etc. This was not accomplished, however, before four Artillerymen and the Adjutant of the Bombay Fusiliers had been beaten to death. A complete rout ensued. The Fusiliers and the Artillery killed about three hundred and fifty in the cantonments, took one hundred and fifty prisoners. The remaining rebels divided, some going towards the Sutlej while others made for Bhawulpore, the Rajah of which is not very friendly to us. Twenty rupees are offered for each head. Some delay seems to have arisen in organising a pursuit. Fourteen hours elapsed before a force was sent. Four hundred men of H.M. 23rd R.W.F. and four guns of the 6th company 3rd battalion R.A., late Major Middleton's, joined us this morning.

September 12th (Sunday). The body of Pandys thought better of their onward move, and have again retired towards the Goomtee. The rebels, whom we heard of on the 15th, after doubling from Sultanpore towards Duriabad, have crossed the road in safety. A force consisting of H.M. 53rd, 7th Hussars, and some guns, are after them, trying to stop them crossing the Gogra.

September 13th. The opening of communication with America by means of the electric telegraph is confirmed. Sundeela is threatened by the rebels. Two Police Corps have gone to reinforce those already there. Awfully hot to-day. Thermometer, at three p.m., 95° in the shade.

September 14th. First anniversary of the assault of Delhi. Banee Madho's force has, it is said, broken up. He himself has gone south to his own district, the hot bed of the Pandys, from which half our old native army was derived. Some emissaries of the Nana's have been attempting to tamper with the fidelity of the 25th Bombay N.I. at Gwalior. The Sepoys informed their officers, and the conspirators were seized. Very hot, 96°.

September 15th. Rebels still very troublesome about Shahabad. They have crossed into Chupprah. It is a regular guerilla war there. The Sepoys and budmashes wander about in parties of four or five hundred and make sudden raids on unprotected districts. The Commander-in-Chief has ordered the assemblage of three thousand Europeans and two thousand Sikhs to clear Shahabad. The natives in this part of Oude appear very badly off for money. They are selling their cows and bullocks for food to the Europeans, a thing that they look on with abhorrence. The rebels captured twenty-five of our camels when out feeding to-day. The drivers and owners do not care; they get compensation from Government. They go out five or six miles towards where the rebels are. If a few were flogged no such thing would occur.

September 16th. The force at Bareilly have received orders to be prepared to march on the 1st October. No word of a move here as yet. English mail, bringing news down to August 17th, arrived. The Queen's visit to Cherbourg has gone off well. The King of Oude, now a prisoner in Fort William, is to come back to Lucknow, and live in the Kaiser Bagh. The crown jewels are all to be returned. This is surely an acknowledgment, tardy, no doubt, of the injustice of the annexation and deposition of the King. Its effect on the people is very doubtful. All sorts of plots and machinations will be hatched in Lucknow unless some stringent laws are laid down, and trustworthy spies obtained. The King's temper must be sadly soured at his ill-treatment, and his hatred for us must be inextinguishable. Strong gale, with clouds of dust blowing all day, ending in the afternoon in rain. Temperature 85°, sinking to 75° after the rain.

September 17th. Sir Colin Campbell has been raised to the peerage by the title of Baron Clyde. It is unfortunate that it must die with him. The Meerut district is being disarmed, already three lacs of arms have been taken. Gale of wind still blowing, but not so hard. Rained heavily for some hours last night. Thermometer only 86° at its highest to-day. The officers of what was formerly the 1st and 3rd N.I. are to be transferred to the new 4th European Infantry. Those of the 5th and 6th to the 5th European, *and those of the 7th and 8th to the 6th European Infantry.* The 35th, 59th and 64th N.I. are being disbanded in parties of twenty.

September 18th. The fugitive mutineers from Mooltan have almost all been accounted for. Above three hundred were killed on a peninsula on the Chinab, over which they could not cross. About seventy were slain on a marshy island by the police. The railway from Allahabad to Cawnpore, the whole distance, was to have been opened by Lady Canning, on the 15th inst. Sir John Lawrence has been made a baronet of the United Kingdom. The Press are raising an outcry against this. He is universally called the "Saviour of India," and as deserving of a peerage as Sir Colin Campbell.

September 19th (Sunday). Letter from England. Thermometer at highest only 87°. Thunder showers. Very cloudy.

September 20th. Letter from Nicholson, at Sasseram. Lieutenant-Colonel Turner, of the 97th, who commands there, is organising an expedition to drive Umur Singh out of the district. He has only about six hundred men at his disposal. He has occupied a place called Bickram Gunge, twenty-two miles from Sasseram, and intends making it the centre of operations. News of a fight near Duriabad. The rebels were caught on an island in the Gogra, about four hundred were slain or drowned, with the loss on our side of one man killed, one officer (Lieutenant-MacGregor) and several men wounded. One gun and two ammunition waggons were captured. A patrol that went out this evening towards Dewah were fired into by the rebels. Their camp, a mile beyond the village, was seen. They number, it is said, five thousand men. A force leaves this to-morrow morning to attack them. Thermometer at highest 93°.

September 21st. On account of the large jungle in which the rebels are, the march of the force was countermanded. The jungle is about forty miles long, and has been for ages a nest for rebels, and into which the King's troops never dare enter. Instead a strong cavalry patrol was sent out. They came across the enemy's Sowars, in the act of burning a village, on the edge of the jungle. The small detachment of H.M. 2nd D.G., charged through and through, killing several; but losing themselves one man killed, whose body was left on the ground, another who was decapitated, but who was brought in, and one man wounded. These men were lost by their horses falling, while the remainder of the corps had to retire from the sudden appearance of hundreds of the rebel's infantry. They were also fired upon by several guns. The Sowars followed up to Dewah. This affair will inspire them with new courage. The leaders of the rebels to the south of this, in the Sultanpore district, are three: Banee Madho, Mehudee Husein, and Moosub Ali. The first has what was formerly called the Nuseerabad Brigade. The thannah of Suftergunge was attacked last night. The brave defenders fled without attempting a stand. Some Sikhs from Duriabad have gone to occupy it. Thermometer at highest 93°.

September 22nd. The thannah of Pertabgunge, about five miles from this, was attacked last night, on the Fyzabad road. The defenders were armed with matchlocks; the assailants had only bows and arrows. They showed considerable pluck. They brought up a ladder, mounted the wall and fired down on the inmates, who offered no resistance. One man was killed, and several camels carried off. The force at Dewah have retired. The Sowars who charged the Bays yesterday, were the 12th Irregulars. They had their standard and kettledrum with them. A sudden order came for a force to leave this and attack the rebels under Moosub Ali, to the south-west of this. A force was also ordered to leave Lucknow and advance on Selimpore, his headquarters, on the other side the Goomtee.

September 23rd. Marched at twelve p.m. The force consisted of four guns, 2nd troop 3rd brigade Horse Artillery; two guns of the Royal Artillery Battery, 6th company 13th Battalion; our troop, H.M. 2nd D.G.; the detachment of Hodson's Horse, two hundred men; H.M. 23rd R.W.F.; two hundred H.M. 90th L.I., and two hundred H.M. 88th. The whole was commanded by Colonel Pratt, C.B., H.M. 23rd. The night was beautiful, a full moon making everything almost as visible as in the day. It was, however, close and warm. Got on very slowly until reaching Luttruck, the course being over a country intersected by numerous nullahs. After passing that place it was one continuous grassy plain, over which the eye could range for miles. It was covered with beautiful mango topes, and recalled the appearance of an English park. As the sun rose we found ourselves in the neighbourhood of the rebels. Our approach was only known by one of their piquets carrying the news. After forming line we advanced. Stray parties of the rebels were seen dispersing, and in one spot about three hundred Sowars were seen making a great noise with tom-toms. They soon retired also. Our course was over a country covered with high crops, and variegated with grassy knolls and hollows. Into these they disappeared, where no round shot could touch them. Our guns kept opening every now and then, where any crowd was seen. From a tope, one gun fired two shots at us without doing harm. This they soon removed, and probably hid, as it could not be found. From this we advanced, passing their encampment, until we reached within a mile of the river opposite Selimpore, where we halted, our further progress being stopped by deep ravines, impassable for guns. The cavalry were sent on, and cut up a few near the river. The artillery and infantry halted beneath trees. When we arrived here, the guns of the other force were heard, and musketry on all sides of the town. The place was soon on fire in several places. It is a large place, with fine stone buildings, and a fort on the side next the river. When halting, a large party of the enemy were seen crossing in an immense barge, the river in this place being very meandearing. The place we saw them on was supposed to be the opposite, instead of the same side as ourselves. When this error was discovered, guns and infantry were sent to join the cavalry, but it was too late, above three hundred men had escaped. They had crossed from Selimpore, when hard pressed, by a ghaut, to our side, then crossed a tongue of land, entered the boat and landed on the opposite side. Communication was opened with our other force. Captain Bunbury reported that all was going on favourably, that he held the whole town, with the exception of the fort, which, however, he had surrounded, with five hundred men inside. Our assistance he did not require; so after burning the barge we again halted for the day. The spies had brought us intelligence of five thousand men and seven guns being on this side of the river, while we did not meet with fifteen hundred, and only one gun. They may have heard of the advance of the Lucknow column and retired into Selimpore. We could see them there, in what appeared a fort, in great trouble, firing off their matchlocks and running about. The fort still held out, up to the time we left, but they would probably retire, if possible, during the night. The day was very warm, and the infantry completely knocked up. We did not start again until seven p.m., having about fifteen miles of a march before us. Several villages were burned by our people, which does not seem a speedy way of pacifying the disaffected. Our course ought to be strictly defined, and no deviation allowed. The infantry were so tired and the night so close, we took about three hours to go as many miles. We got the stragglers mounted on elephants, and, on reaching the grassy maidan, proceeded very smoothly. The night, though beautiful and cloudless, was awfully hot. It was not until three a.m., after innumerable halts, that we reached Nawabgunge, thoroughly tired, after fifteen hours trip, and a march of about forty miles. These rebels, whom we have dispersed, are those who attacked so many thannahs towards Fyzabad. Their flight, without attempting a stand, shows what contemptible foes they are to us, and what a degenerate, chicken-hearted race our police are, who allow themselves to be cut up by them.

September 24th. The Dewah rebels have occupied the thannah there, and have issued a proclamation to the inhabitants, that unless they return in three days, the place will be destroyed. General Michel has come up with Tantia Topee, near Burhi; taken seventy-five guns, and killed a great many. Our cavalry, with guns, have gone in pursuit.

September 25th. We hear that the force that captured Selimpore, killed above five hundred men, including three of their leaders, and took five guns. No particulars as yet. Moosub Ali is mentioned as one of them. Regiments are pouring down country to Cawnpore, to join in the cold weather campaign. The 9th Lancers have left Umballa; the 6th D.G., Meerut, along with the 3rd troop 1st brigade Horse Artillery. No rumours even of a move.

September 27th. Remarkably cool day. Very different from the same last year. Thermometer only 87° at highest. There has been another fight near Sundeela very successful. No signs of a move. The belief in Lucknow is that General Grant will command all the field force in Oude in the cold weather.

September 28th. Thermometer only 84° at its highest. A beautiful comet is now nightly seen at sunset in the west. Its course is south-west, and with the horizon it makes an angle of about 45°. Practising cricket every evening. The enemy's videttes are on this side of Dewah—rather an insulting thing, it being only five miles from this.

September 29th. Raining from twelve p.m. until twelve a.m. this morning. Thermometer 79° at three p.m. Another issue of the Victoria Cross by the Commander-in-Chief. Lieutenants Harrington and F. Roberts, Royal Artillery; Lieutenant H. Gough, L.C.; Gunner Lochlan, 2nd troop 3rd brigade Royal Artillery, etc., etc.

September 30th. This day terminates one of the coolest Septembers ever known. There has scarcely been one warm day, and none you could call oppressive. To-day at highest it was only 86°. The fugitives from Selimpore have been encountered by the Duriabad people. Two guns were captured, and about fifty killed. The police have brought in an ammunition waggon and several hackeries from the scene of our fight. Not a budmash is heard of in that quarter. The Dewah people are rather terrified at this sign of our power, and are dreading a similar fate.

October 1st. A bridge of boats is to be built across the Gogra at Fyzabad. Lieutenant-Colonel Nicholson, Royal Engineers, arrived here to-day, *en route* thither. News of a fight at the other Nawabgunge. The enemy came down upon the camp, but soon retreated, leaving several hundreds behind. The comet was most beautiful this evening. Its tail was very long and bright. It becomes visible at sunset and disappears below the horizon about eight p.m. The natives call it "jaroo," a broom.

October 2nd. A small fort is being laid out here on the open maidan. It is to contain the thannah and police. Similar enclosures are to be made at short intervals along all the roads in Oude. It is rumoured that the general move will take place about the 15th inst., but the delay probably arises from the proclamation annexing India to the British Crown not having been issued yet. It is supposed a general amnesty will be proclaimed at the same time.

October 3rd (Sunday). The great comet, which is at present such a splendid object in the western heavens after sunset, is the same one that appeared in 1264, and again in 1556, but this is a debated point among astronomers. The observers of the first are not trustworthy; of the second appearance we have Haller and Fabricius. From a map and calculations of the former, Mr. Hind, the Astronomer Royal, determined its orbit, and Mr. Bonnel computed that it would attain its perihelion distance in August, 1858. Professor Nichol says of one comet, that "if it were to be compressed until it became as dense as atmospheric air it would hardly occupy a cubic inch of space." The danger of this one—if there really is any—is diminished when we remember that it cannot approach nearer to us than six millions of miles. The rebels are said to be retiring across the Gogra, and that they are greatly disheartened by the slaughter at Goosheyagunge on the 23rd ult.

October 4th. First day of the Nawabgunge races. They were very second-rate. They are only useful in providing amusement for men who are not overburdened with work. General Grant is expected to have arrived at Sultanpore by this time. The rebels to-day came down almost to the Lucknow road, in our rear. A patrol leaves here to-morrow morning to clear it. The report of a fight at the other Nawabgunge is untrue. A force left there to look up some rebels, but the rain came down so heavily that it returned without doing anything. Another clasp is ordered for the capture of Lucknow, making the third up to this time.

October 5th. Thermometer at highest 90½°, so the comet has not increased the temperature as yet. Races again this morning; better on the whole than yesterday. The comet, we hear, is spreading consternation among the rebels. The Begum is ready to fly into Nepal, where she will be welcomed by Jung Bahadoor. Rumours of his hostile intentions against us are rife, but they are probably due to the coldness between him and the Resident from some private matters.

October 6th. Considerable firing heard this morning to he south of this, supposed to be the Duriabad people attacking some body of the enemy. An application for assistance, previous to attacking, was sent us, but declined, because it was twenty miles distant. Thermometer 90 .

October 7th. The fight yesterday was very successful. Two guns captured and four hundred men killed somewhere on the Gogra. Sundeela has again been attacked, and Captain Dawson with his police surrounded. A force has left Lucknow to assist them. By the last accounts the place was holding out. Meeangunge has also been attacked, it being near the other Nawabgunge. A force is marching to relieve it.

October 8th. Thermometer 93°. Nights very cold now. Dysentery consequently very common. In all the cases fever of a remittent type is present. This has only occurred as a rule the last few days. The force that went to relieve

Sundeela, and which only consisted of eighty Europeans and seven hundred cavalry, has itself been surrounded. The rebels, under Hur Pershad, number five thousand men, with nine guns. This shows how ridiculous it was to send such a paltry force. Another large one will be sent from Lucknow, which is now almost empty of British soldiers.

October 9th. The King of Delhi is on his way down country to Calcutta, guarded by H.M. 9th Lancers and a troop of Horse Artillery. His final destination is not known. All his wives and retinue accompany him. Salone is again in our hands, the civil power in force, and the Treasury working.

October 10th (Sunday). Meeangunge has been relieved. One hundred and fifty budmashes killed and one gun taken. The news from Sundeela are very favourable. There have been two fights there—the first on the 6th, and the second on the 8th. Brigadier Barker commanded on our side. On the former date the enemy were driven away from the town, four guns captured, and four hundred men killed, principally in pursuit, by H.M. 2nd D.G. The second fight took place at a place five miles from Sundeela, whither the enemy had fled. It resulted in the further capture of three guns and the destruction of nearly a thousand more of the rebels. The whole of the enemy's baggage fell into our hands.

October 11th. Startling news brought in this morning by spies. The Begum has fled to the foot of the Nepal hills, and the rabble at Boondee have dispersed. The causes of this are as follows:—The Begum and her paramour sent a letter offering terms to us. This was intercepted by one of the rebel chiefs, who returned it to Boondee. The Sepoys were indignant, seized upon Mummoo Khan, and put him under surveillance, where he is at present. The Begum has gone off with the intention of having no more to do with these inconstant followers. This move of hers has caused her Commander-in-Chief, Yusuf Khan, to leave this side of the Gogra and return to the other. The rebels, though still existing in small numbers about Dewah, will probably follow their leader's example. The Chief of Buttai has offered, it is said, to deliver up the fort visited by us on the 27th August. In the Allahabad direction five columns have marched, and are advancing on Roy Bareilly and Banee Madho. Hodson's Horse leave this to-morrow and march to Selimpore, it being the intention to prevent the fugitives crossing in this direction. A great, and it is to be hoped final, clearance of the rebels from the Arrah and Shumshabad districts has been commenced under Brigadier Douglas, H.M. 79th. A despatch from the Chief was brought out this evening. Its importance was so great that it was ordered to be carried to Fyzabad by officers. Captain Fendall, H.M. 53rd D.A.Q.M.G., brought it from Lucknow. It appears that a column under Colonel Kelly has rapidly advanced from Azimgurh up the left bank of the Gogra, and that the enemy are flying in all directions. This despatch contains an order for the regiment to go to Ferozepore under Colonel Brasyer, C.B., to cross the river at Fyzabad and intercept the rebels. We received orders to march at 3.30 a.m. towards Dewah.

October 12th. Started at the appointed time. It was

expected that we might surround the rebels in Dewah, where they were yesterday. Soon after leaving camp, spies brought in word that it was evacuated. The artillery and cavalry went on about a mile beyond Dewah, while the infantry returned to camp. Dewah is a large village surrounded with large jheels and topes of trees. It has several stone buildings, one an old fort. The thannah is on a height surrounded by a deep ditch, and impregnable without guns. About a mile beyond it, on the edge of the jungle, which is very extensive, and in which the fort of Buttai is, we saw several hundred budmashes in great excitement. One party in a tope of trees we saluted with a salvo from the five guns. After doing this much we returned to camp, which we reached about 10.30 a.m., after a march of some sixteen miles.

October 13. The Atlantic Telegraph is broken—all communication stopped. Mehudee Husein, who was driven out of Sultanpore by General Grant, and who has been lurking since then on the other side of the Goomtee, has succeeded in crossing between Pertabgunge and Duriabad to Bahramghat. He had several thousand men and some guns with him. He has probably crossed the Gogra. The officer who carried on the Chief's despatch fortunately escaped them, but was in time to see their rear-guard. The above was, this evening, found to be incorrect. Mehudee Husein is at Pali ghaut, on the Goomtee, preparing to cross. He has given out that he intends making an attack on Duriabad, and that he is to be assisted by some rebels from the east. He has ordered the rebels to make roads for his guns and lay in provisions for him. This looks as if he intended bolting, and that this is a wile to deceive us. Captain Hume, however, commanding there, put such credence in it that he sent an urgent request for assistance. There seems little doubt that some force really did cross the road two days ago. The whole troop was ordered off in the morning, but this was again changed, and two guns with two hundred and fifty of H.M. 88th were ordered to march, making Duriabad on the second day. Our camels are so bad, and our carriage so deficient, that it was found impossible for us all to move.

October 14th. The Moulvie Mahommed, who commanded so long at Futtypore, to the east of this, and Moosub Ali, a rebel chief, were killed in the fight at Sundeela. The Royal Engineers have been suddenly ordered to march from Lucknow to Allahabad.

October 15th. Nothing but news of columns starting and troops marching. The campaign is now commenced. A brigade commanded by Colonel ——, C troop 68th., N.I., was to start from Bareilly about the 13th inst., and advance, clearing the Shajehanpore district. It consists of three guns 3rd troop 3rd brigade Horse Artillery, two guns of Captain Austin's battery, a squadron of Carabiniers, Mooltanee Horse, H.M. 60th Rifles, H.M. 93rd and the 66th Ghoorkhas. Coming southwards: Brigadier Evelegh, from the other Nawabgunge, has advanced south-east to Sissandy, while another brigade from Cawnpore has proceeded to Poorwah. The Selimpore force has made an advance also to the southward. Roy Bareilly, Parsideypore, and Mohungunge, are the three places where the rebels muster strongest. A column is about to enter Oude from Dalamow, on the

Ganges, and near to Futtypore. A sixth force has left Sultanpore and are proceeding up the right bank of the Goomtee towards Mohungunge. General Grant has gone with another towards Azimgurh. This is all that is known as yet, but its object is evidently to give them no place to run to. Their flight will most probably be across the Fyzabad road towards the Gogra, and it will be our duty to try and intercept them.

October 16th. Some firing heard to the south of this to-day, probably the Duriabad force engaged. The Nuseerabad Brigade, our Delhi foes, was only ten miles off from it yesterday, at least so the natives say. The news from Duriabad does not mention any fight as yet, nor any prospect of one. Mohumdee has been occupied by a force from Shajehanpore. Khan Bahadur Khan fled without fighting.

October 17th. No news, although every one is looking anxiously for some from the south, where affairs must be coming to a head. Very cold at nights now; thermometer goes down to 65°, but still mounts to 91° in the day. This change accounts for the prevalence of dysentery, etc. Sunday.

October 18th. The tope that we fired into on the 12th inst., we have heard since contained a small entrenchment, with three small guns. If we had known this, it would have been easy for us to capture them. Since that day they have constant parades, firing of guns, etc., to give them courage. This is the Dusserah, a great Hindoo feast, which accounts for the firing we hear on all sides. The spies say that in the Buttai jungle, there are nine thousand infantry, three thousand cavalry, and nine guns. The first embrace all kinds of budmashes, etc., who rarely fight, but are good at running, the cavalry includes the late 12th Irregulars, who killed their commander, Colonel Fisher; of the guns, five are reputed good, the remainder small and useless. This native report requires, of course, to be halved, when the real number may be approximated.

October 19th. News of a fight near Bunnee, in which the enemy were as usual beaten. No particulars known. The Bareilly column has marched. It is ordered to clear the Fyzabad district of rebels, demolish all forts and reinstate the civil authorities. Duriabad is not now threatened. The rebels are not within twenty miles. No news from any other quarter, but within a few days something ought to be occurring.

October 20th. This day two years I left Southampton. The rumours about Jung Bahadoor preparing to attack Darjeeling do not meet with general belief. That he is preparing for some warlike expedition is certain; but this is said by some, to arise from dissensions among the Nepalese chiefs, and not from any designs upon our territory. The Buttai rebels are getting terrified at the advance of the Shajehanpore column. As this will only increase with the course of events, they will very likely make discretion the better part of valour and retire.

October 21st. Major Money arrived yesterday to resume command of the troop. Still lame from the wound received at Delhi. He saw the Chief at Allahabad, and was told by him that Moir's troop, the 3rd troop 1st brigade, was on its way to relieve us, and that our destination would be Meerut Moir's troop arrived in Lucknow yesterday, but even this does not makes us sanguine of leaving Oude until March. The Begum, we hear, is making a fort at Toolseepore, at the foot of the hills, where she intends flying when we advance northwards. Everyone is looking forward to the general amnesty, which is to be proclaimed the same day as Her Majesty is publicly recognised as Queen of Hindostan. Numbers of the rebels are said to be only waiting for this to come in, and five hundred of the 12th Irregulars are among the number. If such a proclamation is issued, it will be impossible for it to become known to the rebels for months. It is for the interest of their leaders to keep it secret, and what are we to be about in the meantime? It will, most probably, be kept quiet until our army takes the field, when the imposing force, then in motion, will cause a more speedy compliance than any other means.

October 22nd. Mackinnon left to take command of the 3rd company 1st battery F.A. (Bourchier's old battery). Major Raike's, commanding a column in the Azimgurh district, fell in with the rebels near Jullalpore, on the 14th, and defeated them. The disposition of the troops to the south of this, in the Fyzabad division, is at present as follows:—Sir Hope Grant is at Ackberpore, Colonel Kelly is at Atrowlea, not across the Gogra, as formerly stated; Rajah Maun Singh is out with a force, and is at present at Bhadepore.

October 23rd. Letter from Brigadier Horsford commanding at Sultanpore, giving an account of a fight near that place. The Royal Horse Artillery and the Cavalry were the only troops engaged. The enemy, the Nuseerabad Brigade, were met with on an extensive plain, and, on sight of our men, fled. The Horse Artillery captured two guns, English 9-pounders, which this force have retained since the Mutiny commenced. No mention of the numbers slain. The only other English guns known to be in the rebels hands are two with Khan Bahadur Khan, the Bareilly chief, in the Baraitch district. He has also two complete Sepoy regiments with him. Brigadier Barker has captured the fort of Birwah, after a protracted and stubborn fight. The gates had to be blown in with powder bags, as at Delhi, and in doing this, Lieutenant Carnegie, Bengal Engineers, was dangerously wounded. No particulars given, but it is said we have lost fifty killed and wounded. The enemy were probably all killed. Brigadier Barker now goes on to Rooyah, where Brigadier Hope and so many brave men fell in April last.

October 24th (Sunday). Banee Madho has divided his army into five divisions, and has sent them out to stop the forward movement of our Brigades. Instead of keeping a central position and hurling an overwhelming force on the nearest foe, he has split his men into detachments, which will meet with certain defeat *seriatim*. He has shaven his beard and head, visited his father's tomb, and is determined to stand or fall with the cause he has embraced. Spies say that he commands fifty thousand men, with thirty guns, and that his followers have great faith in their leader. Against Colonel Bulwer's force, south of Selimpore, he has sent five thousand men and eight guns. Among all the rebel chiefs there is not one but Banee Madho, for whom you can have any admiration. He is not a murderer, never mixed himself up with the Sepoys, never left his own territory for the sake of plunder, etc., but has remained by himself, refusing all terms, except what are given by the sword. He is truly a patriot, fighting for what he thinks his country's glory, and will probably fall as becomes a brave man, pitied by his enemies. The Commander-in-Chief has started from Allahabad, and has gone on to Pertabgurh.

October 25th. Brigadier Barker's fight seems to have been unfortunate. It commenced at seven a.m., and continued without intermission until four p.m. The enemy in great numbers were in a dense jungle. The chief and about fifty followers were surrounded in a keep within the fort, but when morning dawned, they had all escaped. Our loss was about one hundred, while the enemy scarcely lost more. No further particulars. Colonel Bulwer's force has fallen in with the column sent by Banee Madho to stop his advance; defeated it, and captured four guns. No official news has arrived. Lieutenant Mitford, 3rd Europeans, in command of a detachment of Hodson's Horse, was wounded.

October 27th. A committee has been ordered to assemble at Lucknow, and report upon the expense of restoring the Kaiser Bagh to the state it was in previous to the Mutiny. When this is accomplished, building will commence, and the King return and take up his abode there. What a green individual John Bull is, throwing away precious lives in capturing, and then furnishing it for a king who hates us, and whose object it will be to conspire against us. To show the feebleness and timidity of Lord Canning and Co., the following is authentic. When the "Ram Leila," a feast of the Hindoos, came off, powder was supplied from the British magazine at Cawnpore, to allow the inhabitants of that city to enjoy themselves. These same budmashes have their houses full of plunder taken from European bungalows, yet nothing has been done to compel the disgorgement of this, and these poor ill-treated natives have been compensated for any loss during the Mutiny, while English ladies are starving, having lost their all, refused any equivalent and thrown upon the wide world without a penny. The Chief is still at Allahabad, but champing to be off to the field. Something has gone wrong and delayed the movements. The telegraph is now up to Pertabgurh.

October 28th. The proclamation of amnesty has arrived. It is sealed, and not to be opened until the morning of the first prox. It is to be read out at a parade of all the troops, and all natives, thalookdars, etc., are to be invited to attend. A royal salute will close the proceedings. The Bareilly column have had a skirmish with the enemy near Pusgaon. Two guns were taken, being abandoned. The enemy's sowars attacked the baggage, and killed some camp followers. Another fight by Colonel Bulwer's force at Nugaon. No news as yet come in.

October 29th. Brigadier Barker took eight guns at Ber wah. The fort has not been destroyed, but handed over to a friendly Rajah. Rooyah, where so much opposition was expected, has been found deserted. A force from Futtehgurh advanced from the west under Sir T. Seaton, and this has probably caused the flight. Nothing but movements of the troops recorded in the papers. All the ghauts down the Oude frontier on the Ganges are guarded, to prevent any doubling back of the rebels after defeat.

October 30th. News having arrived from Duriabad that Mehudee Husein was attempting to cross between this and that place with several thousand men and five guns, the whole of our cavalry and two guns were ordered off. Other spies having come in reporting that he was at present forty miles distant, the march was countermanded. Genera Grant has lately fallen in with this chief and defeated him.

October 31st (Sunday). All the cavalry and four guns Horse Artillery started at twelve p.m. to patrol between this and Suftergunge. News came in that the Duriabad force had fallen in with the rebels crossing the road yesterday, and captured five guns. They consisted of the Nuseerabad Brigade, and numbered ten thousand (?) men. Another party of four thousand are still waiting to cross, and are encamped some miles from Suftergunge. Our patrol returned at ten a.m. Brigadier Barker's force has been found by a column from Futtehgurh. Where they go to now no one knows. The budmashes are spreading a report that the sweetmeats, to be supplied to-morrow to the natives, will have the wonderful effect of making those who partake of them Christians. This will be believed by many, and may counteract the effect of the proclamation. Another fight south of Poorwah, in which other five guns were taken.

November 1st. The proclamation and amnesty were

to-day made public all over India, from Cape Comorin to Peshawur. Her Majesty is now the supreme power, and Lord Canning the Viceroy, the title of Governor-General being abolished. The amnesty, the more important subject at present of the two, offers pardon to all Sepoys, Zemindars, etc., who come into us before the 1st January, 1859, and who have not themselves been murderers, or assisted in any massacre of Europeans. Those who have been participators in any such murders will meet with the usual penalty of the law, and all persons who conceal such outcasts will be punished, but their lives will be guaranteed. This amnesty of course abolishes confiscation of estates, etc. A copy of this has been sent by spies to Dewah, and the jungle about Buttai, where only a remnant of the former force is congregated. A parade of all the troops in camp was ordered this morning to hear the proclamation read. The troops were, the 2nd troop 3rd brigade Horse Artillery, No. 14 R.L.F. Battery; detachments of H.M. 2nd D.G., Hodson's Horse, and 4th Oude Cavalry; H.M. 23rd R.W.F.; a wing of H.M. 88th and 90th. After the reading, a royal salute was fired, and the troops marched past the Brigadier. In the afternoon, games among the men were got up. They consisted of running, jumping, etc.; elephant races, hackery and coolie races; Sowars showing their skill in cutting at balls and sticks, lancing at pegs driven into the ground, etc. No sooner had darkness fallen than the villages of Nawabgunge and Bara Bunka, and the stone bridge across the nullah in front of camp, were illuminated. The subscription to the first exceeded two thousand rupees. The show was of a very primitive and simple character. Rows of vessels filled with oil extending along the tops of houses, walls, etc., produced, from the irregularity, a pleasing appearance. A few fireworks on the parade ground terminated the public festivities of this day, although some kept up the amusement until the small hours.

November 2nd. Colonel Bulwer's fight near Jubrowlie was a very extraordinary feat. From good authority he heard that Banee Madho in person was advancing against him with twenty-six thousand (?) men and twelve guns, and to ensure success, they had determined on trying a ruse. Banee Madho with one division was to attack with eight guns, and after a short fight he was to retire, with the hope of leading the cavalry and artillery after him. When this succeeded, the second and third divisions were to advance and annihilate the infantry. Colonel Bulwer made his disposition accordingly. The attack on the first division was so spirited that the flight, instead of being false, became real. He then turned against the second, and treated them in the same way; and the third likewise, capturing two guns. In all the varied combats during the campaign there has been no action where the superiority of Europeans, even against countless masses of rebels, has been so distinctly shown as in this, and it proves how unnecessary is the assemblage of such large armies as Lord Clyde thinks necessary. The commandant of Buttai has sent in his vakeel, offering to come in. This is the first, and he will probably be followed by many more.

November 3rd. Jugdespore has been reoccupied by

Colonel Turner's column. General Grant, after leaving a force at Tandah, is on his way to attack Amethee, the Rajah of which is a fierce enemy to us. A thannah, thirteen miles from Lucknow, was attacked on the night of the 1st by a force under ——— Ali, brother of the late Moosub Ali, killed at Selimpore. They were so well received by the police guard that they retired after losing thirteen men. They looted and burned the village. The Chief left Allahabad on the 2nd. The army has thirty-two heavy guns with it.

November 4th. Letters from home. All well. The rebels, defeated by the Duriabad force on the 30th ult., have joined their friends in the Buttai jungle, and increased their force by five thousand men. The idea of the Bengal ryots about Queen Victoria is very ridiculous. They call her the "Kumpany Ka rand" ("the widow of the Company"). This shows their knowledge of the Company, after a hundred years subjection to it. They imagine it is one man, and her successor will be called the "Kumpany Ka butcha," probably ("butcha," a child).

November 5th. This is the Hindoo Feast of the "Dewalie." The camp, bazaars and houses were brilliantly illuminated in the evening. Brigadier Douglas has cleared the Shahabad district of rebels who have fled to the Rhotas Hills. Colonel Bulwer's force has joined with that under Brigadier Evelegh. This junction was required, from Banee Madho with his whole army advancing in the Poorwah direction. He has again retired, and intends, it is said, making his stand in the Simree jungle, the scene of our fight of the 12th May last. A party of rebels, numbering some six hundred, have taken up their quarters in a dense jungle six miles to the west of this. They will probably be left unharmed at present.

November 6th. The force under Brigadier General Wetherall, but under the personal directions of Lord Clyde, assaulted and captured the fort of Rampore Kusseal on the 3rd instant. Our loss amounted to thirty, chiefly arising from the explosion of a mine, among the number Colonel Farquhar, Beloochees; five guns were taken, and the enemy are reported as having lost a great number of men.

November 7th (Sunday). A few days ago eight hundred Sowars advanced to the Alumbagh, and lived in it for twenty-four hours. After burning and looting all the villages round, they decamped unmolested. Until they were gone no one in Lucknow knew anything of it. This shows how unfriendly and hostile the people of Oude are. They would sooner be plundered by their own countrymen, than live in peace under our rule. The Bareilly Brigade have captured twelve guns, most of them were, however, left behind by the rebels and brought in by the villagers. Banee Madho's army is said to be breaking up and dispersing.

November 8th. A force consisting of four guns, 2nd troop, 3rd brigade, Horse Artillery, all the Cavalry, and four hundred H.M. 90th, started at ten p.m. last night, and proceeded towards Suftergunge. Spies brought in word that a large body of the enemy were on the banks of the Goomtee preparing to cross. We arrived at Dadni, a *coss* from Suftergunge, at 2-30 a.m., and after sending on a patrol halted until sunrise, when we returned to camp, which we reached at 10-30 a.m. The rebels were twenty miles from where we were, and they were stationery. General Grant was, by to-day's letter, at Amethee, the fort of which place he was bombarding. He expected to be master of it in two days, everything being done by the guns and mortars, no risk of failure by assaulting with men being attempted.

November 9th. The battery of Royal Artillery, all the Cavalry, and a wing of H.M. 23rd started at four a.m. to proceed to Suftergunge and remain away three days. Amethee is said to be the strongest fort in Oude, and had defied Kings, Rajahs, etc., with impunity. Its capture will, therefore, have a very beneficial effect. A gunboat, it is said, is to sail up the Gogra and prevent the rebels crossing at Bahramghat. It is more probable, however, that the budmashes will not be stopped going over from this side, as when once in the Baraitch district they will be hemmed in on all sides, and if they do not come in, will all be killed, "a consummation devoutly to be wished."

November 10th. The amnesty is already said to be doing good. From Duriabad, Sultanpore, etc., we hear of rebels laying down their arms. Near Rooyah, a large Talookdar, long our fierce enemy, has come in with five hundred men and one gun. Such cases will, doubtless, be infectious, and when these men are seen to escape, numbers will follow their example. Such fiends as the Nana, Khan Bahadur Khan, etc., will deceive their adherents for long, but they also will ultimately find their followers fall away. A rumour of the Buttai budmashes having attacked Lucknow cantonments last night is current in camp. Whatever truth there may be in this, they fired a salute near Dewah on their return from some place, and its probability is countenanced by the fact that Manow is nearer Buttai than this, and not defended by so many men.

November 11th. The news from Fyzabad is, that H.M. 73rd have been ordered to cross the Gogra, and that the steamer is there to ferry them over. The bridge of boats is still unfinished. Sufficient number of boats have not yet been procured. Until the heavy guns arrive, orders have been received not to finish it. No truth in rumour of attack upon cantonments. The rebels at Buttai are said to number twelve thousand men and twelve guns, of which seven hundred are cavalry.

November 12th. The jungle and village of Simree, Banee Madho's headquarters, have been taken by Brigadier Evelegh, with the loss of one man killed. The enemy were evacuating it when our force arrived. It was here we had our fight on the 12th May, and it would probably have been taken at that time with little loss if our visit had been in the morning. Banee Madho has sent in offering terms, but they are so insulting that it is to be hoped they wont be listened to. His offer has been sent on to the Governor-General for advice. He will surrender, but we must allow him a bodyguard, guns, etc. The method of campaigning now adopted is as follows:—When a chief is found holding out in his fort, the proclamation is sent to him and an answer demanded within a certain time. If this is not favourable, he is at once attacked. No one is ever interfered with until it is known he has rejected the amnesty.

November 13th. Good news from all quarters. The Chief gave Banee Madho twelve hours to come in after his terms were rejected, and when this had elapsed and no answer given, Lord Clyde attacked his position at Shunkerpore with twenty-four heavy guns. Nothing known of the result. The Rajah of Amethee has delivered himself up to Sir J. H. Grant with thirty guns and all his men. Sitapore is now occupied by our troops, probably by Barker's column. This will frighten the Buttai rebels, it having cut off one of their routes to escape by. We heard that eighty of them threw away their arms a few days ago and returned to their homes.

November 14th (Sunday). The Rajah of Amethee did not come in with his men, nor deliver up his guns. He skulked into General Grant's camp one night with one or two followers. His fort is, however, in our hands, and we are busy disarming his people. Ram Bux, the cowardly chief of Doundeakura, whose place we visited and destroyed on the 10th of last May, has escaped across the Ganges, and has as yet eluded our force. The inhabitants of the Mulaon district are coming in numbers and laying down their arms and swearing allegiance to Queen Victoria. Brigadier Troup's column found Mythoolie evacuated, and barely missed capturing the Rajah. Banee Madho still unconquered.

November 15th. Sir John Lawrence is about to leave India, and take his seat in the Indian Council. He is to be succeeded by Colonel H. Edwards as Chief Commissioner of the Punjaub, and Captain James gets the commissioner ship of Peshawur.

November 16th. The Chief is expected in Lucknow about the end of the month, when it is believed arrangements will be made for clearing the Buttai jungle. A large patrol, consisting of two H.A. guns, all the Cavalry, and H.M. 88th, started for Dewah at eight a.m.

November 17th. The Sundeela rebels, under Hari Persad, have joined the force at Buttai. Brigadier Barker, leaving the Futtehgurh column near Rooyah, has advanced to the Goomtee, which he will cross and advance eastward, so as to prevent the rebels from bolting from Buttai, and to assist us in clearing that jungle. Telegraph came from the Chief ordering us to proceed along the Fyzabad road and intercept Banee Madho and his army. Lord Clyde with his immense force had surrounded him on three sides in Shunkerpore, but in spite of this he escaped, after refusing all terms. He says he has sworn allegiance to the King of Oude, and cannot do the same to us. Our information was so bad that nothing was heard of the direction he had taken, and although five columns surrounded him, he, after marching in a zig-zag direction, led his army untouched towards the Goomtee. Although supposed to be coming in our direction, nothing known for certainty.

November 18th. Marched at eleven p.m. Force consisted of two Horse Artillery guns, two Royal Artillery batteries, all the cavalry, H.M. 90th, a wing of H.M. 88th. We proceeded to Dadree, which we reached at three a.m. The Rajah of Kupurtullah's force was at Suftergunge. The news that we got here was that Banee Madho had crossed the Goomtee and was not far distant. This not being believed, spies were sent out. They returned, reporting that he was still on the other side with twelve thousand men and twelve guns. We remained in the same spot all day, and in the evening returned one mile towards Pertabgunge, where we bivouacked for the night. The Rajah's force went a few miles nearer Duriabad, where they were joined by some of the 1st Europeans.

November 19th. At three a.m. a spy brought in word that he had seen about two hundred Sowars escorting some great man on an elephant. The cavalry were dressed in long cloaks, and with steel scabbards, and we found out afterwards that they belonged to our 4th L.C. They were moving at a rapid pace. All the cavalry and two H.A. guns went in pursuit, but instead of our being guided so as to intercept their flight, we went to the village where we had received information of their being seen. We followed at a trot, saw the footsteps of the elephants, and after a chase of about nine miles, which took us towards all points of the compass, we landed on the Fyzabad road, about a mile from camp. The fugitives were two hours ahead, going at a gallop, so that pursuit, with any hope of success, was useless. The great and unaccountable mistake was not having patrols along the road, who would have given timely warning. This individual, supposed at first to be Banee Madho, was found not to be him, but who he was no one knows. Halted all day in the same place.

November 20th. Waited all day for news. Some Irregulars were sent to the only three forces on the Goomtee to collect information. They returned in the evening, reporting that Banee Madho has quitted the banks of the river, and had gone no one knew whither. Our want of reliable news is the drawback in all our movements. The villagers are hostile, and voluntarily tell us lies to deceive us. We started at eight p.m., and reached camp at eleven p.m.

November 21st (Sunday). Found that the 88th were ordered into Lucknow, as the communication between it and Cawnpore was threatened, and this is probably by Banee Madho. General Grant, after destroying Amethee, the Rajah of which, Madho Singh, delivered himself up, was in pursuit of Banee Madho. Brigadier Evelegh's column is in pursuit also. Poorwah has again been invested by the rebels. It is defended by police under Captain Chamberlain. A force consisting of two Horse Artillery guns, two Royal Artillery guns, all the Cavalry, a wing of H.M. 23rd, a part of the 90th, started at nine p.m., to remain on the Fyzabad road in our old position, and await the arrival of the fugitives from the south of the Goomtee. It is rumoured that on Banee Madho's leaving Shunkerpore, he delivered up his son to the care of the British Government.

November 22nd. Kyrut Singh, the chief of Buttai, is coquetting about terms. He has again been offering to Mr. Cavanagh to come in. Mr. Cavanagh very unfortunately told him that a large force was just starting from camp, and that he had better give himself up at once. On hearing this Kyrut Singh decided on attacking us with, it is said, five thousand men and five guns. On spies bringing us this news, the column was immediately ordered back from Pertabgunge, from which place they arrived at eight p.m. The attack was expected on the 23rd.

November 23rd. No attack, and there is little probability of there being one now. Kyrut Singh now says he will keep Buttai until we come, when he will deliver himself up, so as to prevent it falling into any other person's hands. A column of every available man has been sent from Lucknow towards Cawnpore. Brigadier Evelegh has relieved Poorwah, capturing three guns. He is now in pursuit of the assailants. The Dewah force has been largely reinforced. They now number nine thousand men with fourteen guns. The Begum is also crossing at Bahramghat, and intends joining them and burning our camp.

November 24th. Brigadier Horsford's column was to attack Hydergurh on the right bank of the Goomtee to-day. The rebels, who were encamped near it, and who consist of fugitives from Amethee and Shunkerpore, were expected to cross the river last night. This is confirmed by the firing heard in the Suftergunge direction this morning. The Rajah has probably fallen in with them. Brigadier Troup has left his heavy baggage and guns at Mitowlie, and has pushed on with the cavalry and light pieces. Buttai will probably be the final destination of both his and Brigadier Barker's columns. Captain Chamier fell in with the rear-guard of a large body of fugitives crossing the Fyzabad road. He with his Irregulars cut up about one hundred of them. Through some fault information of their march was not brought to him until the larger part were safely across. They had no guns with them. These attempt the passage with a large mob of budmashes this evening, so the spies say.

November 25th. By letter from Jubrowlie we hear that Banee Madho was expected to deliver himself up to the Chief. Where he is no one here as yet knows, but Doundeakeira is spoken of by some. The telegraph wire has been brought here from Lucknow, which looks as if the advent of the Chief was at hand. Very quiet in the Buttai direction.

November 26th. Brigadier Barker's force after crossing the Goomtee have halted. Their destination is said to be Futtypore; but why they are halting where they are, no one can tell. Brigadier Troup has had another fight on the 18th inst. with Ferozeshah, of the Delhi royal family, and captured nine guns. The Horse Artillery and Cavalry under Colonel Brind were alone engaged.

November 27th. Everyone horrified this morning by hearing that Cornet W. Agnew, 2nd D.G., had committed suicide. He was on the sick list, being laid up with fever. He shot himself with his revolver. The first shot missed, the second was fatal. Some money matters are supposed to be the cause. Out on patrol again beyond Pertabgunge. News was brought in that the rebels were crossing. It turned out that four hundred Sowars had passed during the night. We saw no one, and returned at five p.m. General Grant has had an encounter with some rebels across the Gogra at Fyzabad, and captured six guns. They were becoming very plucky, firing into steamers and at our piquets.

November 28th (Sunday). Rumours of a great fight near Doundeakeira are rife, but nothing authentic known.

November 29th. A brigade under Colonel Taylor, 79th Foot, is on its way to Fyzabad. It is the same as that formerly commanded by Brigadier Wetherall. It is supposed they cross the Gogra and advance northward.

November 30th. Lord Clyde with some of the 6th Carabiniers has arrived in Lucknow. Banee Madho's formidable array has disappeared, but where they and the other thousand budmashes have gone no one as yet knows. The fight at Doundeakeira, in which Lord Clyde commanded, resulted in the total defeat of Banee Madho, with the loss of eight guns and five hundred men. Banee is said to have fled down the river Ganges.

December 1st. Lord Clyde has again started from Lucknow with a force to attack a Thalookdar some ten miles from cantonments. His abode is in a strong mud fort, from which he has been cutting up our police, etc., ever since the capture of Lucknow. This probably accounts for the stoppage of Brigadier Barker's column. Disarming the population of Oude and demolishing all forts, and cutting down of jungle is progressing favourably.

December 2nd. Brigadier Evelegh is to command the force with Lord Clyde. It is generally to be believed that Buttai is to be attacked from the west, while the Nawabgunge force will prevent the rebels doubling back towards Lucknow. A road has been marked out and will immediately be commenced, leading from the new fort here to the thannah of Dewah.

23

December 3rd. Mr. Cavanagh, our Commissioner here, has gone to join the Chief, his place being taken by Captain McAndrew. The Chief is still at Lucknow. The brigade under Brigadier Evelegh has gone on. Lord Clyde, with a very large force, comes here on the 5th or 6th, when a general advance will probably be made against Buttai. Orders have been received by the Commissariat here to lay in a supply of thirty days rations for each regiment. We will probably advance on Bahramghat, and, as soon as a bridge is made across the Gogra, into the Baraitch district.

December 4th. A few matchlock-men fired at our cavalry piquet last night. They expected to find the camp unprotected at the flank, and hoped to burn some of us out. After wasting a considerable quantity of gunpowder they retired. General Grant crosses at Fyzabad, and advances northwards. The rebels across the Gogra can, it is said, bring fifty field guns into the field. The Nawab of Banda has delivered himself up.

December 5th. Lord Clyde with all his Staff arrived here this morning. He brings about eight thousand men of all arms. A very large field train under Captain Russell, B.A., also came. The force consists of Brigadier Horsford's Brigade; a battalion of Beloochees, etc., etc. What our destination is no one knows. Those on the Chief's Staff are equally ignorant. Brigadier Evelegh is said to be at Bahramghat. He has the 1st troop 1st brigade Horse Artillery, H.M. 5th Fusiliers, 3rd battalion Rifle Brigade, etc. A bridge of boats also accompanied the force under Lord Clyde, in charge of Colonel Harness, R.E. All day long, baggage, camels, and ammunition were coming up. In the evening we received orders to deliver up all our camels and elephants, as we were to remain behind. The Artillery in Oude being commanded by Colonel Riddell, he chose nothing but Royal Artillery, leaving all the Bengal behind. Whether it was from this cause or not, Lord Clyde ordered him to return to Lucknow, and the 3rd troop 1st brigade H.A., Major Moir, to join him.

December 6th. The force in this part of Oude has been divided into three brigades:—1st, under Brigadier Horsford, consisting of the 2nd Rifle Brigade; 2nd Brigade (Parnell) —H.M. 23rd and 90th; 3rd Brigade (Evelegh)—H.M. 5th and 3rd Rifle Brigade. The cavalry with the Chief consists of H.M. 7th Hussars, Lahore Light Horse, a squadron of H.M. 6th D.G. The Chief, with two brigades, started for Bahramghat at four a.m. Brigadier Evelegh was to clear the Buttai jungle, but last night the rebels all fled towards the ghaut, leaving the jungle unoccupied. The force left here consists of a wing of H.M. 38th; detachment 2nd D.G.; 2nd troop 3rd brigade Horse Artillery; Hodson's Horse, two hundred men. Heavy guns have been coming out from Lucknow to-day. Colonel Maude's 3rd company 8th battalion; Le Mesurier's 3rd company 14th battalion, both with siege guns. The 3rd troop 1st brigade also comes out to-day. Major Fraser with the F troop R.H.A., is with the Chief. To-day the following troops arrived and encamped near Nawabgunge:—a wing of H.M. 80th; Talbot's Royal Horse Artillery company, with heavy guns; the Kumaon Battalion; a battalion of Jezailchees, and a Punjaub Infantry

Regiment. The Chief has left all his heavy pieces behind, and none knows where he has gone.

December 7th. No word from the Chief, and no orders for the heavy guns to go on. We expect to march for Lucknow to-morrow, the doolies for the sick having arrived. A force left Lucknow yesterday, consisting of two guns 2nd troop 3rd brigade Foot Artillery; a wing of H.M. 88th, and some of Hodson's Horse. Destination unknown. This force has gone to Mulleabad in the Sundeela direction. A party of rebels have passed by Barker's column and revisited their old haunts. Barker and Troup have joined together. The former commands the whole. Brigadier Evelegh was only nineteen miles from Nawabgunge to-day. The district is quite clear.

December 8th. The headquarters and two guns of the 2nd troop 3rd brigade Horse Artillery, and the detachment of the 2nd D.G., left Nawabgunge at seven a.m. The troops left behind are a wing of H.M. 38th, two guns Horse Artillery, and two hundred Hodson's Horse. We reached Manow about one p.m., where we found cantoned headquarter's wing of H.M. 88th; one wing of H.M. 38th; 4th Europeans, L.C., and some of Hodson's Horse. Great changes here since our departure in July. The graveyard which was so desecrated, and the wall which was dug up from the foundations, are restored, the tombstones repainted and raised. The church is thatched, and divine service is held in it. Lord Clyde, after occupying Bahramghat without opposition, has found that the pontoon bridge is not complete. Leaving Brigadier Parnell's brigade there, he has started for Duriabad, and has ordered all the troops that have been halting at Nawabgunge, to make the same place in one march. They left this morning with almost all the heavy guns.

December 9th. The Nana has succeeded in crossing the Ganges into the Doab. No intimation of his progress across Oude was reported; the first thing heard of him was a dâk gharrie, near Meeran-ka-Serai, being sent back by some Thannadar, the road being unsafe. The Nana seizing the opportunity of all troops leaving the place, crossed near Kunouge, with Ferozeshah and several thousand Sowars. The telegraph wire has been cut, and all communication with up country is stopped. Except police, we have no troops to pursue. He is, doubtless, making for Central India, and will join with Tantia Topee. Now that he is unearthed, the pursuit will be vigorous; but the immense tract of Rajpootana, with its hills and jungles, will conceal him for some time. His presence in the Peishwa's dominions, if he ever reaches them, will cause us immense trouble, and may prolong the campaign now terminating, through another hot weather.

December 10th. On a committee in Lucknow, consisting of Dr. Brougham, field-surgeon; Dr. Macrae, surgeon, H.M. 97th, and myself. We are ordered to examine all the neighbourhood and Lucknow, and give our opinion where the best spot for a new cantonment is to be found. Four places are spoken of, Dilkusha, Alumbagh, Moosa Bagh, and the old cantonments. Our district, however, extends over six miles circuit of Lucknow. We commence on

Monday. Great changes in the city now. The whole space between the Tara Kote and the Chattur Munzil has been cleared and levelled. Broad roads (military ones) have been made through the native city and commanded by the new entrenchments. It will soon be the Edinburgh of India. General Grant has occupied Gonda without opposition. By this time he will have disturbed the Begum in her den at Boondee. The Chief has also crossed at Fyzabad with a brigade.

December 11th. The Nana was, in the last Government message, reported as being still in the Doab. After crossing the grand trunk road, he made for Russoolabad, and was pushing on for the Jumna, between Kalpee and Etawah. Troops are in pursuit from Agra, Cawnpore, etc., but they will probably be too late. A force under Colonel J. H. Smyth, Artillery, has left Phillibhit and marched northwards, so as to prevent the rebels, defeated by Brigadier Troup, from doubling backwards into Rohilcund. Brigadier Parnell's brigade is reported as crossing at Bahramghat.

December 12th (Sunday). After all it turns out that the Nana is not with the fugitives in the Doab. They are the rebels who were engaged at Biswah on the 1st instant, and include Ferozeshah, Mohsum Ali Khan (who is dressed as a European), Lukkur Shah, etc., etc. Ishmael Khan was the commander at the fight at Biswah, but he has, with numerous followers, delivered himself up to Brigadier Barker. Mr. Hume, with some local levies from Etawah, came in with them, near Henchandpore, but was repulsed, and was obliged to take refuge in a *serai*. The rebels have, when last heard of, gone to Phuppond, near the Jumna. The Nana is said to be still near Baraitch, in a place called Chundah. The Ranees (Bajee Rao's widows) are with him against their will, and are trying to make terms with us.

December 13th. On the committee (medical) to chose a proper site for new cantonments. Our first day's trip was to Dilkusha, and the plateau between it and Alumbagh. We examined the soil, the depth and temperature of the wells, the density and purity of the water, the diseases prevalent, the appearance of the inhabitants, etc., etc. The plateau is ofty and dry, but intersected to the south by numerous nullahs. Its inhabitants do not suffer from spleen disease, and have rarely fever. The Jellalabad jheel, which is several miles in circuit, is a great drawback, and being in the direction from which the prevailing winds blow, must carry malaria over all this plain. For convenience it surpasses all otner places spoken of. The inhabitants are chiefly Hindoos. The large plain between Alumbagh and Buntera, lies so low that it becomes inundated in the rains, hence one of the causes of Havelock losing so many men in this place last year.

December 14th. Colonel Parnell, with his force, is still on this side the Gogra. Large rafts are in course of construction for crossing. The rebels are seen in small numbers on the opposite bank, but they have no guns, consequently our troops are inactive. Nothing doing.

December 15th. On the committee again to-day. Breakfasted at the 97th mess in the Imam Barah. Went over he large hall where the King of Oude used to sit in state, and which we have converted into a barrack. It is one of the finest halls in the world. The span of the arched roof is enormous, and being built by bricks alone, is a style of architecture rarely met with. Lord Valentia, in his travels, describes it as a beautiful specimen of light, elegant, but fantastic architecture. Bishop Heber observes: "I have never seen an architectural view which pleased me more, from its richness and variety, as well as the proportion and general good taste of its principal features." After breakfast rode to the Moosa Bagh along the banks of the river, through a garden of Ali Nucki Khan's house, vizier to Wajid Ali, the deposed King of Oude. I mounted to the roof of the building, from whence an extensive bird's-eye view is obtained of the surrounding country. The house itself is built with its face looking up the river. The ground at the back is enclosed by a high wall, and includes about two acres artificially raised about thirty feet above the surrounding country. The river, which is about half a mile distant, is unconfined by any embankments, and the surrounding country being very low and perfectly flat, becomes at each flood an immense lake. We then proceeded along the Sundeela road to the old cavalry lines of the Oude Irregulars. Hereabouts the ground is raviney, and every here and there small jheels or marshy spots are found. We proceeded out about four miles, through a beautiful, rich, well-wooded country, but with several large jheels scattered about, and with the low-lying banks of the river about two miles distant. Returned down the Mulleabad road, where a large elevated plateau is met with containing wells of very fine water. This is the only spot at all suitable for a cantonment, but the river is too close. Returned across the new bridge of boats at Ali Nucki Khan's house, and struck across the plains to cantonments, which place I reached about 5.30 p.m.

December 16th. The rebels have escaped out of the Doab. Brigadier Herbert, from Cawnpore, was close to them, and the Towana Horse cut up fifty or sixty of their rear-guard as they were crossing the Jumna, and captured their one gun. When last heard of they had crossed the Chumbul at a place called Mahona. General Napier, from Gwalior, was in pursuit. Brigadier Barker has returned with his column from Sundeela. The whole country in and about Baree and Sitapore are quiet. Colonel Brind, with the Horse Artillery and Cavalry, has been detached to pursue some rebels trying to escape.

December 17th. Raining all day. Letter from Sasseram: country all quiet, the Sepoys having come in under the terms of the proclamation. The Chief is at Baraitch. The rebels have fled without attempting to stand. They have entered the Terai and are making for the Nepal hills, while our troops have been pushed on to Toolseepore, where the Begum was forming a citadel. What course will be pursued by Jung Bahadoor, K.C.B., is very doubtful. The remains of the Sepoy army are very numerous, and with a great many guns, but totally disorganized. They are scarcely strong enough to change the Nepal dynasty, if Nepal proves true to itself; and, knowing that he will be assisted by the English, it is probable that Jung will refuse to admit the fugitives to his territory, and oppose their entrance if they attempt to do so by force.

December 18th. Cloudy damp day. On the committee again to-day. Our course was over the cantonments here, and extended north-west towards the lines of the old 7th L.C., near the race-course. This is far the most favourable site for a cantonment, in a medical point of view. It is situated on an elevated sandy plateau, which runs due north, and is of great extent. Except its distance from Lucknow, about three and a-half miles, and its being on the left bank of the Goomtee, nothing further can be brought against it. Water is plentiful, but, from the sandy nature of the soil, the wells fall in unless lined with bricks. The old cantonments were very healthy. The site of the new cantonments must be two miles deep and one in length. The return of Brigadier Barker to Sundeela is owing to rumours of Banee Madho, who is across the Gogra, and other leaders, attempting to follow Ferozeshah in his flight towards Central India.

December 20th. Another meeting of the committee. Our day's trip was to Alumbagh and the plain beyond. The soil here retains moisture more than in any other part. The water in the wells is about thirty feet deep, and of very high specific gravity. That in Alumbagh itself was 1·008, but this was to be expected from the quantity of vegetable and animal matter that must be commixed with it. Water from wells in the plain were 1·006. The average in other places was only 1·003. The Jellalabad jheel lies to the east, distant about a mile. Proceeding down the Cawnpore road on the right hand side, two very large jheels are met with, the further one even now being a mile in length. It becomes perfectly dry about the end of January. The prevailing winds would blow over it in the direction of Alumbagh. This plain is said by the Engineers to be elevated and easily drained, but when Havelock advanced on Lucknow he was unable to leave the road with his guns on account of the water. From this place to Lucknow the ground descends to the canal which bounds this plain to the north. Returned by the Cawnpore road. Reached cantonments about five p.m.

December 21st. Went shooting towards Chinhut. Unsuccessful. Ducks plentiful, but wild. H.M. 68th D.G. came in here last night from Brigadier Barker's column. They had been in pursuit of Ferozeshah, but were too late. They are on their way to join the Chief *via* Bahramghat. Ferozeshah has been met by Sir R. Napier, from Gwalior, his elephants captured, and numbers of his followers, including the Reesaldar of the late 12th Irregulars, killed. The Shazadah had, up to the last accounts, escaped.

December 22nd. Meeting of the committee to draw up the report and record our opinions of the different sites. We agreed that the following was the order of merit of the respective sites:—First, Mairow, and the plain towards the old 7th L.C. lines; second, plain towards Chinhut; third, Dilkusha and the plateau to the west; fourth, Moosa Bagh; fifth, Alumbagh. The favourite place with the civilians is the third; with the Engineers, the fifth. The Nana is reported to have taken refuge in a fort to the north of Baraitch, determined to do or die. It is to be hoped that he will continue in this frame of mind until Lord Clyde can get up to him.

December 23rd. The rebels are said to be hemmed in where they must either fight or deliver themselves up. The Begum is anxious to come in, but the Sepoys refuse to sanction this. Nothing doing.

December 24th. Raining again last night and this morning. A field force is to be formed at Sitapore for next hot weather, ready to march at any moment against any foe that may spring up. Brigadier Barker is reported as likely to be the commander. The permanent garrison of Lucknow is to consist of two and a-half European regiments, one regiment of cavalry, several Native Infantry and cavalry corps, and a numerous artillery. In Oude itself there will be two dragoon regiments, and nine batteries of artillery. Across the Gogra, two batteries of artillery, one Queen's regiment, and two native regiments. One of the dragoon regiments will have two squadrons at Fyzabad, one at Sitapore, and a third at Roy Bareilly.

December 25th. Christmas Day. Rumours of the Begum and Banee Madho having delivered themselves up to the Chief, who is still at Baraitch. Another is, that the vakeel of the former is the only person who has come in, and he has done so to find out what our terms are. The Camel Corps has arrived here. They proceed with the squadron, H.M. 2nd D.G., to Sitapore, where Brigadier Barker is, to prevent the rebels, when the Chief attacks them in their final stronghold, from crossing over again into Oude and Rohilcund. The Carabiniers, after marching to Nawabgunge, received orders to return here. They expect to proceed shortly to Meerut.

December 26th (Sunday). Brigadier Parnell has crossed the Gogra, leaving the 1st Bengal Fusiliers, two guns, 2nd troop 3rd brigade Horse Artillery, and some Sappers, to protect the bridge at Bahramghat. No news from the Chief. The Meerut Light Horse came in here yesterday. They are to be disbanded.

December 27th. The Governor-General is at Cawnpore. Mr. Montgomery has gone to meet him. A large quantity of treasure, amounting to one and a-half lacs, was found in the Begum's Kote last night. The native servants were attracted by a noise in the cellar below the officers' quarters. A party immediately proceeded there, without finding the persons engaged. From a hole having been opened in the ground, suspicions were aroused, and this was enlarged, with the result of first bringing to light an iron ramrod sunk in the ground, and a little deeper this treasure.

December 29th. On a committee for invaliding natives at the field hospital, Lucknow. Lord Clyde has had another fight with the rebels north of Baraitch. Four guns were captured. The Commander-in-Chief, while in pursuit, fell and dislocated his shoulder. He is, however, doing well. The chief body of the rebels are at a place called Chendah, where they were to be attacked a few days later. The English mail has arrived in Calcutta. Lord Lyons is dead. M. Montalembert has been acquitted.

December 30th. Again in Lucknow on the sub-committee. The committee, consisting of the Brigadier, Engineers, Sup.-Surgeon, etc., have made up their minds that the plateau, near the Dilkusha, is the best site. We were ordered to assemble, and after examining a map with the proper situations of the different localities in the neighbourhood, re-examine our report and draw up another report, giving our objections in a sanitary point of view to this place. The map did not change our former opinion. The intended cantonments would embrace almost all the Mahommed Bagh, and approach within six hundred yards of the canal and suburbs of the city. This is an insuperable objection. Others were the vicinity of the Jellalabad jheel, on the south-west; the Goomtee, on the north-east; and the broken raviney ground, full of water in the rains, on the south-east.

December 31st. Colonel Christie, commanding a column near Baraitch, has had a skirmish with the enemy. While making a road the troops were attacked. The enemy were easily beaten back, but they escaped with their guns. With the Chief there are two brigades, an infantry one under Brigadier Horsford, C.B., and a cavalry one under Colonel Jones, C.B., 6th D.G. Every day news of a final fight is expected. Peace, or rather the termination of the campaign in Oude, it is generally supposed, will be proclaimed by Lord Clyde to-morrow. Small-pox has broken out in cantonments. The cases are as yet few and mild.

January 1st, 1859. The year that has just expired, has been an eventful one in the history of British India. It found us with Oude and Rohilcund in arms, numerous bodies of rebels in Central India, Behar, etc., who defied our authority, who murdered us and our followers, whenever they had an opportunity, and who, by their continued existence in arms, swelled their ranks with all the disaffected and evil-inclined of the district. The beginning of January saw us in possession of Futtehgurh, the rebels driven from the right bank of the Ganges, and retreating across the Ramgunga, as soon as our troops advanced. This advance into Rohilcund was evidently the first step to the reoccupation of the province. Lord Clyde intended recapturing it, and leaving Oude untouched until the end of the year. This advice was not followed, and orders were received from the Governor-General to advance on Lucknow, with the whole army, and recapture that stronghold. The reason for this was, the belief that the loss of the capital would have such a moral effect on the people of Oude that thousands would lay down their arms and come in. From Futtehgurh the army retraced its steps to Cawnpore, and from there marched on Lucknow. General Franks, and the Ghoorkhas, under Jung Bahadoor, advanced from the south-east to join in the siege. By the beginning of March, the army was assembled in front of the city. On the 6th, the Goomtee was crossed, and a flank movement, under Sir J. Outram, turned the flank of all the enemy's works, they having neglected the defence of the river side, which exposed them to an enfilading fire, thus rendering defence impossible. They evacuated the first line, which we occupied without loss, and retired on the second or Kaiser Bagh line of works. On the 11th, the Kaiser Bagh, the centre of the enemy's position, was captured with little loss. One position after another was captured, the enemy never attempting a stand; and, on the 22nd, the whole of Lucknow was in our possession. Pursuit was delayed. Sir E. Lugard, with a strong brigade, left to relieve Azimgurh; another, under Brigadier-General Walpole, proceeded towards Shajehanpore and Bareilly. The Commander-in-Chief joined the latter from Futtehgurh. The repulse at Rooyah, and death of Brigadier A. Hope, exasperated the army against their commander. Sir C. Campbell joining, drove the enemy from one place after another, and Bareilly was finally captured with the assistance of Brigadier J. Jones. Rohilcund soon became quiet. Towards the Oude frontier, numerous maurauding bands, the chief of which was commanded by the Moulvie, who lost his life while attacking the Rajah of Powayne's fort, made incursions into our districts, and surrounded the garrison of Shajehanpore. These rebels being driven back, affairs settled down for the hot weather. Now and then a skirmish alone gave proof of the continuance of the campaign. In Oude, General Sir J. Grant made several expeditions; one towards Sitapore; another towards Roy Bareilly. It was intended to occupy the latter place, but the approach of the Begum and her followers to Nawabgunge, caused the return of the column. On the 13th June, the fight at Nawabgunge took place. The enemy were defeated, and fled across the Gogra. A cantonment was formed at that place to preclude another assemblage of rebels, and prevent the inhabitants of Lucknow from deserting their homes. The straits in which Râjah Maun Singh was placed, near Fyzabad, by the rebels, again caused General Grant to take the field in July. Maun Singh was relieved and his co-operation with us was confirmed. August found us across the Goomtee, in spite of the enemy occupying Sultanpore, thus limiting the enemy to the district between it and the Ganges. The remainder of the month and September were passed without any stirring news. Skirmishes with the enemy were frequent, with uniform success to us. Banee Madho was the only formidable foe south of Lucknow. He, the Rajah of Shunkerpore in Biswanah, the most warlike district in Oude, was an implacable and consistent rebel, alike defying our power, and scorning our terms. Around his standard flocked all the old Sepoys and malcontents, attracted by his name; second only in their estimation to their Queen, the Begum. Early in October the campaign commenced. Pertabgurh and Salone were again annexed. Columns from Allahabad, on the south, and from Sultanpore, on the south-east, were ready to march. Another delay occurred. A proclamation and amnesty were about to be proclaimed over the length and breadth of India. November 1st was the eventful day. Pardon was offered to all who came in before the 1st January, 1859; except such persons who had murdered or taken part in the massacre of Europeans. As soon as this royal proclamation was issued, the campaign commenced. It was, however, decided that it should be carried on slowly, and without the intention of destroying our enemies. As soon as the army approached a fort, the proclamation was sent to the commandant, allowing him twenty-four hours to consider it.

Bahnee Madho gave out that he had sworn to hold out or

die. The same terms were offered. He refused them with contempt, but fled with all his men and guns. To what point of the compass he had fled, was for some time a mystery. At Doundeakeira, he was met, however, and his army dispersed. The whole of the country to the Gogra was thus cleared of any formidable force. While these events were being transacted to the south of Lucknow, Brigadier C. Troup had advanced from Bareilly, driving the enemy before him. Brigadier Barker from Lucknow relieved Sundeela, captured Berwah with considerable loss, and found Rooyah evacuated. All opposition was thus confined to the east of the Gogra. Brigadier Rowcroft had cleared the Azimgurh district and advanced northward. Lord Clyde with his army advanced to Bahramghat, left a brigade to cross there, and proceeded to Fyzabad, where the river was crossed. An extended line being thus occupied, a general advance was made, with the object of hemming in the rebels between the Terai and the Gogra. No opposition was met with. Gonda was occupied. Baraitch found evacuated. The enemy fell back on the Terai, where they are by the last intelligence. Shahabad and the Jugdeespore jungle had been cleared by Brigadier Douglas, in October, and things were becoming settled in that quarter. Central India, which was overrun by bands and armies of Mahrattas and Rajpoots, etc., was left to Sir H. Rose and his army. Kotah was captured, Jhansi assaulted. On every occasion he was successful; the enemy dared not oppose him. He advanced on Kalpee, and drove the rebels from it. Tantia Topee with some of the fugitives fled to Gwalior, excited a revolution among Scindiah's troops, drove the Maharajah to Agra, and proclaimed the Nana the Sovereign. Vengeance shortly overtook him. Gwalior, one of the citadels of India, was taken by Sir H. Rose, and Tantia Topee had again to seek shelter in flight. Since that time he has been perseveringly followed throughout his erratic flight, but has as yet escaped, through his rapid movements and unexpected doublings. Thus ends the Indian Mutiny, the severest trial ever undergone by any nation. The revolt of the Prætorian Guards, fixed the day of Rome's decline. England, in spite of the fiery ordeal through which she has gone, has sprung up like the phœnix from the ashes, to remain the wonder and admiration of the world. What nation in existence could have carried on a such a war, at such a distance from home; landed and conveyed to the other side of the world, some 80,000 men, leaving behind enough to protect her island home. On this day the amnesty ceases. Some suppose it will be extended, and this is in accordance with the weakness of the Government. It has up to this time been disregarded, disbelieved, and despised. The remaining rebels find themselves too much implicated, their chiefs are outlaws and murderers, and knowing that no pardon awaits them, they stimulate the minds of their retainers to future success.

January 2nd. It is rumoured that the termination of the Oude campaign will be immediately proclaimed, so that Ministers will be enabled to congratulate the people on the restoration of peace when Parliament meets. This bears marks of truth, but the country will awaken and find that the embers of the Mutiny still smoulder, and that here and there the flames will break out for years to come when opportunity offers. The people of India are discontented, and dislike us, but fear our power, and look with longing eyes on their old families, regretting the splendours of bygone days.

January 3rd. No news from the Chief. He has advanced towards Toolsepore, where the rebels are in force. Brigadier Evelegh is at Gonda awaiting the issue of events, and preventing the rebels passing back again towards Azimgurh, where the population is friendly to them.

January 4th. An expedition in pursuit of the Nana has terminated in failure and loss of life in a very melancholy and sudden way. The 7th Hussars, with Major Home, were in pursuit, and about to cross the river Raptee, over which our guns had previously gone, when the Major and several men were swallowed up in a quicksand, horses and all disappearing. Some of the bodies have been recovered. The rebels are trying to enter into Nepal, but Jung Bahadoor has opposed them and driven them back. If he remains firm, the rebels must soon yield or deliver up their arms.

January 5th. A grand display of fireworks. A nautch and splendid supper were given by a rich banker of Lucknow last night. Officers in great numbers attended, and the show went off well, although a heavy fall of rain rather dimmed the pyrotechnic show. Letters from home dated 13th November. All well.

January 7th. By the last accounts the Chief was about thirty miles north of Baraitch in the Terai. About twenty-five guns had been taken, but no rebels killed. Troops have been left behind at a place called Nunpoora, and it is rumoured a cantonment is to be laid down there. At Sitapore they are fixing on a suitable locality. Nothing stirring; not even a flying report to enliven one. Rumour is silent, and hides itself.

January 8th. The 97th Foot are under orders to proceed to Roy Bareilly. H.M. 88th occupy the great Imam Bara, and a wing of H.M. 80th is to proceed to Cawnpore, which is now destitute of troops. The 1st Madras Fusiliers have been sent to Futtypore. A column has left Agra under Brigadier Showers, C.B.; its destination is Bhurtpore, it being rumoured that Tantia Topee is bending his steps towards that place.

January 9th (Sunday). Another fight north of Baraitch at Bankee. A body of the rebels passed Brigadier Rowcroft, but were pursued by a force from the Chief's camp. The rebels were defeated; fifteen guns taken. A great many rebels were killed, and, but for the dense jungle into which they ran, the slaughter would have been immense.

January 10th. Shooting. No sport. Days very warm now. The 97th Queen's march towards Banda. The 38th go to Roy Bareilly. H.M. 6th D.G. proceed to Agra to-morrow *via* Sundeela and Futtehgurh. They are to be joined on their way to some troops from Brigadier Barker's column. Tantia Topee is evidently the cause of this. Some design on the part of some Rajah is, perhaps, expediting the assemblage of troops.

January 11th. It is said that the Chief intends returning

to Lucknow in a few days. The rebels are said to have crossed the Nepal frontier, so the game lies in Jung Bahadoor's hands. A small army of observation is to watch the Terai from some spot north of Baraitch.

January 12th. Rumour still rife that the Begum has delivered herself up, and that she is now on her way to Lucknow. It is doubtful whether this is *the* Begum who has so long striven to keep up the spirit of her followers. She, some say, has gone into Nepal. Tantia Topee and his confrères are reported as on their way to a place called Kuntumpore, where there is a strong fort amply provided with munitions of war. The Rajahs of Mohumdie and Mithowlie have delivered themselves up under the terms of the proclamation to Brigadier Troup.

January 13th. The Chief on his way to Lucknow. Sir J. Grant has taken command of the troops in the field. Conjectures are busy about the probable person to succeed Lord Clyde, who goes home this year. Sir Hugh Rose is the most admired of any general out here. The Lucknow cantonments are fixed on. The Dilkusha plateau is the site chosen. The Engineers are busy laying out the ground.

January 14th. The Nawab of Faruckabad is a prisoner in our hands, having delivered himself up. He is on his way hither escorted by a wing of H.M. 80th, two guns, 2nd troop 3rd brigade Horse Artillery, under Captain M'Leod, and a detachment of Sowars. He is to be tried, and will, it is to be hoped, be hanged; but the sentimental feelings that are so much in vogue may cause this sentence, which the murderer of English women and children so richly deserves, to be commuted to imprisonment. The 3rd battalion Rifle Brigade have been ordered to Agra. It is believed the Chief intends himself to enter Central India, and direct in person the hunt after Tantia Topee.

January 15th. On the committee for examining medical subordinates in Lucknow, kept the whole day on it. The Begum and Co. are said to be in the valley of the Raptee, north of Bankee, beyond the first range of hills. They are in a bad plight for want of provisions. They will be left alone; disease and want will soon thin their ranks. Mr. Montgomery has been appointed Lieutenant-Governor of the Punjaub in succession to Sir J. Lawrence, who proceeds to England.

January 16th (Sunday). The order precluding officers from resigning or retiring, which was issued during the Mutiny, is withdrawn. A camel driver fell into a well in the compound last night and was drowned. The Nawab of Sultanpore has delivered himself up, as well as Nazim Mehudee Hoosein, of whom we used to hear so much about Selimpore.

January 17th. Lord Clyde arrived this morning with the headquarters of the 6th D.G. Some squadrons of Madras Light Cavalry, a wing of the Beloochees, and other two guns also came in, and the whole troop is once more together for the first time since July. The 23rd Royal Welsh Fusiliers are encamped near the Kokeal Nuddee. The Nawab of Feruckabad goes to Allahabad to be tried. We go to Umballa shortly.

January 18th. The headquarters 6th D.G. and the F Troop

Royal Horse Artillery leave to-morrow for Meerut. We march from here with the 24th Punjaub Infantry (Sappers and Miners) on the 20th. News of an unsatisfactory affair near Moradabad. A detachment of the 42nd Highlanders, numbering about sixty men, were attacked by an overwhelming force of rebels—about four thousand—and, before assistance came, fifty casualties had occurred. No particulars known, but that the rebels were never supposed to be so numerous, and scarcely believed to be in existence.

January 19th. Making farewell calls in Lucknow, on Dr. Brown, etc.; also on Major Norman, Assistant Adjutant-General, to request I may be posted to the 2nd troop 3rd brigade. This is to prevent my being sent off with the first detachment requiring an assistant surgeon.

January 20th. Marched from cantonment at five a.m., and encamped about two miles beyond Alumbagh, near the Chand Jheel. With us are the F Troop Royal Horse Artillery, who are on their way to Meerut, and the 24th Punjaub Infantry, who go to some place in the Punjaub. Cold, windy day; very different to the last week at Murrow. On account of our short march to-day, only five miles from Lucknow, we make a long one to-morrow.

January 21st. Started at five a.m. Marched twenty-one miles to Nawabgunge, reaching about eleven a.m.

January 22nd. Started at 6-30 a.m. Marched twelve miles to Oonao, which place we reached at about ten a.m. Here a civilian lives, and it is the headquarters of a police district.

January 23rd (Sunday). Same hour as yesterday marched.

Reached our encamping ground at Subadar's Talao, Cawnpore, about ten a.m., having come about twelve miles. Cawnpore is forty-seven and a half miles from Lucknow. The bridge of boats is now situated on the other side the canal, at the new fort. News of a fight near Phillibhit; the rebels crossed the Chonka river, and attacked Cureton's Sowars, and De Kantzow's levy. The Sowars were defeated with considerable loss. This so elated the rebels that they attacked the Phillibhit column. The fight was long and bloody. We captured their two guns and drove them back, but not until two officers and about twenty men were killed and wounded. Cawnpore is two hundred and sixty miles from Delhi, *via* Etawah and Allygurh.

January 24th. Orders from the Chief to reduce our hospital establishment from the war to the peace footing.

THE END.